Social Work in Ireland

Social Work in Ireland

Changes and Continuities

Edited by

Alastair Christie

Brid Featherstone

Suzanne Quin

Trish Walsh

 macmillan education palgrave

First published 2015 by
PALGRAVE

Palgrave in the UK is an imprint of Macmillan Publishers Limited,
registered in England, company number 785998, of 4 Crinan Street,
London, N1 9XW.

Palgrave Macmillan in the US is a division of St Martin's Press LLC,
175 Fifth Avenue, New York, NY 10010.

Palgrave is a global imprint of the above companies and is represented
throughout the world.

Palgrave® and Macmillan® are registered trademarks in the United States,
the United Kingdom, Europe and other countries.

ISBN 978–1–137–38320–4

This book is printed on paper suitable for recycling and made from fully
managed and sustained forest sources. Logging, pulping and manufacturing
processes are expected to conform to the environmental regulations of the
country of origin.

A catalogue record for this book is available from the British Library.

A catalog record for this book is available from the Library of Congress.

Contents

List of Tables

Notes on Contributors

Chapter 1 Revisiting our History post-'Celtic Tiger': So, What's New?

Caroline McGregor is Professor at NUI Galway School of Political Science and Sociology and is Director of Social Work. She is also a senior research fellow at the UNESCO Child and Family Centre, NUI Galway. Caroline previously worked as a lecturer (1999–2003) and senior lecturer (2003–12) at Queen's University Belfast. She studied for her social work degree (1992) and her PhD (2000) at Trinity College Dublin, where she also worked as a contract lecturer and researcher (1994–99). One of Caroline's main interests has been the history of social work in general and child protection and welfare in particular, with an emphasis on how critical understandings of history inform the present and the future. She has published extensively on this subject, initially under the name of Caroline Skehill and, since 2012, as Caroline McGregor.

Suzanne Quin is an Associate Professor and Dean of Social Science at University College Dublin. Her areas of teaching and research are social work in healthcare, health policy, the psychosocial effects of illness and disability in children and adults, and working with groups. Suzanne is a member (and former chairperson) of the Social Workers Registration Board and a member of the Policy and Practice Committee of the All Ireland Institute for Hospice and Palliative Care. Before joining the staff of the School of Applied Social Science (formerly the Department of Social Policy and Social Work), she was Head of the Social Work Department in the National Rehabilitation Hospital.

Chapter 2 Social Work in a 'Globalized' Ireland

Alastair Christie is the Professor of Social Work at University College Cork (UCC). He is currently Head of the School of Applied Social Studies and the Joint Course Director of the Doctor of Social Science. He worked as a social worker and social work manager in England and Canada before working at Lancaster University, England. In 1997, Alastair moved to live in Ireland and work in the School of Applied Social Studies, UCC. His research interests include globalization and social work, social work as a profession and children in care.

Trish Walsh is a lecturer at the School of Social Work and Social Policy, Trinity College Dublin (TCD). She practised as a social worker and senior practitioner in London and Dublin, specializing in child and family and mental health social work. She has worked at TCD as a social work academic for over 20 years, developed a new Masters in Social Work programme in 2002 and was appointed member and then vice-chair of the former National Social Work Qualifications Board (2007–11). Her current research interests include transnational families, migrant carers, bereavement and end of life care, and therapeutic social work approaches.

Chapter 3 Putting Ethics at the Heart of Social Work in post-Celtic Tiger Ireland

Brid Featherstone is Professor of Social Work at the Open University. She has researched in and written extensively on gender, family support and child protection. Brid worked in social work in the areas of juvenile justice and child protection and has taught social work students in Ireland, England and Germany.

Fred Powell is Professor of Social Policy at University College Cork, where he served as founding Head of the School of Applied Social Studies (1989–2014) and Dean of Social Science (2008–14). He has published a number of books, including *The Politics of Irish Social Policy 1600–1990* (1992), *The Politics of Social Work* (2001), *The Politics of Community Development* (2004), co-authored with Martin Geoghegan, *Youth Policy and Civil Society in the Modern Irish State* (2012), co-authored with Martin Geoghegan, Margaret Scanlon and Katharina Swirak, *The Politics of Civil Society* (2013), and *Continuing Professional Development in Social Work* (2014), co-authored with Carmel Halton and Margaret Scanlon. Fred has also contributed articles to the *British Journal of Social Work*, *Community Development Journal*, *Society and Social Policy*, and *International Social Work*.

Chapter 4 Child Welfare and Protection in Ireland: Déjà Vu All Over Again

Helen Buckley is an Associate Professor at the School of Social Work and Social Policy, Trinity College Dublin, where she coordinates the PG Diploma in Child Protection and Welfare. She is currently the chair of the National Review Panel, which examines the deaths of children in contact with statutory social work services. Helen's main research interests are child protection practice and policy, service user perspectives and knowledge transfer. She recently led a project commissioned by the Department of Children and Youth affairs on making child protection inquiry recommendations more effective.

Kenneth Burns is a college lecturer, Deputy Director of the Master of Social Work course at University College Cork and a research associate with the

Institute for Social Science in the 21st Century. He has worked as a social worker and social work team leader in child protection and welfare. Kenneth's recent publications include *Children's Rights and Child Protection: Critical Times, Critical Issues in Ireland* (2012), co-edited with Deborah Lynch, *Strengthening the Retention of Child Protection Workers: Career Preferences, Exchange Relationships and Employment Mobility* (2012) and 'Employment mobility or turnover? An analysis of child welfare and protection employee retention' (2013), *Child and Youth Services Review*, 35(2), 340–6, co-authored with Alastair Christie.

Chapter 5 Adoption in Ireland: Exploring the Changing Context

Simone McCaughren is a lecturer at the School of Applied Social Studies, University College Cork. She is currently the Director of the Bachelor of Social Work programme and has a keen interest in fourth level education. She previously worked as a social worker with the adoption department of the former Health Service Executive in Cork and continues to do some occasional practice with a Dublin-based adoption information and tracing unit. Simone's research interests include adoption law and practice, children's rights. She has written a number of articles on the subject area of adoption and regularly engages in media discussion and debates.

Muireann Ní Raghallaigh is a lecturer in social work at University College Dublin (UCD). She previously worked as a social worker with separated asylum-seeking children and as a family worker offering psychosocial support to children and parents. Prior to moving to UCD, she worked in the Dublin Institute of Technology and Trinity College Dublin. Muireann's main research interests are various aspects of international social work, particularly cross-cultural social work and the experiences of asylum seekers and refugees. Her publications relate to separated asylum-seeking children, primary care social work, intimate partner violence in developing contexts, and teaching methodologies.

Chapter 6 Fostering the Future: A Change Agenda in the Provision of Alternative Care

Mairie Cregan is a part-time lecturer in the School of Applied Social Studies at University College Cork and is a practising social worker in the field of adoption. She was raised as a birth child in a fostering family and fostered herself for over 30 years. Mairie has been involved in creating alternative care systems in Eastern Europe since 1990 and is currently involved in setting up search and reunion services in Romania for Romanian children adopted into Ireland, as well as support services for birth families. She is a founder member of Féileacáin, the Stillbirth and Neonatal Death Association of Ireland, and serves as a training and research officer with this organization.

Valerie O'Brien is a college lecturer at the School of Applied Social Science at University College Dublin and an Associate at Clanwilliam Institute, Dublin. She is a social worker, systemic psychotherapist and supervisor. Valerie served for 12 years on the Irish Adoption Board and is currently a member of a number of boards in the child welfare domain, including the Irish Foster Care Association, Social Workers in Foster Care, the Family Therapy Association of Ireland and the Irish Council of Psychotherapy. Her main areas of interest are family group conferencing, kinship care, and adoption practice and policy. Clinically, Valerie works with complex blended families (kinship, adoption, reformed) and consults on complex multiparty cases.

Chapter 7 Responding to Family Violence: New Challenges and Perspectives

Declan Coogan is a lecturer in social work in the School of Political Science and Sociology at the National University of Ireland (NUI) Galway and a Research Fellow with the UNESCO Child and Family Research Centre at NUI Galway. He is a registered social worker and psychotherapist with practice experience in community child and adolescent mental health and child protection and welfare services. Declan is the NUI Galway/Ireland Lead for the EU-funded Responding to Child to Parent Violence Project team, set up to develop awareness of, and intervention programmes for, child to parent violence.

Stephanie Holt is a lecturer in social work in the School of Social Work and Social Policy, Trinity College Dublin. Prior to coming to Trinity, she worked as a child and family social worker in West Dublin. Stephanie has held the post of Director of Postgraduate Teaching and Learning in the School since 2011 and has had lead responsibility for the development of Trinity's first fully online postgraduate programme – the Postgraduate Diploma in Applied Social Studies. Her primary research interests include domestic violence, intimate partner homicide, and family support.

Chapter 8 Intellectual Disability: Responding to the Life Course Goals and Challenges for Individuals and their Families

Anna Jennings was employed as a social work manager in the area of intellectual disability for a number of years. Since coming to University College Dublin in 2000, she has held the post of Director of MSocSc (Social Work) for five years and is currently employed as Director of Professional Practice. Anna's research interests include disability and practice learning.

Bairbre Redmond is Dean of Undergraduate Studies and Deputy Registrar, Teaching and Learning at University College Dublin. She is responsible for the development and maintenance of high-quality teaching and learning across the university and supporting academic development in this area. In 2014, Bairbre was appointed Chair and Academic Lead for Educational Innovation for Universitas 21, a leading global network of research universities that collaborates in areas of common interest. As well as researching and developing new reflective teaching and training, Bairbre has also been involved, for over a decade, in a series of studies on stress, job satisfaction and retention of social workers working in the area of child protection and welfare, funded by the IRCHSS (2003) and the HSE (2008).

Chapter 9 Responding to Psychosocial Aspects of Illness and Health: Challenges and Opportunities for Social Work

Erna O'Connor is an Assistant Professor at the School of Social Work and Social Policy, Trinity College Dublin. She is Course Director of the Master in Social Work programme and Fieldwork Coordinator. Prior to working in social work education, Erna worked as a social worker in drug services and as a social worker and social work team leader in hospital-based social work in Dublin. Her research interests include health-related social work, social work responses to trauma and bereavement, reflective learning and practice, and social work and migration.

Elaine Wilson is a lecturer and placement coordinator in the School of Applied Social Science, University College Dublin. She worked as a senior medical social worker and Acting Head of Department in St Vincent's University Hospital, Dublin. Having worked as an oncology social worker for a number of years, Elaine took up a Research Fellowship position with the Cancer Clinical Research Trust. Her PhD research examined the psychosocial effects of early-stage breast cancer on young women exiting treatment. Elaine's research interests include the psychosocial needs of people with cancer, the needs of people as they make the transition from treatment to survivorship, and the social construction of illness. She is also interested in social work education and adult learning.

Chapter 10 Opportunities for Social Workers' Critical Engagement in Mental Health Care

Liz Brosnan recently completed a doctorate in sociology on mental health service user involvement, examining the inherent tensions for service users, service providers and movement actors in involvement practices and policies. Liz qualified as a clinical psychologist in 1987, and in 2000 became a core member of 'Pathways', the first user-led research project in Ireland. She has been an activist in the national survivor/service user movement since 2003. A former Director of the Irish Advocacy Network and the National Service User Executive, Liz presented a service user perspective to advisory committees with national statutory bodies and NGOs, including the National Disability Authority, the Mental Health Commission and Amnesty International Ireland. She was a lay member on the panel for Mental Health Tribunals for seven years. A founder member of Recovery Experts by Experience, Liz has many interests, including yoga, gardening and sharing her life with a beautiful old dog, who helps maintain sanity.

Lydia Sapouna is a lecturer at the School of Applied Social Studies, University College Cork. Her teaching, research and community contributions are primarily in the area of mental health, with particular emphasis on recovery approaches, community development, and user participation. Over the years, she has worked collaboratively with service user groups in the areas of advocacy and human rights. Lydia and Liz Brosnan (who co-authored a chapter in this book) have worked together for over a decade seeking to inspire critical, self-reflexive practice, which gives social work students the tools to understand emotional distress as a human experience in a social context. Her research focuses on the importance of user-defined outcomes in the evaluation of mental health care. Lydia has been centrally involved in the establishment of the Critical Voices Network Ireland, a network for people from diverse backgrounds who want a mental health system that is not based on the traditional biomedical model.

Chapter 11 Reforming, Reframing or Renaming Irish Probation Practice in the 21st Century?

Anthony Cotter is a former regional manager with the Probation Service and a former member of the National Social Work Qualifications Board. He has wide experience in many areas of social work and probation practice and has a special interest in social work education and report writing. Anthony is an occasional lecturer at the School of Applied Social Studies, University College Dublin, a registered member of CORU and a certified mediator.

Carmel Halton is Director of the Master of Social Work Programme and Director of Practice at the School of Applied Social Studies, University College Cork. Her research activities span a broad range of educational and professional interests, including professional and post-qualifying social work education, social work practice and practice teaching, reflective inquiry and reflective practice, professional peer supervision, portfolio assessment and development, deviance/offending, and probation.

Chapter 12 Substance Misuse and Social Work in Ireland: Must Do Better?

Shane Butler is Associate Professor at the School of Social Work and Social Policy, Trinity College Dublin, where his teaching and research activities are mainly focused on mental health and addictions. Prior to working in TCD, he worked as a mental health social worker with the Eastern Health Board. Shane is the author of *Alcohol, Drugs and Health Promotion in Modern Ireland* (2002) and *Benign Anarchy: Alcoholics Anonymous in Ireland* (2010).

Hilda Loughran is a senior lecturer at the School of Applied Social Science, University College Dublin and is currently the Director of Social Work. She has taught and researched a range of topics, including crisis work, solution-focused work and groupwork but has a particular interest in alcohol and drug-related policy and practice. Hilda has specifically researched the role of social work in 'addiction' and has been involved in preparing social workers for working with alcohol and drug issues for over 20 years.

Chapter 13 Growing Old with Dignity: Challenges for Practice in an Ageing Society

Sarah Donnelly is a lecturer in social work at the School of Applied Social Science, University College Dublin. Prior to this, Sarah was employed as a medical social worker in Tallaght Hospital for 13 years and worked in a variety of clinical areas, including neurology and age-related healthcare. During this period, Sarah was seconded to work on the 'Care and Connect' project for Trinity College Dublin, which led to the completion of her PhD on the topic of care planning meetings with older people with a cognitive impairment. Her research interests include ageing, dementia, care planning meetings, capacity and decision making, and practitioner-based research.

Anne O'Loughlin is principal social worker at St Mary's Hospital, Phoenix Park, Dublin. Throughout her career, she has worked as a social worker based in Departments of Medicine for Older Persons in several Dublin hospitals. Since 2012, Anne has also been senior social worker for the protection of older persons in the Dublin North City area. She has a strong commitment to the central role of social work advocacy, and has focused her efforts in particular to drawing attention to the issue of the mistreatment of older persons. Anne has combined social work practice with continuing academic studies, and holds a Higher Diploma in Health Care (Risk Management), a Masters of Social Science Degree (Social Work), and a PhD (Social Work) from University College Dublin.

Foreword

Global definition of the social work profession, as approved by the IASSW General Assembly, 10 July 2014, Melbourne, Australia

Social work is a practice-based profession and an academic discipline that promotes social change and development, social cohesion, and the empowerment and liberation of people. Principles of social justice, human rights, collective responsibility and respect for diversities are central to social work. Underpinned by theories of social work, social sciences, humanities and indigenous knowledges, social work engages people and structures to address life challenges and enhance wellbeing.

Critical self-reflection is a core social work skill and essential to professional development. This book not only provides a comprehensive analysis of social work as it has developed in the Republic of Ireland, but does so in a way that demonstrates the considerable capacity that academic social work in the country has for critical self-reflection. In a bold project, a learning community of academic staff from all the Irish universities where social workers are trained has been constructed. They have come together to consider a set of key questions from a range of vantage points based on their varied knowledge and experience:

- In what ways is social work in Ireland responding to rapidly changing social, cultural and economic circumstances?

- How will the new relationships between the state, voluntary and private sectors impact on the provision of social services?

- How can social work advance a critical analysis and a progressive politics within post-Celtic Tiger Ireland?

- How does, and will, social work respond to the needs of specific service user groups?

These are questions sharply posed in a society that has undergone the rapid economic and social change associated with the rise and fall of the Celtic Tiger economy – a period in which the number of social workers and social work students more than doubled, professional registration became a legal requirement, managerialism took hold, and the needs of service users deepened, diversified and, for the first time in some cases, found a voice.

From my vantage point in the neighbouring jurisdiction of Northern Ireland, I can see the pertinence of these 'questions for our time and place' and appreciate the informative and thoughtful answers given. For anyone wanting to gain a view of and engage with the challenges and opportunities of contemporary Irish social work, this book will prove an invaluable 'primer' or foundation text. The wide lens perspective of the first three chapters, on ethics, globalization and history, along with the sweep of the nine specific service group chapters that follow provide an excellent, up-to-date overview of Irish social work. The detailed information, explanation of core concepts, and well-worked arguments will pay revisiting by those with a particular interest in any of the areas covered – from the ethics of resistance, child welfare and protection, to social work across the healthcare spectrum.

The book also deserves attention as a case study in the interweaving of social work as a global profession with a particular set of national history, knowledges, needs and circumstances. The needs identified, the services described, the knowledges, values and skills discussed resonate with the newly agreed global definition of social work. That resonance has, however, a distinctly Irish tone, well captured by the contributors to this book. They convincingly demonstrate that Irish social work has developed in its own particular way, while giving due regard to the impact of globalization – its costs and its benefits. The ability of the contributors, and the social work they describe and discuss, to develop and connect local policies and practices to a global context inspires confidence in the future of social work in Ireland.

John Pinkerton
Queen's University Belfast

1

Revisiting our History post-'Celtic Tiger': So, What's New?

Caroline McGregor and Suzanne Quin

Introduction

The past decade has been a time of unprecedented change in Irish society, which has had a significant impact on the organization and practice of social work. Global trends in the structure of work in the public sector, and the focus on statutory registration and monitoring of professions within the EU have also been of major relevance. A key theme has been the impact of privatization and 'market think' on the provision of social services in general, and social work in particular. Overarching the discourses of managerialism has been the challenges to developing and maintaining a quality service in the context of globalization and neoliberal responses by governments to defining and responding to economic crises (Broadhurst et al., 2010; Lees et al., 2013).

Certainly, the economy has been the dominant feature in Irish society during these years, with the swift change from 'boom to bust' resulting in the bailout and its programme of austerity. Writing at the peak of the Celtic Tiger, Fahey et al. (2007, p. 10) described a now unrecognizable Irish society thus:

> Subjective well being and national morale are among the highest in Europe; living standards have risen and have done so more or less for everyone; jobs have become astonishingly abundant and have improved in quality; people are now flocking into rather than out of the country; young adults are forming couples and having children at an exemplary rate by rich country standards; and people are physically healthier and as far as we can tell from the rather patchy evidence, generally feel good about their lives and the society around them.

At the same time, these authors pointed out that life was not equally good for all and that public services had considerable room for improvement. Moreover, there was the underlying concern as to whether or not the good times would remain, as reflected in Fahey et al.'s (2007, p. 10) comment that 'there is the niggling worry that the whole edifice of economic growth may come crashing down about our ears at some time in the future'. This, of course, is exactly what has happened. Evidence of the impact of this crash on the wellbeing of individuals and the socioeconomic context of a range of service users is plentiful. Data for the Growing Up in Ireland study, as just one example, shows that between late 2008/early 2009 and 2011, families (with children aged three years old) reporting financial difficulties rose from 44% to 61%. Indeed, if we consider the changes in Irish society generally over the past decade, whether politically, culturally, socially, intellectually or institutionally (in other words, the genealogical context), it seems fair to say they have been immense. But when considering 'transformations' care must be taken that we are not overpolemic about the enormity of change, because in and among the acknowledged major shifts and developments of the past decade, some persistent and enduring continuities are also evident, as shown in this chapter. This relationship with history and the present is an approach well rehearsed and applied to social work (e.g. Skehill, 2004, 2007; Garrity, 2010). While this chapter does not explicitly carry out an archaeological or genealogical discourse analysis consistent with a history of the present (see Foucault, 1977, 1980; Dean, 1994), the general principles of the approach have been integrated to illuminate some important observations about the present by reference to key moments in the past (see Garland, 1992; Skehill, 2007; Garrity, 2010). In particular, we are interested to consider present challenges in terms of the extent to which they represent continuity through our history or a shift away (discontinuity). We are interested in considering the construction of discourses of social work (archaeology) in terms of its main activity, nature and potential, as well as the dominant social, political, institutional, intellectual and cultural discourses (genealogy) that surround and shape both the potential and limit of the profession at any particular moment in time (see Skehill, 2007). We are using history of the present as a conceptual device to emphasize that the present cannot be totally separated from the past but neither is it a mere product of it. We should be neither progressive nor revisionist in our approach (Dean, 1994) but rather seek to problematize the present using the past as a critical device. Thus, the interest in history is not to generalize or judge if things are 'better 'or 'worse' but something more complex. For example, in some ways we see progressive developments in social work, while in others we can observe 'reversals in historical pathways'. Through identifying key moments or themes, we are able to illustrate and illuminate elements of social work that appear significant at present. In so doing, we are mindful of making the distinction between what social work aspires to be and how it actually appears to be now. Such an assessment provides a sound basis on which to consider possibilities and limitations as we look to the future.

With this framework in mind, what follows are a set of themes that illustrate some of the main developments in social work in the past decade. In each instance, we comment on the changes and then connect this back to other key moments in the history of social work to get a sense of the nature of that 'change' or 'continuity'. The discussion that follows draws on this analysis to address the core questions that are of central concern for this book. This will inform our conclusion as to how history can continue to offer us a critical tool for analysing the various new 'presents' we find ourselves in. The four themes we focus on are: demographic change and its impact; service expansion and retraction; managerialism, registration and accountability; and champions of social justice and human rights.

Demographic change and its impact

The so-called 'Celtic Tiger' was responsible for immense changes in the demographic profile of Irish society within a short space of time. After decades of net emigration, Ireland became an immigrant nation (Office of the Minister for Integration, 2008). Net immigration was at its peak in 2006 when over 100,000 immigrants came to Ireland, the majority coming from countries that had joined the EU since 2004, the remainder being returned Irish emigrants and 'rest of the world' category, mainly from Africa and Asian countries (Considine and Dukelow, 2009). The vast majority were 'economic migrants' attracted by the relatively high wages and work opportunities Ireland could offer. Social work migrants formed a small cohort of this category. Within the two-year period 2004–05, the National Social Work Qualifications Board accredited 259 social workers with non-national qualifications (NSWQB, 2006).

By 2006, 10% of the overall population was non-Irish and, while demographic change occurred throughout the state, it was particularly evident in the Dublin area where the migrant population accounted for 13.3%, resulting in an immigrant population that was five times greater than it had been in the previous decade (Fahey and Fanning, 2010). Ireland had changed from an almost monocultural society to a multicultural society within one generation. Moreover, while the majority were economic migrants, others had come seeking refuge, often alone and leaving behind in their country of origin family members in vulnerable circumstances. Social workers and their employing agencies have had to engage in a steep learning curve on service provision to what has become an ethnically and culturally diverse community. It is welcome to note the increase in grounded and relevant research into important fields from Irish scholars and practitioners related to this, such as experiences of asylum seekers and refugees in the child protection and welfare system in Ireland (Dalikeni, 2012), practice with unaccompanied asylum seekers (Christie, 2002, 2011; Christie and Burns, 2006) and asylum seekers and resettlement (Kinlen, 2013). Publications regarding the wider field of cultural competence, such as the work of Ní Raghallaigh (2011, 2013; Ní Raghallaigh and Sirriyeh, 2014), have opened up challenging themes such as cultural diversity and spirituality in social work. Indeed, when we look back to the history of social work (e.g. Skehill, 1999), the monocultural nature of society – and thus practice – meant that the cultural diversity theme in practice was often limited to indigenous ethnic minorities such as the Travellers and overly broad aspirations towards 'anti-racist' social work as required by the Central Council for Education and Training in Social Work, the UK organization responsible for accrediting social work in the Republic of Ireland up to the early 1990s (see Kearney, 2005).

Service expansion, retraction and social work expertise

The provision of social work services grew, albeit from a low base, during the era of the Celtic Tiger. A survey of social work posts (NSWQB, 2006) found that there were a total of 2,237 whole-time equivalent posts, with the Health Service Executive (HSE) being the largest employer of social workers. It was still a predominantly female profession and, linked to the discussion of immigration above, nearly one-third of social work practitioners had qualifications obtained outside the state. In spite of the economic high tide of the time, 'budget allocation and employment ceilings' were cited as obstacles to getting much needed additional posts sanctioned. As well as the established areas of practice, new developments indicated the need for increased numbers of social workers; for example, the projected need for up to 600 social workers in primary care as the plan for establishing primary care teams throughout the country unfolded (Department of Health and Children, 2004). However, this was not to be. The economic crisis of 2008 put a stop to ambitious plans for this and other such expansion. In relation to primary care, the projected roll-out of primary care teams was greatly curtailed so that by 2010, only 350 teams in varying levels of development had been established. Moreover, not all the primary care teams had social workers attached and there was evidence to suggest that social workers were increasingly under threat of redeployment to the similarly underresourced child welfare and protection services (Ní Raghallaigh et al., 2013).

It was not only in the area of primary care that social work services were curtailed by the catastrophic economic downturn. Public service embargoes prevented even existing posts being filled when they became vacant or, if considered essential, they were only filled on a temporary contractual basis. Those in permanent posts were less likely to move to another social work post than in the boom years (Redmond et al., 2011). This at least promised better continuity of service but was offset by the increasingly larger caseloads of the remaining staff and severe cutbacks in social services more generally. There is little prospect this will change in the short term despite some improved economic indicators. The HSE had to be given a supplementary budget in December 2013 to enable it to provide essential services while facing a further budget cut for the following year, thus making 2014 a challenging year for health service providers and users.

Looking at this issue from a present perspective suggests retraction and reversal in historical pathways. As social workers, we are sharing the experiences of those across the public sector, and indeed much of Irish society more generally, of retracted services and protracted growth. However, in terms of the areas of expertise of social work, the primary care developments also point to an important discontinuity with the more recent past (that is, from 1970 to 2000). Taking a longer look back to the *Committee on Social Work Report* (Department of Health, 1985), for example, an incredible shift has occurred, long advocated for by many in social work, whereby primary care and adult community care services finally received the recognition so lacking during the 1970s and 80s, when the primary focus was on the developments within the child and family field of practice. While the argument developed by Skehill (2004, 2005) around expertise in childcare and protection continues to hold sway (addressed more fully in Chapter 4), it is also a notable shift in social work developments in the past decade to observe a wider expansion of the profession within primary care services.

It is interesting that while primary care developments have been arrested in light of the wider socioeconomic context, developments in the child and family arena of practice have progressed despite the recession, although of course not unaffected by this in terms of employment restrictions, public service pay cuts and so on. Skehill (2005, p. 141) argued that

> it is difficult to deny the impact of genealogical factors in the 1990s which created major opportunities for social work in the field to expand. However, by looking further back in history, one might also attribute the present positioning of social work in part to its own archaeological construction as an expert strategy and mediator in the 'social'.

Both possibilities remain when we consider developments since, and a simplistic deductive approach is to be avoided. However, it would seem that, through the rise and fall of the Celtic Tiger, another momentous process occurred alongside this in the wider genealogical context, resulting in massive challenges to the cultural, social, political, intellectual and institutional discourses of our child welfare service at multiple levels. This included:

- disclosures of horrific abuse and human rights violations in Catholic-run institutions (see Government of Ireland, 2009; Holohan, 2011), leaving Church and state culpable of unacceptable wrongdoing by their actions or lack thereof (see Powell et al., 2012; McGregor, 2014a)

- exposure of failures and limitations within the child protection and welfare system in terms of responding to serious child neglect and abuse concerns (e.g. HSE, 2010)

- deaths of children known to the child protection and welfare services (Shannon and Gibbons, 2012).

The *National Children's Strategy* (Department of Health and Children, 2000) highlights the explicit attempt to move from a residual, reactive discourse of child welfare to a proactive, children's rights orientation. This shift is reflected in the plethora of developments relating to independent representation for children via the Office of the Children's Ombudsman in 2002 to the 2012 Referendum on Children's Rights and the Children and Families Bill, which legislated for the establishment of an independent agency to deliver comprehensive child and family services. Such developments are detailed in Chapter 4. For this chapter, a few points can be emphasized.

First, the greater social and public profile of child abuse as a political and social issue has resulted in increased media attention to social work in the past decade. In terms of media focus on social work, a review of Irish print media by Gaughan and Garrett (2011, p. 276) found that 'reporting of social work and social services was focused on work with children and families and, more specifically, child abuse cases'. Media reporting of the deaths of Sharon Grace and her two children (2005) and the Dunne family (2007) highlighted the lack of social work out-of-hours service as well as the repeated calls by social workers for the establishment of such a service to try to prevent such tragedies from occurring (Gaughan and Garrett, 2011). The *Roscommon Child Care Case: Report of the Inquiry Team to the Health Service Executive* (HSE, 2010) drew negative media attention to the fact that social workers had been involved with a family over a prolonged period of time during which the children continued to suffer severe abuse inflicted by their parents. Cumulatively, reports such as these 'raised public awareness, increased demands for better protection and placed child protection social work under increased scrutiny' (Featherstone et al., 2012, p. 56). However, McNulty (2008) points out that, with some exceptions, social workers have not been at the receiving end of negative publicity compared to that experienced by social workers in the UK.

Second, it seems that, as in the case of the 1991 Act and its implementation being largely influenced by the outcry after the *Kilkenny Incest Investigation*, the current emphasis on developments in child and family services, over primary care for example, can likewise be best understood within the wider social and political context in which the change is occurring. The simplistic discourse of 'purging the past' in this new development is palpable and in need of problematization (McGregor, 2014a).

Third, while not denying the dominance of a political discourse on the development of the new agency for child and family services, its implementation also confirms a continuity of the now well-recognized expertise of professional social work as frontline practitioners in child protection and welfare practice, especially at the socio-legal interface of risk management and family support (Skehill, 2004). Tusla, the Child and Family Agency established on 1 January 2014, poses a number of challenges and opportunities for professional social work but has not questioned the centrality of the profession to the front line of the risk management dimension of the service. This leadership role implies the need to ensure that child protection is maintained as part of a continuum of family child and service interventions (using Meitheal, for example, the Tulsa-led national practice model), and not a marginalized 'end point' of the 'rainbow' of intervention. This is a responsibility social work and its managers must prioritize. And finally, those 'outside' the agency, such as those in HSE primary care, have the potential to be leaders in promoting interagency cooperation and ensuring against segregation of services, one of the concerns of social work and social care practitioners reflected in a recent survey (McGregor, 2014b).

In considering how this leadership can be maximized, one significant and positive factor for social work in Ireland within the past decade has been the increase in social workers who have moved on to senior management positions within the HSE and the NGO sector, giving the profession a stronger leadership position than has been evident in any moment in its past (see Skehill, 1999). This has brought a more pronounced social work perspective on the development of services within the agencies. In terms of structures, as detailed above, it is planned to dissolve the HSE at some unspecified future date, with the Department of Health taking direct responsibility for service provision. For many social workers, however, this change will be immaterial, as they now form part of Tusla (a conjunction of the Irish words for new (tús) and day (lá)).

Managerialism, registration and accountability

Alongside the positive potential indicated in the increased visibility of social work at management level (to some extent), the discourse of managerialism is, in itself, one that has been a matter of major concern in Ireland in the context of the introduction of new business processes, the Health Information and Quality Authority and the general ethos of managerialism that has imbued social services. Of course, this is a matter of concern far beyond current Irish developments. Since the 1990s, focus has been placed on the impact of managerialism on social work practice in many jurisdictions. Referring to social work practice in the English context, for example, Rogowski (2012, p. 928) comments that 'recent changes to social work's organization and practice have amounted to deprofessionalization because the overriding concerns have been with encouraging managerialism and the social work business'. This echoes earlier concerns raised by Munro (2004) about the impact of audit on social work practice. Similarly, in relation to social work in Australia, Burton and van den Broek (2009, p. 1328) refer to the 'abundance of process, procedures, monitoring and audit systems which feature strongly in much of the new public management schema'. Moreover, they argue, 'increased scrutiny by the media has also exacerbated focus on benchmarks and performance indicators'.

The landscape of business process modelling, quality assurance and increased accountability denotes a significant discontinuity in the history of social work and represents a wider neoliberal trend reaching far beyond the country and the profession. Indeed, it is remarkable to note, for example, the interface between social work developments in the four UK jurisdictions, especially England, and the Republic of Ireland. At one and the same time, debates in the UK emphasize the overreliance on procedures and the need to re-emphasize relationships (e.g. Munro, 2011), while debates in Ireland lament the potential loss of the same. Both positions require a historically informed context to avoid polemic positioning that regulations and procedures are, in themselves, good or bad and show the benefit and importance of opportunities for shared learning across jurisdictions, especially neighbouring ones. Featherstone et al. (2012, p. 59), for example, argue that Ireland can gain the benefit of hindsight by considering the consequences of England's decision to 'privilege the management of institutional risk over the improvement of practice'. Such shared learning would help problematize the issue and avoid overly simplistic or deductive analyses that wrongly imply that procedures, regulations and accountability are bad things. This would hardly be sustainable in light of the shocking evidence we have of what can happen in an unregulated system, as highlighted in the report on child abuse (Government of Ireland, 2009; see also Skehill, 2011), and equally myopic arguments about the importance of relationships, as if it were a newly derived contemporary concern as opposed to a historically continuous feature of social work, taking particular prominence at certain moments in time (e.g. Perlman, 1979; see also McGregor, 2014c).

A related area where social work can benefit directly from prior experience, and cross-border collaboration in particular, is that of registration, as this has been required in the UK and Northern Ireland for some years. The Northern Ireland Social Care Council, which is responsible for the registration of social workers and social care workers, was established under the Health and Personal Social Services (Northern Ireland) Act 2001. In the Republic of Ireland, the Social Workers Registration Board (SWRB) was set up in 2010, the first such board to be created under the Health and Social Care Professionals Act 2005. This Act provided for the establishment of 12 separate professional boards in the so-called 'allied health professions', under one umbrella council. Unlike the UK, separate boards are to be created for social work and social care.

The overall objective stated in the 2005 Health and Social Care Professionals Act is to 'protect the public by fostering high standards of professional conduct and professional education, training and competence among registrants of that profession' (Article 27(1)). The SWRB comprises 13 members, the majority of whom are lay, with the remaining representing managers, educators and social workers delivering frontline services. The register for current practitioners closed on 31 May 2013, from which date only those registered, or who had applied for registration, are able to use the protected title of 'social worker'. The SWRB is also the competent authority for qualifications obtained outside the state. Its Annual Report 2012 lists the number of applications received/processed for that year as a total of 29, the majority of whom came from Great Britain or Northern Ireland, with the next highest proportion coming from Poland. This relatively low number of international applications is in marked contrast to figures for 2006 quoted above. Over 3,000 social workers were registered by the SWRB by the end of 2014.

The main reason why the Social Workers Registration Board was the first board to be established under the Act was that its role was partly preceded by the National Social Work Qualifications Board and its predecessor, the Central Council for Education and Training in Social Work (CCETSW), showing a strong continuity in the professional accreditation of social work as a strategy. As far back as the 1970s, there had been pressure to establish a national board to oversee social work education and training (Kearney, 2005). In 1990, the UK's CCETSW withdrew from the accreditation of social work courses in the Republic of Ireland, which resulted in the setting up of the National Validation Body on Social Work Qualifications and Training, to be replaced by the National Social Work Qualifications Board (NSWQB) in 1997. In turn, the NSWQB ceased to function on 9 March 2011, the date on which the Social Workers Registration Board was formally established. In its last Annual Report, the then director of the NSWQB commented that 'the landscape of social work is a changing one, it requires national oversight to ensure relevant and comprehensive information is gathered to inform policies and decisions' (NSWQB, 2010).

However, the Health and Social Care Professionals Act does not allow for this broad scope. In this way, social work has lost out on the capacity to contribute to policy by engaging in projects such as those undertaken by the NSWQB in relation to social work posts (NSWQB, 1999, 2001, 2006), the mobility of social workers in Ireland, North and South (O'Brien, 2001), and the induction study on the needs of newly qualified social workers (NSWQB, 2003). What has been gained, on the other hand, by the creation of the SWRB is the formal system of registration, the protected title and the inbuilt requirement of continuing professional development, which will help to ensure that practitioners will be up to date in their knowledge and skills.

Linked to this, fitness to practice is obviously an area for concern for social workers, given the difficult and complex situations with which they must engage. Evidence from England and Northern Ireland, however, would indicate that there is less to fear than might be thought. In Northern Ireland, where over 21,000 social workers and social care practitioners are registered, there were just 258 complaints, 22 of which were the subject of conduct hearings (NISCC, 2014). In the same year, the Health & Care Professions Council (England) (HCPC, 2014) pointed out that only 0.64% of registrants had a complaint made against them. Further interrogation of these figures did show that, of the range of professional groups included, social workers (including those engaged in social care work) had a higher percentage than average, with a complaint rate of 1.22%, but also had the largest number of cases closed because the concerns raised did not meet the standard of acceptance.

Champions of social justice and human rights

Social work as a profession defines itself internationally as a practice of promoting social justice and human rights (IFSW, 2014). Likewise, in an Irish context, we have always (rightly) aspired to emphasize our advocacy, value-based and justice orientation. The past decade has tested the profession in this regard and in many ways helped to expose our persistent continuity as well as the major changes we have found ourselves affected by, or influencing. While there are different views on the extent to which promoting social justice and human rights has ever been a core practice of Irish social work, it seems fair and accurate to say that the voice of the social work profession has not been evident in highlighting the devastating effects of cutbacks in services to its most vulnerable clients. It must be acknowledged that this is partly a governance issue, whereby individual social workers are limited from speaking about specific practice by their employee status. It is also evident that the Irish Association of Social Workers has had limited success in engaging media interest in social work issues and, more generally, representing the critical voice of social work during times of key social debates – such as the cuts to respite care for persons with disability or the lack of political will to address the increasing number of families experiencing serious deprivation as a result of the ongoing impact of the recession and the associated austerity measures. Other organizations have emerged to make some contribution in this regard, for example the Social Work Action Network, founded in the UK and now with established branches in Ireland. An important factor that influences the limited involvement of social workers in promoting social justice outside their individual day-to-day practice is that Irish social workers are not required to join their professional association and many choose not to do so; for some, their union provides the necessary representation they require. Thus, a relatively small professional voice is further diminished. This is not unique to Ireland. Marston and McDonald (2012, p. 1030) point out social work's 'relative lack of profile compared to other professions'. They comment that 'the British Association of Social Workers has not been able to operate as an effective mass-membership organization, thereby limiting its ability to affect the destiny of the profession'.

Conclusion

The ethos of using history to inform the present that has informed this discussion is perhaps best reflected in the following statement from McGregor's recent commentary on the use of history to critically reflect on social work in the UK (McGregor, 2014c). Here, McGregor (2014c, p. 10) argued that to develop a critical and informed understanding of the present with reference to the past 'necessitates an engagement with history that acknowledges both achievements and failures ... some reasons to be ashamed ... and other reasons to be proud', and that 'it necessitates the promotion of history not as an "add on" contextual dimension but as a core and central element that informs social work research, education and practice' (Shaw, 2008, cited in McGregor, 2014c, p. 10).

This chapter has allowed us to only briefly highlight some of the major changes in social work that have happened in the past decade. In so doing, we have taken an embedded history of the present approach to ask what are the main issues and challenges in social work post-Celtic Tiger that represent our 'key moments'. We chose four illustrative themes that highlight some of the continuities, discontinuities and challenges. It seems we can say that, to some extent, there has been a transformation in the nature and form of social work in recent times, with some notable discontinuities from the past, such as the impact of managerialism and the relatively greater power to influence gained by social work's professional status and recognition. Alongside this, some persistent continuities remain in the core nature and form of social work. We hope that our discussion has contributed to each of the questions posed in this book. However, by way of a focused discussion and conclusion, we have chosen here to concentrate in more detail on one particular question: How can Irish social work advance a critical analysis and a progressive politics? In response, we wish to respond to this with a summary of how a critical engagement with the past can indeed advance such critical analysis.

There are a number of messages arising from the themes considered in this chapter that indicate how social work can contribute to the advancement of a critical analysis and progressive politics. With regard to the impact of demographic change, it would seem that it can be through a continuation of research on this topic, and the development of education and training around cultural competence, diversity and the promotion of rights of marginalized ethnic groups and asylum seekers that we can advance a critical approach. This work can build on excellent resources from elsewhere (e.g. Sue, 2001; Laird, 2008) as well as lead on the particular challenges in practice in Ireland, specifically in light of its monocultural and rather unchallenged past experience of ethnic diversity outside the indigenous population.

Regarding the second theme, service expansion, retraction and social work expertise, it seems that a major contribution we can make to informed critical analysis and a progressive politics (with a small p) is to engage more critically and assertively with the historically continuous tension that seems to have occupied too much space in our past: that is, the question of whether we are best to develop as a specialist (child welfare oriented) or generic profession. Too explicit a distinction between both dimensions of social work offers an unhelpful dichotomy that seems to have become part of our received history and thus our present distinction between 'child protection and welfare' and the 'rest'. The genealogical conditions of social work at present, in light of new structures of delivering services for children and families and primary care, offer a great opportunity to lead in breaking down the false dichotomy between supporting adults through primary care/mental health services and working with children/families, embracing and accepting that it is a bit of both (generic and specialist). The challenge is ensuring that we contribute to enhancing and leading on interagency cooperation between the independent Child and Family Agency and the HSE primary care services and embrace a life course approach, whereby we promote and recognize the importance of expertise across the life course for generic practice while valuing the expertise that has already been well established (e.g. in child protection and welfare).

Regarding the third theme, this is an area where we can genuinely attempt to connect wider critical theory (e.g. the impact of neoliberalism, globalization, managerialism, the risk society and so on) and social work practice to help problematize the current developments within this wider societal context. One continuity in the history of social work generally, and indeed a defining characteristic of social work education and training, is the balance required between a form of 'academic learning' and 'practice learning'. How knowledge has been transmitted and applied over time and space is a subject for a paper in itself. Just focusing on the specific problem in the present, adapting to more overt managerial contexts for practice, it would seem there is the possibility to create opportunities for shared learning about the wider dynamics of this context, including a re-establishment of a closer critical relationship between Irish and UK educators and practitioners, wherein the potential for mutual learning and advancement of critical perspectives is immense.

Finally, regarding the fourth theme, we are unsure of the answer to this. It is challenge, because a look back to history shows two elements:

1. An aspiration towards this wider justice role reinforced by the international definition of social work (IFSW, 2014).

2. Evidence that, notwithstanding some excellent pockets of evidence of human rights and social justice practice, at almost every point in its history, this has not been the dominant discourse of social work practice and training.

While appreciating the challenges for the profession during the past decade, we must not be overly 'rose-tinted' to deny that we also have to question if enough has and is being done to advocate within the profession, to the wider social and political context, for those most affected by the recession. The overt contexts of utter injustice are alarming and difficult sometimes to comprehend from a 21st-century perspective. Sadly, some scenarios seem too closely reminiscent of periods in the past where the economic circumstances of the vast majority of services users was the most pronounced influence on all aspects of their lives and wellbeing. The IFSW statement of ethical principles (2012) is unequivocal about the responsibility of social workers to seek the redress of such scenarios. Article 4.2.4 stipulates that 'social workers have a duty to bring to the attention of their employers, policy makers, politicians and the general public situations where resources are inadequate or where the distribution of resources, policies and practices are oppressive, unfair or harmful'. The renewed definition of social work by the IFSW in July 2014 states that:

> Social work is a practice-based profession and an academic discipline that promotes social change and development, social cohesion, and the empowerment

and liberation of people. Principles of social justice, human rights, collective responsibility and respect for diversities are central to social work. Underpinned by theories of social work, social sciences, humanities and indigenous knowledge, social work engages people and structures to address life challenges and enhance wellbeing. The above definition may be amplified at national and/or regional levels.

This statement sets a strong challenge for us to aspire towards practice underpinned by human rights and social justice, although we have some way to go before the laudable principles are clearly evidenced in dominant mainstream practice.

References

Broadhurst, K., Hall, C., Wastell, D. et al. (2010) 'Risk, instrumentalism and the humane project in social work: identifying the informal logics of risk management in children's statutory services', *British Journal of Social Work*, 40(4), 1046–64.

Burton, J. and van den Broek, D. (2009) 'Accountable and countable: information management systems and the bureaucratization of social work', *British Journal of Social Work*, 39(7), 1326–42.

Christie, A. (2002) 'Responses of the social work profession to unaccompanied children seeking asylum in the Republic of Ireland', *European Journal of Social Work*, 5(2), 187–98.

Christie, A. (2011) 'White children first? Whiteness, child protection policies and the politics of "race" in Ireland', in Lynch, D. and Burns, K. (eds) *Children's Rights and Child Protection: Critical Times and Critical Issues*, Manchester, Manchester University Press.

Christie, A. and Burns K. (2006) 'Special Edition of Journal: Community and social service responses to asylum seekers', *Irish Journal of Applied Social Studies*, 7(2), 6–17.

Considine, M. and Dukelow, F. (2009) *Irish Social Policy: A Critical Introduction*, Dublin, Gill & Macmillan.

Dalikeni, C. (2012) The Views and Experiences of Asylum Seeking Families within the Child Protection System in Ireland, PhD, Queen's University Belfast.

Dean, M. (1994) *Critical and Effective Histories*, London, Routledge.

Department of Health (1985) *Committee on Social Work Report*, Dublin, Department of Health.

Department of Health and Children (2000) *The National Children's Strategy: Our Children, Their Lives*, Dublin, Stationery Office.

Department of Health and Children (2004) *The National Primary Care Steering Group: Progress Report*, Dublin, Stationery Office.

Fahey, T. and Fanning, B. (2010) 'Immigration and socio-spatial segregation in Dublin, 1996-2006', *Urban Studies*, 47(8), 1623–42.

Fahey, T., Russell, H. and Whelan, C.T. (eds) (2007) *Best of Times? The Social Impact of the Celtic Tiger*, Dublin, IPA.

Featherstone, B., White, S. and Wastell, D. (2012) 'Ireland's opportunity to learn from England's difficulties? Auditing uncertainty in child protection', *Irish Journal of Applied Social Studies*, 12(1), 48–62.

Foucault, M. (1977) *Discipline and Punish*, Harmondsworth, Penguin.

Foucault, M. (1980) 'Questions of method', in Faubion, J.D. (ed.) (1994) *Michel Foucault: Essential Works*, vol. 3, Harmondsworth, Penguin.

Garland, D. (1992) 'Criminological knowledge and its relation to power: Foucault's genealogy and criminology today', *British Journal of Criminology*, 32(4), 403–22.

Garrity, Z. (2010) 'Discourse analysis, Foucault and social work research: identifying some methodological complexities', *Journal of Social Work*, 10(2), 193–210.

Government of Ireland (2009) *Report of the Commission to Inquire into Child Abuse* (Ryan Report), Dublin, Stationery Office.

Guaghan, L. and Garrett, P.M. (2011) 'The "most twisted and unaccountable force in the state"? Newspaper accounts of social work in the Republic of Ireland in troubled times', *Journal of Social Work*, 12(3), 267–86.

HCPC (Health & Care Professions Council) (2014) *Fitness to Practice Annual Report 2014*, London, HCPC.

Holohan, C. (2011) *In Plain Sight: Responding to the Ferns, Ryan, Murphy and Cloynes Reports*, Dublin, Ireland Amnesty International.

HSE (Health Service Executive) (2010) *Roscommon Child Care Case: Report of the Inquiry Team to the Health Service Executive*, Dublin, HSE.

IFSW (International Federation of Social Work) (2012) *Statement of Ethical Principles*, http://ifsw.org/policies/statement-of-ethical-principles/.

IFSW (2014) *Definition of Social Work*, http://ifsw.org/policies/definition-of-social-work/.

Kearney, N. (2005) 'Social work education: its origins and growth', in Kearney, N. and Skehill, C. (eds) *Social Work in Ireland: Historical Perspectives*, Dublin, Institute of Public Administration.

Kinlen, L. (2013) 'Welcome to Ireland: seeking protection as an asylum seeker or through resettlement – different avenues, different reception', *Refuge*, 28(2), 31–47.

Laird, S.E. (2008) *Anti-oppressive Social Work: A Guide for Developing Cultural Competence*, London, Sage.

Lees, A., Meyer, E. and Rafferty J. (2013) 'From Menzies Lyth to Munro: the problem of managerialism', *British Journal of Social Work*, 43(3), 542–58.

McGregor, C. (2014a) 'Why is history important at moments of transition? The case of "transformation" of Irish child welfare via the new Child and Family Agency', *European Journal of Social Work*, 17(5), 771–83.

McGregor, C. (2014b) 'The Child and Family Agency 2014: initial views and experiences of social work and social care practitioners', *Irish Social Worker*, spring/summer, 2–5.

McGregor, C. (2014c) 'History as a resource for the future: a response to "Best of Times, Worst of Times: Social Work and Its Moment"', *British Journal of Social Work*, doi:10.1093/bjsw/bct197.

McNulty, F. (2008) 'Radical or redundant? Irish social workers, the print media and the Irish Association of Social Workers', in Burns, K. and Lynch, D. (eds) *Child Protection and Welfare Work: Contemporary Themes and Practical Perspectives*, Dublin, A & A Farmar.

Marston, G. and McDonald, C. (2012) 'Getting beyond "heroic agency" in conceptualising social workers as policy actors in the twenty-first century', *British Journal of Social Work*, 42(6), 1022–38.

Munro, E. (2004) 'The impact of audit on social work practice', *British Journal of Social Work*, 34(8), 1075–95.

Munro, E. (2011) *The Munro Review of Child Protection: Final Report – A Child-Centred System*, London, TSO.

Ní Raghallaigh, M. (2011) 'Relationships with family, friends and God: the experiences of unaccompanied minors living in Ireland', in Darmody, M., Tyrrell, N. and Song, S. (eds) *The Changing Faces of Ireland: Exploring the Lives of Immigrant and Ethnic Minority Children*, Rotterdam, Sense Publishers.

Ní Raghallaigh, M. (2013) 'The causes of mistrust amongst asylum seekers and refugees: insights from research with unaccompanied asylum seeking minors living in the Republic of Ireland', *Journal of Refugee Studies*, 27(1), 82–100.

Ní Raghallaigh, M. and Sirriyeh, A. (2014) 'The negotiation of culture in foster care placements for separated refugee and asylum seeking young people in Ireland and England', *Childhood*, doi: 10.1177/0907568213519137.

Ní Raghallaigh, M., Allen, M., Cunniffe, R. and Quin, S. (2013) 'The experiences of primary care social workers in Ireland', *Social Work in Health Care*, 52(10), 930–946.

NISCC (Northern Ireland Social Care Council) (2014) *Annual Report and Accounts for the Year Ended 31st March 2014*, Belfast, NISCC.

NSWQB (National Social Work Qualifications Board) (1999) *Social Work Posts in Ireland*, Dublin, NSWQB.

NSWQB (2003) *Induction Study: A Study of the Induction Needs of Newly Qualified and Non-nationally Qualified Social Workers in Health Boards*, Dublin, NSWQB.

NSWQB (2006) *Social Work Posts in Ireland*, Dublin, NSWQB.

NSWQB (2010) *Final Report 2010*, Dublin, NSWQB.

O'Brien, A. (2001) *Crossing Borders: Social Work Mobility Study*, Dublin, NSWQB.

Office of the Minister for Integration (2008) *Migrant Nation: Statement on Integration Strategy and Diversity Management*, Dublin, Stationery Office.

Perlman, H. (1979) *Relationship: The Heart of Helping People*, Chicago, University of Chicago Press.

Powell F., Geoghegan, M., Scanlon, M. and Swirak, K. (2012) 'The Irish charity myth, child abuse and human rights', *British Journal of Social Work*, 43(1), 7–23.

Redmond, B., Guerin, S. and Nolan, B. (2011) *The Retention of Social Workers in the Health Services: An Evidence-based Assessment*, Dublin, HSE/UCD.

Rogowski, S. (2012) 'Social work with children and families: challenges and possibilities in the neo-liberal world', *British Journal of Social Work*, 42(5), 921–40.

Shanon G. and Gibbons, N. (2012) *Report of the Independent Child Death Review Group*, Dublin, DCYA.

Shaw, I. (2008) 'Merely experts? Reflections on the history of social work, science and research', *Research, Policy and Planning*, 26(1), 57–65.

Skehill, C. (1999) *The History of Social Work in Ireland: A Historical Perspective*, Lampeter, Edwin Mullen Press.

Skehill, C. (2004) *History of the Present of Child Protection and Welfare Social Work in Ireland*, Lampeter, Edwin Mellen Press.

Skehill, C. (2005) 'Child protection and welfare social work in the Republic of Ireland', in Kearney, N. and Skehill, C. (eds) *Social Work in Ireland: Historical Perspectives*, Dublin, Institute of Public Administration.

Skehill, C. (2007) 'Researching the history of social work: exposition of a history of the present approach', *European Journal of Social Work*, 10(4), 449–463.

Skehill, C. (2011) 'The origins of child welfare under the poor law and the emergence of the institutional versus family care debate', in Crossman, V. and Gray P. (eds) *Poverty and Welfare in Ireland 1838–1948*, Dublin, Irish Academic Press.

Sue, D.W. (2001) 'Multidimensional facets of cultural competence', *Counselling Psychologist*, 29(6), 790–821.

2

Social Work in a 'Globalized' Ireland

Alastair Christie and Trish Walsh

Introduction

Ireland has been identified as one of the most globalized countries in the world through its engagement in global trade, global capital movements, global exchanges of technology and ideas and global labour movements. In this chapter, we explore some of the different claims made about globalization, and examine the impact of the activities and processes of globalization on the contexts in which social workers practise and the shifting roles and definitions of social work.

As discussed in Chapter 3, this 'openness' to international flows of capital has resulted in Ireland being particularly vulnerable to fluctuations in the global economy and heavily reliant on international foreign investment. The government's free-market political ideology that promoted deregulation, its inappropriate fiscal stimulation of the housing boom (leading to the eventual bust), and the unethical relationship between property developers, politicians and bankers were all major contributors to the dramatic downturn in the Irish economy and deep cuts in public sector spending (Drudy and Collins, 2011). The collapse of particular areas of the private sector and the intro-duction of 'austerity politics' led to cutbacks in public sector funding and resulted in a return to high levels of emigration – 89,000 people emigrated from Ireland between April 2012 and March 2013 (Glyn et al., 2013). As job opportunities for social workers have shrunk, an increasing number of newly qualified workers will have emigrated. While globalization processes have not necessarily led to the retrenchment of welfare spending in 'mature' welfare states (Swank, 2005), in Ireland the historically underfunded, fragmented and patchy welfare system has been particularly hard hit by the economic/politi-cal crisis, with the resultant cuts in public spending on social services.

However, globalization presents more than merely economic and political challenges to individual nation states, and has led to fundamental shifts taking place in the relationships between a global order based on sovereign nation states and new formations shaped by expanding numbers of cultural, social, political and economic networks and increasing movement of people across national borders, all aided by technological advances. The phenomenon of globalization also has profound implications regarding the emergence of highly differentiated migration regimes, thereby increasing inequality and complexity in transnational family forms (Ní Laoire et al., 2010). More and more often, social workers are required to adopt a transnational way of working with individuals, families and communities who 'reside in different countries, but sustain active, regular links and connections with one another across state borders' (Yeates, 2009, p. 23).

Globalization has increased the social, cultural, political and economic interconnectedness of our lives. Held et al. (1999, p. 16) considered it to be a transformational phenomenon and 'a process (or set of processes) which embodies a transformation in the spatial organisation of social relations and transaction, expressed in transcontinental or interregional flows and networks of activity, interaction and power'. Central to their analysis is an emphasis on the positive impact of globalization. However, Pugh and Gould (2000, p. 124) caution against an uncritical adoption of globalization as a phenomenon, in that 'the omnipresence of the term [globalization] contributes much to the "taken-for-granted" acceptance of the idea'. Midgley (2008, p. 7) argues that no one perspective on globalization can accurately capture 'the complexities of contemporary, global, cultural dynamics', instead, social workers need to appreciate 'the fluid, multifaceted, and multidirectional character of contemporary cultural exchanges'. So, for social workers practising in a globalized Ireland, a central aspect of practice should be appreciating the potential of such diversity and mobility, while not underestimating the complexity they may add to many organizational contexts where normative standards and a social control function may be premised on the inaccurate assumptions of Ireland as essentially monocultural and 'white' (Christie, 2010).

Globalization and welfare

The 'global turn' in social sciences has fundamentally challenged the view that welfare and social services can be understood as exclusively happening within the borders of nation states (Yeates, 2008). The assumption that welfare regimes are automatically linked to nation states has been increasingly questioned, with new linkages being made by the nation state and welfare regimes (Clarke, 2005). The question for social work is: How do these realignments between institutions, policies and practices impact on social work and how can social work influence them? The globalization of welfare is not a new phenomenon. Colonial powers often 'tried out' welfare policies to regulate colonized populations (Midgley and Piachaud, 2011); national systems of education and policing were developed in Ireland before being established in countries within the UK (Akenson, 1970). However, the current phenomenon of globalization is having a much more profound impact on the provision of social services as:

- the territorial nature of nation states becomes less secure and traditional boundaries have become more permeable and 'leaky'

- the power and authority of the nation state has become more readily challenged by international, regional and local forms of governance

- new forms of family and community life are shaped by new patterns of migration, mobility and technological 'connectedness' (Clarke, 2005).

Social workers are having to respond to new forms of living, in which service users' lives are 'characterized by dense, extensive forms of networks of interconnections and interdependencies that routinely transcend national boundaries' (Yeates, 2008, p. 3), with some increasingly 'trapped' within local areas, isolated by poverty. Globalization has created new forms of poverty and inequality, in which services users have to rely on connections outside the nation state and, at the same time, are being made increasingly immobile through poverty, being denied access to new forms of mobility and technology. Welfare states and nations are constitutively linked, as welfare is one of the ways in which nations are created and sustained (Lewis, 1998). Welfare states

> *attempt* to reinforce or enforce certain 'ways of life'; they regulate forms of being and behaviour; they categorize and classify the population (and deal with its different segments); and they manage the relationship between the public and private realms. (Clarke, 2005, p. 412)

It is questionable how far Ireland is a 'welfare state' (particularly when compared to social democratic welfare states in Europe); however, even in Ireland arrangements for welfare have an important role in constructing 'difference' (see Christie, 2004) – gendered, racialized and sexualized differences, and differences between those identified as able-bodied and those identified as disabled. Many of the struggles social workers have experienced are concerned with challenging these categorizations and giving voice to those who have been 'othered' by welfare state policies. In Ireland, the combination of the Catholic Church and the state have had a particularly powerful, if now more often challenged, role in reproducing the 'other' in Irish society. Welfare policies have a role in managing internal boundaries within states but an equally important role in managing the boundaries of the nation state, and in particular the differential access routes for citizens and 'non-citizens' to welfare services, including health, education, housing and personal social services, while facilitating processes that determine individuals' rights to citizenship or potential deportation. Social workers have been most clearly drawn into these processes through the provision of state care to separated children (see Chapter 6) and through differential access to social services depending on individual citizenship/residence/migration status.

In considering how social work is positioned and might want to position itself in the new 'globalized' welfare regimes, we identify five areas that require further analysis and action:

- migration, mobility and differentiated migration regimes

- social work with asylum seekers, refugees and the 'undocumented'

- the global care chain

- the feminization of migration and transnational family forms

- the development of an international social work profession and new forms of resistance.

Migration, mobility and differentiated migration regimes

'Historically, Ireland has never had to deal with large-scale immigration, whether of refugees and asylum-seekers or labour migrants' (Torode et al., 2001, p. 42). Reasons for this include:

1. Ireland, because of its geographical and political isolation in the first part of the 20th century, was not as accessible to migrants as other European countries.

2. The weakness of the Irish economy resulted in high levels of unemployment and predominately outward migration.

Significant changes came about in the 1990s, when *local* factors, such as a more buoyant economy, increased communication and international transport links, and a more liberalized cultural and political environment, combined with *global* factors, such as increased demands on European countries to address the needs of refugees and asylum seekers resulting from dramatic political changes internationally, the increasing presence of multinational and global companies requiring highly skilled workers, and a general increase in worker mobility. Domestically, the global plight of asylum seekers began to elicit a more proactive and sympathetic response from the Irish government, but it was only with the steady increase in the numbers of asylum seekers arriving in Ireland that policies and services were developed. From 1994, when 39 applications for asylum were made, the numbers peaked in 2000, when 10,938 applications were made. By 2008, applications had declined to less than 4,000 per year (ORAC, 2013). Although the implementation of the 1996 Refugee Act led to the development of a more structured system for processing applications, the Irish regime continues to attract much criticism for the extremely high level of refusals, with only 1% of applications granted on initial application, the lengthy period applicants have to wait for decisions (www.intercultural.ie), the harsh conditions endured by applicants in direct provision hostel accommodation and the ban on employment, and the specific treatment of unaccompanied minors seeking asylum (Christie, 2003). It is hardly surprising, then, that the numbers seeking asylum in Ireland have continued to plummet, with only 869 applications received for the year up until the end of November 2013 (ORAC, 2013).

The decrease in inward migration through the asylum-seeking process in the past decade has been matched by an increase in working migrants registered with government departments. It is worth noting that until 2000, no work permit system existed in Ireland and for those from outside the EU, 'those who wished to enter the country, either as refugees or as labour migrants, could do so only through the asylum process' (Torode et al., 2001, p. 42). Despite the worsening unemployment figures since the global financial crisis in 2008, levels of inward migration have continued to increase year on year, with the annual figure up to April 2013 at 55,900 (up from 52,700 in 2012) (www.cso.ie). Even taking into account the continued increase in outward migration of foreign nationals and Irish nationals (up from 87,100 in 2012 to 89,000 in 2013), the Irish population continues to increase, aided by a relatively high birth rate. The population of the country was estimated at 4,593,000 in April 2013, of which over half a million people identify as non-Irish born.

An analysis of the official statistics available from government departments confirms that Ireland is now encountering a differentiated migration regime. There is sustained inward migration of highly skilled workers alongside sustained outward migration of Irish nationals seeking better job opportunities and citing quality of life factors as motivation. The percentage of the population born outside Ireland remains at 12%, but 'while being born outside Ireland is a clear indicator of immigration, it is not necessarily an indicator of nationality, since a significant number of people born outside Ireland self-identify as Irish' (Gilmartin, 2012, p. 5).

Castles and Miller (2009, p. 7) described contemporary international migration as part of a 'transnational revolution that is reshaping societies and politics across the globe'. Several factors have contributed to this, including:

- a general increase in international mobility

- binding European directives on the free movement of labour and students

- the increasing ease with which people can now keep in contact through communication technologies

- the ubiquity of modern telecommunications, where 'alluring images of life in the privileged developed countries are beamed into the most remote and materially impoverished corners of the world' (Walsh et al., 2010, p. 83).

The transformation of migration policy, from a situation in 2000 when Ireland lacked even the facility of work permits, to the one in 2013 where Immigrant Investor schemes have been launched, citizenship ceremonies developed, and Irish Visa Waiver programme implemented, is nothing short of dramatic. Yet it appears to be economic priorities alone that have driven such changes, as Alan Shatter, minister for justice, equality and law reform, said: 'I am prioritizing initiatives to reform the immigration system to contribute to investment in the State and to assist in economic development' (INIS, 2014). In other words, official Irish policy towards migration seeks to discourage asylum-seeking applicants, while incentivizing international companies to establish bases in Ireland, and in the minister's words, prioritizing the global labour demands of such companies through work visas and residency schemes, all to assist in the economic rebuilding of the country. In Ireland, as elsewhere, 'differentiated migration regimes have been set up, to encourage the highly-skilled to be mobile, while low-skilled workers and people feeling persecution are excluded ... in the globalized world, mobility has become the most powerful and most coveted stratifying factor' (Bauman, 1998, p. 9). Welfare rights have been restricted for some time for migrant workers from some Eastern European countries, in addition to a more active monitoring of transnational marriage patterns in order to identify and repress the 'exploitation' of EU citizenship and marriage rules. The presence of such a differentiated migration regime has significant implications for social work practice, as it contributes directly to inequality and the risk of unfair treatment of people in need who are dependent on the citizenship status they hold. For example, since the collapse of the construction industry in 2007/08, homeless services have reported a marked increase in vulnerable homeless Eastern European men, originally employed in such industries. The official government response to the plight of such destitute men is to offer assistance with the cost of repatriation. According to figures released by the Reception and Integration Agency (RIA, 2013), there was a 52% increase on those repatriated to European countries in 2013 compared with 2012. Of the 313 people repatriated in 2013, over 275 were from Eastern European countries.

As professionals committed to the principles of anti-oppressive practice and social justice, how should we respond? How feasible is it for practitioners in different fields of practice and organizational contexts to work in a genuinely anti-oppressive way, tackling inequality at the personal, cultural and structural levels (Dalrymple and Burke, 1996)? Do we need, as a start, to assess the extent to which our existing practices and organizational mandates recognize the constantly shifting and complex character of cultural exchanges (Midgley, 2008)?

Central to the debate has to be a recognition that social work already has a substantial body of knowledge, both practised and taught, which recognizes and seeks to understand the complexity and rewards of working with diversity and multiculturalism. The anti-racist perspective (Dominelli, 1997, 2002) in the UK and cultural competence approaches in North America attempted to address these issues at a practice level, although often also charged with a neglect of wider global social justice issues (Midgley, 2008). The changes over the past 20 years in the pace and spread of populations on the move is a phenomenon with which we need to grapple more actively, given the differentiated migration and welfare regimes now creating new forms of hardship in our society.

Social work with asylum seekers, refugees and the 'undocumented'

There is no one 'migrant experience' – individuals and families cross national borders with differing motivations and resources. The vast majority of migrants coming to Ireland in recent years have been a combination of citizens from a range of EU member states and returning Irish citizens. Migrants who come to Ireland seeking asylum (asylum seekers) and those who have recently gained rights to remain in Ireland (e.g. those who have been granted refugee status or 'leave to remain') are particularly vulnerable. Migrants who move to live in Ireland are rendered vulnerable through their lack of access to Irish citizenship and associated rights and services, exposure to racism, and lack of support networks in Ireland. This leads to migrants living in poverty and being denied basic human rights. Social workers can have an important role in working with migrants as individuals and groups as well as demanding social justice for migrants who are discriminated against by current policies and practices.

Asylum seekers and refugees will have experienced different degrees of loss and trauma prior to arriving in Ireland. They may have suffered from the death of and/or separation from family and friends and witnessed various forms of violence. In addition, some have been trafficked and/or 'smuggled' into Ireland. While those who cross national borders to seek asylum and refugee status have diverse backgrounds, they all share the experience of having little choice in having to leave, and suffer from the associated physical and emotional loss of having to leave (Sales, 2007). This involves a loss of possessions and economic resources as well as the loss of status and 'a profound loss of individuality, self-esteem and independence' (Sales, 2007, p. 86). These losses can result in high levels of depression and anxiety and a strong sense of being isolated and excluded from Irish society.

Three groups of migrants are particularly vulnerable in Ireland: adults and children living in direct provision; separated children; and those migrants that live in Ireland without legal right to remain (undocumented migrants). Social workers have direct and indirect contact with all these groups.

The system of direct provision, which requires asylum seekers to live in accommodation centres, was officially introduced in 2000. Approximately 4,500 asylum seekers (one-third of this number are children) currently live in direct provision, which is designed to meet asylum seekers' basic needs for accommodation and food. Asylum seekers are not allowed to work or study, or prepare their own food, and are dependent on an allowance of €19.50 (adults) and €9.60 (children) per week. Children are allowed to attend school. The accommodation centres vary considerably; two centres have been specially built for asylum seekers, but most centres are reconditioned hostels, hotels or guest houses run by private companies (FLAC, 2009). The average waiting time for a final decision on refugee status is four years (IRC, 2015). Asylum seekers spend long periods of inactivity in cramped conditions, often leading to depression, social isolation and poverty. Families are usually housed in one room, and singles share a room with others of the same sex. Shower and toilet facilities are usually shared and meals are cooked for the residents and served at a set time each day. There are no facilities for preparing meals in the vast majority of centres. There is little space for children to play or study. While there are interagency meetings that include RIA local social services, there is a lack of monitoring of accommodation centres, and they tend to remain largely outside the concern of social work services. Accommodation centres are part of a 'hidden Ireland' where few services, including social work, are provided. The years spent in these centres, waiting to be granted refugee status or 'leave to remain', or to be deported, are highly detrimental to the wellbeing of adults and children.

Social workers have a more direct role with separated children (some-times referred to as unaccompanied minors), who are children under the age of 18 years, living outside their country of origin and separated from both parents or legal/customary carer. When separated children are identified in Ireland (often by customs officials), they are placed in the state's care. There were 5,952 children referred to the specialist social work service between 2000 and 2010 as separated children. While the number of separated children has reduced in recent years, social workers' engagement with separated children raises a number of issues, mainly created by the tensions between child-centred and migration-centred policies:

- How far should separated children be treated as children and/or as migrants?

- Are social workers expected to prioritize the rights of children or support government policies to identify, isolate, detain and potentially deport migrants?

- How far do social work practices with separated children support the 'policing' of the state's national boundaries (Christie, 2002)?

- What role should social workers have in supporting separated children to apply for refugee status?

- What kinds of social work services should separated children be offered when they reach 18 years of age and are placed in adult accommodation centres?

- How should social workers respond to the significant number of separated children who go missing from their accommodation?

- To what extent should social workers cooperate in providing services to separated children that are substandard compared to services for other children (Horgan et al., 2012)?

While the position of separated children has improved, having been removed from largely unsupervised hostels and now being placed primarily with foster carers, there are still concerns about the adequacy of social work and fostering services, and in particular the return of separated children, when they reach 18 years of age, into the direct provision system.

The third group of migrants particularly vulnerable to exploitation are those migrants who are outside the asylum system and have no legal status to live in Ireland. 'Undocumented' migrants without legal status live a precarious existence in Ireland, largely without any form of social protection from the state, and increasingly forced to rely on under-funded voluntary sector groups (Lightman, 2012). These 'undocumented' migrants include:

- adult and child migrants who have left direct provision because of the conditions in the accommodation centres and/or their applications for refugee status or leave to remain have been turned down

- separated children who have left local authority care

- adults and children who may have been trafficked into Ireland but have not been identified by the police or migration services.

Trafficking in human beings is recognized as a growing phenomenon, but because of its clandestine and fluid nature, it is difficult to quantify and make more visible (Horgan et al., 2012). Some indication of the number of people trafficked into Ireland is seen in the number of possible victims reported to An Garda Síochána (the Irish police) – 66 in 2009, 78 in 2010 and 57 in 2011. The majority, 66%, were adult women, 24% were children and 10% were men (Group of Experts on Action against Trafficking in Human Beings, 2013). People are trafficked for two main reasons: forced labour and sexual exploitation. Forced labour can take the form of domestic servitude or working in industries such as tourism, agriculture, manufacturing and construction. Sexual exploitation takes place through prostitution and various forms of pornography. Busch-Armendariz et al. (2014) argue that social workers are going to play an increasingly important role in anti-trafficking initiatives, both in preventive work and through contact with potentially vulnerable groups, such as people who are homeless. Social workers working in the state, private and voluntary sectors increasingly face decisions about whether they can offer support to individuals and groups who are excluded from 'official' sources of social protection.

The global care chain

Already recognized as a phenomenon across the Middle East, North America and Europe, recent Irish studies have confirmed the extent to which migrant workers now form a significant proportion of the workforce in acute and community hospitals, and in particular in residential care settings for older people (Walsh and O'Shea, 2010). Migrant care workers made up approximately a third of all care workers in the elder care settings surveyed in this extensive study (Walsh and O'Shea, 2010, p. 1):

> the prevalence of foreign national carers in the long-stay sector for older people is marked by the fact that 49% of nursing staff and 36% of all staff in private nursing homes are from another country ... The public sector has also seen an increase in migrant care workers, as have agencies providing market-based home care services.

While these figures related to 2007, Walsh and O'Shea (2010, p. viii) consider the projected future need for migrant care workers would be strong despite the economic decline experienced since 2008, given that

> the strongest determinant of the demand for foreign national care workers is the difficulty in hiring and retaining Irish carers ... This difficulty appears to be linked to negative perceptions of caring for older people, lack of career pathways, general underfunding in the sector and a reluctance to work shift hours.

In Walsh and O'Shea's study, carried out in 2010, the top three primary source countries for nurses were India, the Philippines and Poland; and for care assistants, Poland, the Philippines and Nigeria.

The public childcare sector in comparison does not appear to have difficulty hiring and retaining Irish carers. The development of specialist childcare courses, the elevation of some childcare roles improving career pathways, and the increase in private for-profit organizations employing childcare workers have all contributed to this. Only in the private childcare sector and at-home care is the presence of migrant workers more visible. The lack of regulation of workers in this sector results in potentially high levels of exploitation and abuse of migrant workers.

An analysis of comparative figures from regulatory social work bodies demonstrates a different trajectory and composition for qualified migrant social workers. The number of workers with qualifications gained outside Ireland peaked in 2001, when over 300 applications for recognition were received at a time of expansion and investment in social services. The primary source nations over the period 1996–2007 were the UK (352), Australia (206) and the US (198) (Walsh et al., 2010). Since the economic downturn in 2008, the numbers have plummeted. The latest figures available from CORU (2013) indicate that only 29 applications for recognition of qualifications gained outside Ireland were received in 2012. The majority of applicants continue to be from Anglophone countries, with a slight increase in applications from Poland and Slovakia. Little work has yet been done in the Irish context to examine the extent to which transnational migration into Ireland is characterized by the systematic devaluing of skilled migrants, a phenomenon noted elsewhere (Danso, 2009, p. 539):

> Even as developed countries lure and vie for high-calibre immigrants in order to gain or maintain a competitive advantage in the 'knowledge-based' global economy, structural barriers in the labour markets of these countries exclude and deny immigrants access to occupations and jobs commensurate with their training and expertise.

While the needs of new migrant communities continue to be promoted by NGOs such as the Migrant Rights Centre Ireland (MRCI, 2012), there appears to be less national or organizational action or recognition of the specific needs and assets of diverse workforces in care work. Neither professional organizations and inspection/regulatory bodies nor national employers have yet explicitly addressed such fundamental changes in the composition of the social work and social care workforce and the ethical issues that ensue for us as employers, colleagues, neighbours and friends of migrant care workers. It is in the arena of the voluntary sector where more enlightened practices are emerging. For example, Age Action in Ireland in 2014 commenced a pilot project, funded by a European grant, to promote good intercultural practices in residential homes for older people in one area of Dublin, following research findings that indicated high levels of racism towards migrant workers in the sector (MRCI, 2012).

The feminization of migration and transnational family forms

The changing profile of international migration can be difficult to map accurately, given the range of mobility routes via work, study or asylum-seeking processes as well as the movement and presence of the 'undocumented' across the globe. Despite this, definitive studies have now established the extent to which this phenomenon exists not only across North America (Parrenas, 2008; Boris and Parrenas, 2010), but also across Europe, including Ireland (Walsh and O'Shea, 2010; Lutz, 2011). As Lutz (2011) points out, housework and care work continue to be viewed as women's work despite all the advances in women's emancipation and equal opportunity policies over time. As more women enter the paid workforce and more Irish women avail themselves of educational opportunities to upgrade qualifications and skills, fewer are available for traditional care work, especially that which is undervalued and poorly paid. This work is now 'outsourced' by women to primarily other women, mainly migrants from economically disadvantaged parts of the globe. Many of the women who migrate as global care workers are parents themselves. Parrenas (2008) documents the phenomenon of 'parenting at a distance', focusing on the experiences of Filipino migrant mothers and fathers as well as the children left behind. Levitt (2009) challenges the orthodox view that first- and second-generation immigrants differ in their continued bonds to their homelands. Rather, she asserts that, increasingly, children of immigrants are raised in a transnational social field with strong social networks, and the newer generations have the social skills and competences to negotiate multiple and fluid identities and relationships.

Communication technologies are, arguably, the 'social glue' that facilitates the transnational actions and identities of migrants (Vertovec, 2004).

Keeping contact with children through Skype, text messaging, Facebook and other communication technologies enables 'parenting at a distance', yet the concept of such transnational parenting patterns remains invisible in our official guidance and assessment frameworks for working with such families. The most recent HSE practice guidance for family assessment (HSE, 2011) makes no reference to the needs of such families, yet according to Castles and Miller (2009, p. 33):

> increasing numbers of international migrants do not simply move from one society to another, but maintain recurring and significant links in two or more places. They form transnational communities which live across borders. This trend is facilitated by globalization, both through improvements in transport and communication technology, and through diffusion of global cultural values.

The presence of new transnational family forms has profound implications for how social workers assess and support parenting 'at a distance'. If families are kept apart through unjust differentiated migration regimes, do our more traditional frameworks for understanding parenting work? In recent media reports of Irish family law proceedings (Gartland, 2014):

> counsel for the father of two young children in State care asked [the judge] to reinstate access via Skype. The court heard both parents were living outside the State and one was ill … the Child and Family Agency agreed to two Skype sessions from the foster parents' home and two emails on the children's progress before the next hearing of the case.

How do traditional theories of bonding and attachment work in such circumstances? Should social workers be introducing new frameworks for assessing transnational families that explicitly incorporate the impact of migration rules on how transnational families can function? How can they maximize the potential of technological communications to maintain family bonds, when many social work offices lack the necessary equipment?

Doyle and Timonen (2010) studied the reconciliation of work and family life for migrant workers in Irish long-term care settings. Their study confirms the powerful role immigration laws play in perpetuating inequality as they 'serve to stratify the population of migrant carers into those who have the freedom to remain in the country indefinitely, change employer easily and bring their children to Ireland and those who do not have these rights' (p. 33). Of the 40 female migrant care workers Doyle and Timonen (2010, p. 48) interviewed, many 'confronted a range of obstacles which included discrimination, conditional residency and limited financial resources'.

A poor understanding of the phenomenon of transnational parenting and the particular pressures encountered by such families risks triggering social work patterns of engagement and intervention that may be actively unhelpful or destructive. Particularly alarming therefore is the finding by Coulter (2013), reporting on childcare law proceedings, of the relatively high proportion of African families involved in such proceedings as they comprised 11.4% of respondents surveyed. Coulter (2013, p. 20) observes that 'this is totally disproportionate to their presence in the population as a whole … according to this data, African families are 20 times more likely to find themselves in the childcare courts than other members of Irish society'.

Development of international social work and new forms of resistance

What responses can and should social workers make to the threats of globalization as a part of 'compassionate' national welfare states? Since the global financial crisis of 2008, some note that there has been a weakening of the forces of globalization, accompanied by a reassertion of the nation state, sometimes accompanied by increased levels of xenophobia and particular hostility to migrant workers (Lightman, 2012, p. 20). Such a phenomenon is now seen across many parts of Europe, with political instability fuelled by the politics of austerity. Transnational networks of academics/researchers, such as the Canadian/German partnership on Transnational Social Support (Chambon et al., 2013), are producing new theoretical insights into comparative and increasingly common experiences across the globe. These analyses of common concerns articulate the unique blends of local cultural practices and free-market fundamentalist principles, which are still negotiated primarily through nation state welfare regimes and continental political alliances, such as the EU and US/Canadian alliances. Through dialogue and reflection about the commonalities and disparities at national and local levels, we can aim to create a stronger, more visible presence as a profession in challenging the global inequalities and oppressive practices evident in current migration regimes. Through new European fora, such as the annual European Conference on Social Work Research, founded in 2010, scholarship and practices are shared and examined and new alliances formed. Leadership is also important as professional organizations, educators, employers and practitioners have a role to play in developing stronger positions on cultural diversity and complex issues around cultural relativism. One example of the international resources that Irish social work can

avail itself of is the depth of knowledge and practice wisdom available elsewhere, such as family therapists in North America. Family and systemic
therapists from North American centres familiar with decades of migration
argue for reformulated theoretical and intervention models for transnational families:

> The complexity of relationships that arise from transnational connections calls
> into question dominant discourses about family bonds and requires that we adopt
> new theory and treatment considerations. The relational stresses and the almost
> untenable choices that economic immigrants face take the form of separations
> and reunions of parents and children, and difficult gender or generation trans-
> formations that need to be considered against this new transnational backdrop.
> (Falicov, 2007, p. 157)

Yet, given the increased interdependence of populations and countries, the consistent calls for more international collaborations in social
work practice need to be tempered with a recognition of the paradoxical
and contradictory dimensions of globalization in order to avoid the risk of
oversimplifying or reducing the scale of the phenomenon. The unthinking
importation of dominant or popular frames of reference may unwittingly
replicate oppressive regulatory social work practices, underpinned by dominant forms of neoliberalism. An approach advocated by Bohnisch and
Schroer (2012, p. 34) as a genuine transnational sociopolitical perspective of
understanding is Amartya Sen's capability approach, at the centre of which
is 'the ideal of a good life, the attainment of which must be measured by the
relation between opportunities of realization and barriers to such opportunities'. Reframing the good life as that of a 'better life' within the paradigm
of neediness, Bohnisch and Schroer (2012, p. 39) argue that 'transnational
processes of socialization generate a new dialectic of neediness' and social
workers need to be cautious in their adoption of a position that might lead
them to determine the 'right' needs and stigmatize 'wrong' ones. Bohnisch
and Schroer (2012, p. 39) call for:

> a conceptual framework for a future, transnationally reflexive form of social work,
> which is not offered to people from an external source but is derived from the
> socio-historical and socio-structural developmental conditions of the relevant
> social conditions of life – and which does not leave it to individuals to decide how
> to recognize and develop their abilities.

This offers us a starting point in the construction of more ethical practices
within these transnational times. Globalization not only offers lucrative
rewards and opportunities, but also creates new forms of poverty and disadvantage. Social work needs to grapple with it in all its complexity.

References

Akenson, D. (1970) *The Irish Education Experiment*, New York, Routledge & Kegan Paul.

Bauman, Z. (1998) *Globalization: The Human Consequences*, Cambridge, Polity.

Bohnisch, L. and Schroer, W. (2012) 'Social policy in a transnational world: the capability approach, neediness, and social work', in Chambon, A., Schroer, W. and Schweppe, C. (eds) *Transnational Social Support*, London, Routledge.

Boris, E. and Parrenas, R.S. (eds) (2010) *Intimate Labors: Cultures, Technologies and the Politics of Care*, Stanford, CA, Stanford University Press.

Busch-Armendariz, N., Nsonwu, M.B. and Heffron, L.C. (2014) 'A kaleidoscope: the role of the social work practitioner and the strength of social work theories and practice in meeting the complex needs of people trafficked and the professionals that work with them', *International Social Work*, 57(1), 7–18.

Castles, S. and Miller, M.J. (2009) *The Age of Migration*, 4th edn, Basingstoke, Palgrave Macmillan.

Chambon, A., Schroer, W. and Schweppe, C. (eds) (2012) *Transnational Social Support*, London, Routledge.

Christie, A. (2002) 'Responses of the social work profession to unaccompanied children seeking asylum in the Republic of Ireland', *European Journal of Social Work*, 5(2), 187–98.

Christie, A. (2003) 'Unsettling the "social" in social work: responses to asylum-seeking children', *Child and Family Social Work*, 8(3), 223–31.

Christie, A. (2004) 'Difference', in Fanning, B., Kennedy, P., Kiely G. and Quinn S. (eds) *Theorising Irish Social Policy*, Dublin, UCD Press.

Christie, A. (2010) 'Whiteness and the politics of "race" in child protection guidelines in Ireland', *European Journal of Social Work*, 13(2), 199–215.

Clarke, J. (2005) 'Welfare states and nation states: some conceptual reflections', *Social Policy and Society*, 4(4), 407–15.

CORU (Regulating Health & Social Care Professionals) (2013) *Annual Report*, Dublin, CORU.

Coulter, C. (2013) *First Interim Report, Child Care Law Reporting Project*, Dublin, Child Care Law Reporting Project.

Dalrymple, J. and Burke, B. (1996) *Anti-Oppressive Practice: Social Care and the Law*, Maidenhead, Open University Press.

Danso, R. (2009) 'Emancipating and empowering de-valued skilled immigrants: What hope does anti-oppressive social work practice offer?', *British Journal of Social Work*, 39(3), 539–55.

Dominelli, L. (1997) *Anti-racist Social Work: A Challenge for White Practitioners and Educators*, Basingstoke, Macmillan.

Dominelli, L. (2002) *Anti-oppressive Social Work Theory and Practice*, Basingstoke, Palgrave Macmillan.

Doyle, M. and Timonen, V. (2010) 'Obligations, ambitions, calculations: migrant care workers' negotiations of work, career and family responsibilities', *Social Politics: International Studies in Gender, State and Society*, 17(1), 29 –52.

Drudy, P.J. and Collins, M.L. (2011) 'Ireland: from boom to austerity', *Cambridge Journal of Regions, Economy and Society*, 4(3), 339–54.

Falicov, C. (2007) 'Working with transnational immigrants: expanding meanings of family, community and culture', *Family Process*, 46(2), 157 –71.

FLAC (Free Legal Advice Centres) (2009) *One Size Doesn't Fit All: A Legal Analysis of the Direct Provision and Dispersal System in Ireland, 10 Years On*, Dublin, FLAC.

Gartland, F. (2014) 'Father of two children in State care asks judge to reinstate access via Skype', *Irish Times*, 23 January.

Gilmartin, M. (2012) *The Changing Landscape of Irish Migration, 2000–2012*, NIRSA Working Paper No. 69, 1–19.

Glyn, I., Kelly, T. and MacÉinri, P. (2013) *Irish Emigration in an Age of Austerity*, University College Cork, Émigré.

Group of Experts on Action against Trafficking in Human Beings (2013) *Report Concerning the Implementation of the Council of Europe Convention on Action against Trafficking in Human Beings by Ireland*, Strasbourg, Council of Europe.

Held, D., McGrew, A., Goldblatt D. and Perraton, J. (1999) *Global Transformations: Politics, Economics and Culture*, Cambridge, Polity Press.

Horgan, D., O'Riordan, J., Christie, A. and Martin, S. (2012) *Safe Care for Trafficked Children in Ireland: Developing a Protective Environment*, Dublin, Children's Rights Alliance.

HSE (Health Services Executive) (2011) *Child Protection and Welfare Practice Handbook*, Dublin, HSE.

INIS (Irish Naturalisation and Immigration Service) (2013) Immigration in Ireland – 2012 in Review: Minister Shatter outlines priorities for 2013.

IRC (Irish Refugee Council) (2015) *Proposal: One-off Scheme to Clear Asylum Backlog*, Dublin, IRC.

Levitt, P. (2009) 'Roots and routes: understanding the lives of the second generation transnationally', *Journal of Ethnic and Migration Studies*, 35(7), 1225–42.

Lightman, E. (2012) 'Transnational social policy and migration', in Chambon, A., Schroer, W. and Schweppe, C. (eds) *Transnational Social Support*, London, Routledge.

Lutz, H. (2011) *The New Maids: Transnational Women and the Care Economy*, London, Zed Books.

Midgley, J. (2008) 'Perspectives on globalization and culture: implications for international social work practice', *Journal of Global Social Work Practice*, 1(1), 1–11.

Midgley, J. and Piachaud, D. (2011) *Colonialism and Welfare: Social Policy and the British Imperial Legacy*, Cheltenham, Edward Elgar.

MRCI (Migrant Rights Centre Ireland) (2012) *Who Cares? The Experiences of Migrant Care Workers in Ireland*, Dublin, MRCI.

Ní Laoire, C., Carpena-Méndez, F., Tyrell, N. and White, A. (2010) 'Introduction: childhood and migration – mobilities, homes and belongings', *Childhood: Global Journal of Child Research*, 17(2), 155–62.

ORAC (Office of Refugee Applications Commissioner) (2013) *Annual Report*, Dublin, ORAC.

Parrenas, R.S. (2005) *Children of Global Migration: Transnational Families and Gendered Woes*, Stanford, CA, Stanford University Press.

Pugh, R. and Gould, N. (2000) 'Globalization, social work and social welfare', *European Journal of Social Work*, 3(2), 123–38.

RIA (Reception and Integration Agency) (2013) *RIA Annual Report 2013*, www.ria.gov.ie/en/RIA/Pages/AnnualReport2013.

Sales, R. (2007) *Understanding Immigration and Refugee Policy: Contradictions and Continuities*, Bristol, Policy.

Swank, D. (2005) 'Globalisation, domestic politics, and welfare state retrenchment in capitalist democracies', *Social Policy and Society*, 4(2), 183–95.

Torode, R., Walsh, T. and Woods, M. (2001) *Working with Refugees and Asylum-Seekers: A Social Work Resource Book*, Dublin, Department of Social Studies, TCD.

Vertovec, S. (2004) 'Cheap calls: the social glue of migrant transnationalism', *Global Networks*, 4(2), 219–24.

Walsh, K. and O'Shea, E. (2010) *The Role of Migrant Care Workers in Ageing Societies: Context and Experiences in Ireland*, Galway, Irish Centre for Social Gerontology.

Walsh, T., O'Connor, E. and Wilson, G. (2010) 'Local, European and global: an exploration of migration patterns of social workers into Ireland', *British Journal of Social Work*, 40(6), 1979–95.

Yeates, N. (2008) 'The idea of global social policy', in Yeates, N. (ed.) *Understanding Global Social Policy*, Bristol, Policy.

Yeates, N. (2009) *Globalizing Care Economies and Migrant Workers: Explorations in Global Care Chains*, Basingstoke, Palgrave Macmillan.

3

Putting Ethics at the Heart of Social Work in post-Celtic Tiger Ireland

Brid Featherstone and Fred Powell

Introduction

> What constitutes a good life? What is necessary to human flourishing? What kinds of human capabilities do particular societies value, encourage, genuinely enable, or block? What conceptions of human nature and the good society underpin our contemporary economic discourse? Can we, as ordinary citizens, enter the discourse on economic policy issues, or are we too economically illiterate for that? Are the issues so complex as to require their being lifted out of the democratic parliamentary system? These are but a few examples of the questions our times require us to raise. Posing the problem in such terms encourages us, I hope, to take a step beyond critical analysis in order to think positively about a set of principles by which we might live and explore the contemporary possibilities for developing ethical arts of economic government. (Higgins, 2013)

In this quote from a speech he gave at Dublin City University, Michael D. Higgins, Irish president, has placed ethics squarely at the heart of the kinds of conversations he considers vital in a time of acute crisis. In this chapter, we explore some of the contours of the crisis and offer some thoughts on how a call to ethics of the type envisaged by President Higgins can promote a social work project that is rooted in offering hope and concrete help to the citizens of Ireland. We suggest that an important historic mission of social work has been to speak for, and alongside, those most marginalized, but it has also acted as a handmaiden to the powerful and operated to silence and/or further harm those most powerless. In times of crisis and austerity, we argue that we need robust ethical tools to resist such a project.

36

In this chapter we identify some of these tools. But first, we offer some background to the current context.

A world torn apart?

Historically a small, poverty-stricken country on the periphery of Europe without many natural resources, Ireland's metamorphosis into what became known as the 'Celtic Tiger', from the late 1990s onwards, was startling and its performance was remarkable (see Featherstone, 2011). Kevin Gardiner (1994), UK economist, coined the term 'Celtic Tiger' in 1994, comparing Ireland's economic take-off to the Asian tiger economies. What lay behind this 'success story'? O'Toole (2009) notes that any analysis must recognize the low starting place Ireland occupied. Its performance was remarkable partly because it had been so poor before. As Considine and Dukelow (2009) note, assessments of the factors involved vary in emphasis. There was an improvement in external economic conditions generally and an intensification of global economic activity. The upturn in the global economy was crucial as, for some time, the Irish state's policy had been directed at encouraging high-skill, high-tech international companies to locate in the country. Low corporation taxation rates, government grants and, at that stage, relatively low wages were powerful inducements to companies to locate in a country that was part of the European Union (EU) and had access to large markets. A young, well-educated English-speaking workforce was an important 'selling point' to foreign investors (Considine and Dukelow, 2009). In particular, the development of a social partnership model involving the trade unions contributed to a stable industrial relations climate that was attractive to international companies. Moreover, EU membership and the attendant funding benefits were significant in supporting growth. Ireland was promoted as a centre for the international finance sector, with government policy favouring light touch regulation and oversight. Indeed, in 2005, *The New York Times* described Ireland as the 'Wild West' of European finance because of its lax regulatory regime (O'Toole, 2009).

Momentum slowed in the early 2000s after nearly a decade of high growth. This coincided with a downturn internationally, particularly in the IT industry, which impacted significantly on Ireland. The return of economic growth in subsequent years was based on what proved to be unsustainable and highly problematic economic and political practices. Excessive property values fuelled a construction boom reliant on lending from the banks. The banks, in turn, became locked in competition about who could lend most, and they abandoned crucial safeguards in relation to managing risk. There were no robust regulation and inspection systems to halt the recklessness. Indeed, a small closed circle of men (mainly) were able to lend to each other, regulate each other and rule the country in what was to prove a disastrous version of 'crony' capitalism (O'Toole, 2009; Cooper, 2010). Because money appeared to be flowing freely, there was little interrogation of its sources or the assumption behind much of what was happening, which was that property prices would continue to rise. Moreover, dissenting voices were treated with derision (Ihle, 2010).

The construction boom unbalanced the economy and government spending became heavily reliant on tax revenues from it. A fair and sustainable taxation system was not developed and there was a continuation of troubling practices in relation to tax evasion, particularly by the super-rich. Government spending rose based not on a sober assessment of the housing, health, welfare and infrastructure needs of the country but rather on securing electoral success. The failure to build a sustainable infrastructure in a range of domains, for example healthcare, is one of the more serious problems now facing society (Leahy, 2009). While social work did grow substantially in those years, it is interesting that the areas of growth involved child protection and probation, areas where the assessment and management of risk have been foregrounded (see Chapter 1).

The global financial crisis in 2008 impacted immediately and dramatically on Ireland. While banks all over the world were in trouble, Irish banks were extremely vulnerable. They were dependent on securing funding from other banks worldwide and this funding dried up almost overnight. Moreover, having lent in a reckless fashion to property developers and the building industry, they faced crises in relation to liquidity and solvency.

The Irish government's decision in September 2008 to guarantee the deposits, loans and obligations of the six Irish banks (a total sum of €400 billion, at the time more than twice the country's gross national product) was to prove catastrophic. The guarantee was not based on a clear understanding of the levels of bad debt the banks were carrying and was to lead ultimately to the need to seek a bailout from the EU, the International Monetary Fund and the World Bank. Under the terms of the bailout, Ireland, alongside other countries such as Greece and Spain, was obliged to embrace a wide-ranging array of austerity measures, with particular policies directed at cutting welfare payments and services for the most vulnerable (O'Toole, 2012). Alongside the material consequences of paying off the bad debts of reckless businesspeople, the psychological consequences of surrendering financial sovereignty have been no less devastating for a country with a history of foreign domination.

As Mercille (2014) notes, there have now been nine austerity budgets in Ireland since 2008, and there is extensive evidence that the human consequences have been devastating. A major report from the Organisation for Economic Co-operation and Development (OECD, 2014), exploring the impacts of the economic crisis and austerity, notes that three eurozone countries – Ireland, Greece and Spain – have seen a doubling of the number of people living in households with no income from work. The report concludes that austerity hampers progress in reducing inequality and poverty and that the economic losses resulting from austerity are not shared equally. Labour incomes appear to fall more strongly than profits or rents, and losses suffered by workers also persist for longer.

Income inequality in Europe has risen since 2008, but more drastically since 2010, when the general shift towards austerity took place. There has been a shift towards part-time precarious jobs, which is fuelling the deconstruction of labour laws, with a complete disregard for existing labour standards enshrined in international, EU and national laws.

Mercille (2014) highlights the findings from Social Justice Ireland on the impact of austerity on the population. The 'at risk of poverty rate' of young Irish adults between 18 and 24 years of age has nearly doubled since 2008 and it stands at almost 27%. The overall unemployment rate in Ireland is about 12%, but, if emigration is factored in, it would be around 20%, and if involuntary part-time workers are included, it would be above 24%. A report from the European Foundation on Living and Working Conditions (2014) found that, in Ireland, nearly one in five young people have experienced serious deprivation, which is twice as many as in 2007, while 51% of young people have difficulty accessing healthcare because it is too expensive.

A network of 30 Irish groups in the community and voluntary sector (Community Platform, 2014) surveyed people on the impact of the recession and government policy on their lives. It concluded that austerity has been devastating for people who are on low incomes, unemployed, marginalized, or dependent on welfare. It warned that the dual attack of unemployment and relentless cuts, at national and local level, has pushed individuals, families and communities into poverty. It documents parents going hungry to feed their children, people unable to heat their homes, and a young generation at serious risk of being lost to unemployment, drugs and crime.

The issue of homelessness achieved prominence in 2014 because of the death of a man sleeping 'rough' not far from the Irish parliament. Mercille (2014) notes the growing concerns from charities that homelessness is out of control. According to research in Dublin alone, six people become homeless every day and, as in other big cities, it is hard to enter the rental market because there are 2,500 people chasing 1,500 accommodation units. Rents have increased by 18% since 2011, while the rent allowance payable by the Department of Social Protection has fallen by almost 30% in the same period. There is a significant waiting list for social housing. While the current government committed to building some new homes over the next two years, its plans would only reduce the waiting list by 2% (Mercille, 2014).

Overall, sources as varied as the OECD and Social Justice Ireland argue that austerity was and still is the wrong solution to Ireland's woes and has intensified pre-existing vulnerabilities and inequalities. This is not surprising. Clark with Heath (2014) have likened the impact of austerity on the UK to that of a tornado whipping through a city, decimating already vulnerable areas and leaving the richer areas untouched. Austerity has intensified already existing inequalities in the UK. When we consider the kind of society Celtic Tiger Ireland was, the devastation wrought by austerity is indeed explicable.

Vulnerability, inequality and the building of a care-less society

Kirby (2002, 2006, 2010) has argued that economic success in Celtic Tiger Ireland was accompanied by social failure. Kirby (2010) uses the notion of 'vulnerability' to capture the destructive impact on society caused by the freeing of the markets from controls that serve the social good. Indeed, he argues that Irish society grew more vulnerable over the course of the Celtic Tiger era. Despite the myth of the boom years that a great levelling in relation to inequality had occurred, as the Think-tank for Action on Social Change (TASC, 2009) notes, Ireland was among the most unequal societies in the developed world.

Levels of inequality need to be located within an understanding of the neoliberal trajectory taken by its politicians. Ireland, in the last decade of the 20th century, quickly shifted towards the standard neoliberal model of an increasingly deregulated trade in goods, services and labour, and the relentless promotion of the market as an arbiter of efficiency, distribution and appropriate responses to needs, private and collective. Kirby (2009) suggests that the growth of the power of the market over Irish society did not happen by accident but was the outcome of a determined politics across the globe.

Harvey (2005) noted the turnaround in the share of national income going to top income earners in a range of countries between the late 1970s and 1999. Extraordinary concentrations of wealth and power emerged in countries as diverse as Russia, Mexico, Latin America and China, with a similar process happening in the UK. The work of epidemiologists Wilkinson and Pickett (2009) has illuminated the impact of this rise in inequality, bringing an array of evidence in their book, *The Spirit Level: Why More Equal Societies Always Do Better*, to reach important conclusions. They have collected internationally comparable data on health and a range of social problems: levels of trust, mental illness (including drug and alcohol addiction), life expectancy, infant mortality, obesity, children's educational performance, teenage births, homicides, imprisonment rates and social mobility. Their findings suggest that there is a strong link between ill health, social problems and inequality. Differences in average income between whole populations or countries do not seem to matter, but differences within those populations or countries matter greatly. The amount of income inequality in a country is crucial. Wilkinson and Pickett (2009) note strong findings from the data that levels of trust between members of the public are lower in countries where income differences are larger. For example, people trust each other most in the Scandinavian countries and the Netherlands, and least in very unequal countries.

A linked insight from Wilkinson and Pickett's work concerns how inequality within a society quite literally 'gets under the skin' of individuals, leaving them feeling unvalued and inferior. They note the work of sociologist Thomas Scheff (1988), who argued that shame is the key social emotion. 'Shame and its opposite, pride, are rooted in the processes through which we internalize how we imagine others see us' (Wilkinson and Pickett, 2009, p. 41). Greater inequality heightens our anxieties because it increases the importance of social status. We come to see social status as a key feature of a person's identity in an unequal society.

The debates around poverty during the Celtic Tiger years illustrate the failure to engage with inequality and the implications for individual and societal health and wellbeing. The measuring of poverty was subject to considerable debate as different methods told different stories (Kirby, 2009). Those who sought to claim the Irish story as one of success pointed to the decline in 'consistent' poverty. Their critics pointed out that the measure they were using was concerned with 'absolute' poverty as it concentrates on material survival only. An alternative measure is that of 'relative' poverty. This measure is rather more embarrassing for proponents of the Irish 'success' story as it shows an increase in such poverty over the years of the economic boom. However, during the boom, the fact that relative poverty increased was of little concern to policy makers. Indeed, some politicians openly argued that inequality was a necessary requirement for a dynamic liberal economy.

In Ireland, the welfare of market players was placed as a priority over the welfare of its citizens and Ireland coped with globalization first and foremost by competing. Crucially, social policy remained subordinate to economic priorities and this is now what President Higgins is signalling needs to change. Free-market economics trumped all other considerations with a lack of attention to what constituted the 'good life' in a holistic sense. Ireland had never developed a postwar welfare settlement as happened in other countries and, unsurprisingly, given its neoliberal leanings, the Celtic Tiger did not develop robust social protection systems. While levels of welfare payments were high, the cost of living was too. Healthcare was largely a private good and a strong, universal system freely available to all citizens was not developed. As highlighted above, housing became divorced in the most extraordinary way from social or environmental concerns about affordability or sustainability.

As Culpitt (1999) notes, across a range of countries where postwar social protection systems had been successfully established, neoliberalism successfully eclipsed the former moral imperatives of mutual obligation that sustained political support for welfare states. A new rhetoric of governance argued for the lessening of risk, not the meeting of need. Indeed, a diverse cast of people and issues became known only through the language of risk. Kemshall (2002) noted that social work shifted from a preoccupation with need to one of risk, and Webb (2006) argued that need and risk became conflated with social work taking on a role in risk regulation and as an expert mediator for problematic populations and vulnerable people. Webb (2006) noted an ambivalence here, which was manifest through instrumental rationality in terms of calculating and regulatory practices, and substantive rationality in securing personal identity through dialogic and expressive face work. We explore the implications of this analysis for the shape of Irish social work throughout this book but especially in Chapter 4 on child protection where, as in other countries, the tensions between instrumental and substantive rationality have become pronounced (Featherstone et al., 2014).

Unsurprisingly, perhaps, a 'care deficit' was a feature of the Celtic Tiger with the move of considerable numbers of women into the paid labour force and a failure on the part of the state to build a robust infrastructure to support care relationships and practices. As the National Economic and Social Council (NESC, 2005) noted, historically when large numbers of women remained in the home, the family was arguably the single most important pillar of Ireland's national system of social protection. In a large number of instances, the care of young children, older people and other household members with special needs hinged around the full-time presence of a fit and capable household member, usually a woman. Relatively residual roles were played by the state and organizations in civil society, and an even lesser one by commercial bodies. However, the rise in women's employment rates from the 1970s onwards began to weaken this pillar of caring and, during the 1990s, the rates jumped further to open a significant deficit between the diminished capacity of families to provide care and the development of a new caring capacity on the part of the state, not-for-profit bodies and commercial bodies.

Lynch (2010) has argued that the care deficit in Ireland needs to be located within a broader understanding of how interlocking inequalities were reproduced. She suggests that there are four key systems or sets of social relations that need to be understood and transformed: economic, political, cultural and affective. A key system clearly is the economic and, as indicated above, levels of economic inequality were very high. Gender, age and region were all important aspects of this picture. In relation to gender, Duvvury (2011) notes that, while during the Celtic Tiger era, there was a rapid advance of women's entry into education alongside high levels of entry into the workforce, particularly among married women, there was, however, a persistent gender wage gap, with a concentration in low-paid jobs and vulnerable employment. Women were consistently overrepresented in lower paid, atypical, part-time, flexi and contract work (NCWI, 2010). Moreover, 62% of women adjusted their working patterns on becoming a parent, in comparison to 27% of men (CPA, 2007).

The political system is the set of relationships involved in making and enforcing collectively binding decisions and it is important to note that, in Ireland in the formal political system, representation of women in the last parliament before the last general election in 2011 was 13.9%. This placed Ireland in the bottom half of representation of women across 160 countries and significantly below most of Europe, where Spain is at 36.6%, Germany 32.8%, Netherlands at 42% and Sweden 46.5% (Women in Parliaments, World Classification, 31 May 2010, quoted in Lynch, 2010).

The cultural system is concerned with the production, transmission and legitimation of cultural practices and products, including forms of symbolic representation and communication. It generates differences in social standing and status, and Lynch (2010) has pointed out a range of ways in which the Irish education system, in particular, has reproduced inequality and also contributed to a discrediting of alternative thinking about more socially just ways of ordering society. The latter point is of considerable significance in a society where there has not been a history of robust intellectual thought on social matters, with a long legacy of a repressive Catholic influence that is now in tatters but yet to be replaced by an alternative.

The affective system is concerned with providing and sustaining relationships of love, care and solidarity. Lynch (2010) has noted that inequality in the affective domain takes two primary forms: when people have unequal access to meaningful, loving and caring relationships and when there is inequality in the distribution of care work (emotional and physical). Those who are likely to be deprived of love and care (due to war and famine, for example) are generally different from those who experience affective inequality due to undertaking a disproportionately high level of care work. Overall, according to Lynch, in Ireland, women's unequal relationship with men has been generated in this latter form of the affective domain and reinforced in the economic, political and cultural domains.

Because of the economic transformation from the 1990s onwards, an unprecedented set of debates began about the role the state should play in caring for families and supporting them to meet their childcare responsibilities. Many inadequacies such as those in relation to the provision of quality affordable childcare places and the reconciliation of work and family life were highlighted (Hayes and Bradley, 2007). This was also linked to a growing international consensus about the beneficial effects of high-quality care and education in the early years and a social investment state rationale in relation to social cohesion and future economic prosperity (Featherstone, 2004). However, despite all the debate, there was a slow and fragmented approach especially when compared with developments internationally. Levels of childcare provision were poor and there was a consistent preference for market-led solutions rather than state-provided services. Thus, childcare in Ireland has been extremely expensive by comparison with other countries (see Lynch and Lyons, 2008).

In relation to the reconciliation of work and family life, here, too, policies were underdeveloped and it is not surprising, therefore, that research on the distribution of caring, housework and employment among women and men in Ireland found that women did a month's more housework per year than men and substantial inequalities remained (McGinnity and Russell, 2008).

More generally, according to Lynch and Lyons (2008), the picture of care work varies with the sources of data. One of the major sources has been the national census, which only measures unpaid caring for adults and children with disabilities. Thus, it gives an incomplete picture of how much unpaid care work is undertaken in Ireland. When combined with other sources of data, it would appear that 28% of the adult population have care responsibilities and 85% are caring for children only, while a further 7% (all of whom are women) are caring for adults and children with care needs. Overall, the disparity in unpaid caring stands at a ratio of 2.5:1 – 40% of women aged 16+ have some care responsibilities, mostly for children, compared to 16% of men, with women much more likely than men to carry the primary responsibility for children without pay. Further analysis of the figures indicates that women are much more likely to be working longer hours in care work than men.

During the boom time, a robust infrastructure in relation to supporting care was not put in place to be invested in emotionally and practically by the general population. Constructions of care as a private responsibility were promoted by neoliberal policy makers. As Rush (2007) has noted, there was a nascent critique that he locates within an ethic of care. For example, there was a critique of an ongoing emphasis on economic growth and universal paid employment especially from those in disability organizations and carers' organizations. He noted that the advocacy of an ethic of care did not necessarily mean advocacy of public sector expansion but rather greater public investment in the quality of care in Ireland's mixed economy of welfare. This was a nascent critique, however. Thus, when the economic crash came, there was no publicly available discourse to support, for example, demands that rather than making people unemployed, working hours could be reduced to support the sharing of care responsibilities. Large numbers of men who lost their jobs in the construction industry, for example, were not publicly supported to take on care responsibilities. Many of them did so, but in the absence of public recognition of the value of doing so, they were often left with a profound sense of inadequacy and failure (Featherstone, 2012).

Ethics, social work and a 'new' Ireland

The roots of Irish social work are in social crises and date from the 19th century. Kearney (1987) notes that the first trained social worker was appointed to a position in housing management in 1899, and records the establishment of a settlement movement at Trinity College in 1901, known as the Dublin University Social Service Union. It was no accident that the first social work appointment was in housing management as Dublin had the worst slums in the (then) UK (Powell, 1992). Celia Harrison (1863–1941), social worker, feminist and artist, became the voice of civic protest against slum conditions, notably championing tenant rights at the Dublin Housing Inquiry in 1914, following the Church Street disaster in 1913. Harrison had established the Dublin City Labour Yard in 1905 to provide work for the unemployed. She was subsequently elected in 1912 to the Dublin Corporation on an anti-corruption platform (Powell, 1992; Ferriter, 2009). The connection between slum conditions and child abuse was direct. Overcrowded conditions in tenement buildings made children vulnerable to child abuse (Ferriter, 2009). But then the term 'child abuse' did not exist.

The establishment of the Irish Free State in 1922 was followed by the Catholicization of civil society. Only the Irish Society for the Prevention of Cruelty to Children (as it became known in 1956) retained a significant role in the area of child protection, an issue with which the Catholic Church had ideological problems, seeing it as an invasion of family rights. It was not until the Health Act 1970, which established eight regional health boards, later transformed into the Health Services Executive (HSE), that the state became the main employer of social workers. Since 1970, the role and task of professional social work in Ireland has been transformed from a peripheral activity into a key statutory service mainly engaged in child protection and probation work (see Chapter 1).

As Banks (2014) notes, there is a long history of discussions on ethics in social work. In Ireland, the Irish Association of Social Workers, established in 1971, set out the principles of social work practice in its code of ethics (IASW, 2007). These principles travel a well-trodden path with their attempt to straddle a range of domains. The first principle states that the social worker's primary focus is the needs of the people using the social work service. While respecting the social, cultural and environmental context in which they live, this focus must recognize, take account of, and balance possible conflicts between their needs and the human rights of different individuals and the communities in which they share their lives. This focus must take precedence over the self-interest and personal convictions of the social worker. Second, poverty, inequality or discrimination may constrain service users' ability to fulfil their needs. These constraints cannot always be resolved at the level of the individual. Social workers will advocate with, and on behalf of, those whom society excludes and, in doing so, should engage with service users and facilitate them in contributing their views to such developments. In addition, social workers should use their professional association as a forum for critical debate and dialogue with other professional agencies, the government and the public at large, to advocate for and promote positive social change. In focusing on the individuals, groups and communities in which they live, social workers will be aware of the potential power imbalance in the relationships that follow. Social workers will strive to use their power appropriately within such relationships and will place special emphasis on the consideration and promotion of service users' views in all decisions related to the quality of their lives. Social workers will promote the participation of service users in order to maximize the potential of any service user or group for self-determination now and in the future. The practice of social work operates within systems that have a regulatory function. Social workers must be cognisant of the inherent tensions between support and control that may arise. In addressing such tensions, social workers will, at all times, strive towards the objective of the service user maximizing their own ability to make and carry out decisions affecting their quality of life.

In many respects, the IASW code of ethics is a model for good practice. Banks (2014, p. 18) argues, however, that in a climate of austerity and neoliberalism, we need to extend the topic of ethics beyond the focus on professional codes of conduct and the individual moral agent acting rationally on the basis of ethical principles:

> Whilst ethics in social work certainly covers matters of professional responsibility, accountability and discretion, the subject matter of ethics cannot be divorced from personal commitments and values or from the wider political and social context in which it takes place.

In terms of personal commitments and values, there has been an influential contribution from those concerned with Aristotelian virtue ethics in the past decade. Webb (2006) argues that, in a neoliberal context, where a preoccupation with knowing and eliminating risk has hollowed out the social work project, the moral identity of the social worker needs to be recast in terms of virtue ethics. Classically juxtaposed and contrasted with Plato's utopian engineering, which is characterized by a rigid attachment to a blueprint for changing society, virtue ethics suggests that what we need instead is something much more dialogical. The right answers must be negotiated in context, with attention to the particulars of this individual or this family in this situation, not an appeal to what are inevitably fictitious universals held in place by expert discourses (MacIntyre, 1997).

Virtue ethics is a normative theory emphasizing a person's character and the way they reach judgements. It is usually seen as running counter to rule-bound or duty-bound conceptions of moral principles and the hierarchical basis of Plato's worldview (Plato, 2007). Derived from the classical writings of Aristotle, virtues are admirable human dispositions that can be learned, and distinguish good people from bad people (Webb, 2006, p. 22). Thus, the basic question to be asked is not just what constitutes good social work, but rather what is a good social worker?

Webb (2006) has argued for the importance of locating ethical discussions within an understanding of neoliberalism and especially the way in which risk becomes individualized and central to the social work project. Who is a risk to themselves or others and how can they be managed? By contrast, there is another approach to engaging individuals and families which, we would suggest, is pertinent in a context of crisis and was central to the preoccupations of President Higgins in the quote at the start of this chapter.

President Higgins asks us to consider the following questions. What constitutes a good life? What is necessary to human flourishing? What kinds of human capabilities do particular societies value, encourage, genuinely enable, or block? He argues that the contemporary response to our present crisis reflects the gaps that were created during the Celtic Tiger years between morality and ethics and economic and social policy. The depeopled economy was the creation of a split between the values of each of the branches of human reflection and existence. He argues that we have to recover from this and regain ground lost at the level of public discourse. Thus, he signals the need for a paradigm shift that places a different set of concerns and conversations at the heart of a range of domains in contemporary Ireland. We would suggest that this offers unprecedented opportunities for social work to work alongside other constituencies in building a different settlement.

The idea of 'human flourishing' is traceable to Ancient Greece. It is a positive idea that envisages every citizen achieving their innate potential to live a fulfilled and dignified life. It has proved central to an important literature on capabilities, a literature that has been influential in development studies, health and education and to a lesser extent in social work internationally (Gupta et al., 2014).

The capabilities approach was originally developed by the Nobel prizewinning economist Amartya Sen and further explored by feminist philosopher Martha Nussbaum. It provides a theoretical framework concerning wellbeing, human development and social justice. The capabilities approach is generally conceived as a flexible and multipurpose framework, rather than a precise theory. It can be used to assess individual wellbeing, the evaluation of social arrangements, and develop policies and practices to effect social change. It emerged as an alternative to resource or income-based approaches to evaluating human welfare. It challenged orthodox neoclassical economics and neoliberal ideologies that focused on economic growth and per capita income, and was influential in the development of the United Nations Human Development Index in 1990.

The capabilities approach focuses directly on the quality of life that individuals are actually able to achieve, and proposes that we consider not just resources but rather the valued things people are able to do or be as a result of having them – the capabilities they command. Thus, it offers an important way into exploring the possibilities for individuals to live a good life as well as the constraints at play.

While Sen and Nussbaum have worked together and separately to develop thinking about the capabilities approach, they differ in relation to whether an overarching list of 'human capabilities' can and should be developed. Sen (2005, p. 157) questions whether a definitive list can be chosen without reference to contexts and suggests that this would result in a 'substantive diminution of the domain of public reasoning'. Nussbaum (2011) argues for the compilation of a list of the core, fundamental capabilities necessary for human wellbeing, which must be guaranteed in order for a society to be just. She suggests that the list is subject to ongoing revision and the list of ten 'central human capabilities' is sensitive to gender and cultural difference. While being closely related to human rights, Nussbaum sees capabilities as requiring more affirmative and proactive state support. The central human capabilities relate to the following domains: life, bodily health, bodily integrity, senses, imagination and thought, emotions, practical reason, affiliation, other species, play, and control over one's own environment. This work is being used in social work to inform thinking about what is required by service users to live a good life and support those they care about, and to move beyond the individual/structural binary that has bedevilled not only Irish social work but also international practices and debates (see Gupta et al., 2014).

Conclusion

In this chapter we have explored the key aspects of the neoliberal trajectory taken through the Celtic Tiger years and discussed the inequalities that scarred the landscape. We note the calls for a differing settlement that challenges the privileging of a particular form of economic thinking over all else. We draw from the ethical traditions concerned with human flourishing and capabilities to signpost alternative sources of thinking generally and inform social work theory and practice in particular. We suggest that the capabilities approach offers possibilities in the current Irish context as well as internationally, as it offers a systematic framework for highlighting the unevenness and gaps in structures and supports as well as an ethical language and pointers towards differing policy and practice choices.

References

Banks, S. (2014) *Ethics: Critical and Radical Debates in Social Work,* Bristol, Policy.

Clark, T. with Heath, A. (2014) *Hard Times: The Divisive Toll of the Economic Slump,* London, Yale University Press.

Community Platform (2014) The human face of poverty in Ireland, http://communityplatform.ie/index.php?mact=News,cntnt01,detail,0&cntnt01articleid=55&cntnt01origid=15&cntnt01returnid=114.

Considine, M. and Dukelow, F. (2009) *Irish Social Policy: A Critical Introduction,* Dublin, Gill & Macmillan.

Cooper, M. (2010) *Who Really Runs Ireland?* London, Penguin Books.

CPA (Crisis Pregnancy Agency) (2007) *Research on Crisis Pregnancy, Parenting and Employment Policy,* Dublin, CPA.

Culpitt, I. (1999) *Social Policy and Risk,* London, Sage.

Duvvury, N. (2011) 'Gendering the recession', paper presented at seminar at National University of Ireland, Galway, 14 April.

European Foundation for the Improvement of Living and Working Conditions (2014) *Social Situation of Young People in Europe,* Luxembourg, Publications of the European Union.

Featherstone, B. (2004) *Family Life and Family Support: A Feminist Analysis,* Basingstoke, Palgrave Macmillan.

Featherstone, B. (2011) 'The current economic crisis in Ireland: why social work needs to be part of the challenge to a discredited system', *Comunitania,* 1(1), 17–29.

Featherstone, B. (2012) 'Can a crisis become an opportunity? Gender and care in Ireland', in Richter, M. and Andresen, S. (eds) *The Politicization of Parenthood,* Heidelberg, Springer.

Featherstone, B., White, S. and Morris, K. (2014) *Re-imagining Child Protection: Towards Humane Social Work with Families,* Bristol, Policy.

Ferriter, D. (2009) *Occasions of Sin: Sex and Society in Modern Ireland,* London, Profile.

Gardner, K. (1994) 'The Irish economy: a Celtic Tiger', *MS Euroletter,* 31 August.

Gupta, A., Featherstone, B. and White. S (2014) 'Reclaiming humanity: from capacities to capabilities in understanding parenting in adversity', *British Journal of Social Work,* doi:10.1093/bjsw/bcr188.

Harvey, D. (2005) *A Short History of Neoliberalism,* Oxford, Oxford University Press.

Hayes, N. and Bradley, S. (2007) 'The childcare question', in Fanning, B. and Rush, M. (eds) *Care and Social Change in the Irish Welfare Economy,* Dublin, UCD Press.

Higgins, M.D. (2013) 'Toward an Ethical Economy', Dublin City University speech, 11 September, www.president.ie/speeches/toward-an-ethical-economy-michael-d-higgins-dublin-city-university-11th-september-2013/.

IASW (Irish Association of Social Workers) (2007) *Code of Ethics,* Dublin, IASW.

Ihle, J. (2010) 'We warned you: critics of government proved right', *Sunday Tribune,* 10 October, p. 50.

Kearney, N. (1987) *Social Work and Social Work Training in Ireland: Yesterday and Tomorrow,* Occasional Papers Series no 1, Dublin, Department of Social Studies, Trinity College.

Kemshall, H. (2002) *Risk, Social Policy and Welfare,* Buckingham, Open University Press.

Kirby, P. (2002) *The Celtic Tiger in Distress: Growth with Inequality in Ireland,* Basingstoke: Palgrave Macmillan.

Kirby, P. (2006) 'The changing face of the Irish state: from welfare to competition state', in O'Connor, T. and Murphy, M. (eds) *Social Care in Ireland: Theory, Policy and Practice,* Cork, CIT Press.

Kirby, P. (2009) 'Contesting the politics of inequality', in Ging, D., Cronin, M. and Kirby, P. (eds) *Transforming Ireland: Challenges, Critiques and Resources,* Manchester, Manchester University Press.

Kirby, P. (2010) *Celtic Tiger in Collapse,* Basingstoke, Palgrave Macmillan.

Leahy, P. (2009) *Showtime: The Inside Story of Fianna Fáil in Power,* Dublin, Penguin.

Lynch, K. (2010) *From a Neo-liberal to an Egalitarian State: Imagining a Different Future,* Dublin, TASC Annual Lecture.

Lynch, K. and Lyons, M. (2008) 'The gendered order of caring', in Barry, U. (ed.) *Where Are We Now? New Feminist Perspectives on Women in Contemporary Ireland,* Dublin, New Island/TASC.

McGinnity, F. and Russell, H. (2008) *Gender Inequalities in Time Use: The Distribution of Caring, Housework and Employment among Men and Women in Ireland,* Dublin, The Equality Authority/Economic and Social Research Institute.

MacIntyre, A. (1997) *After Virtue,* London, Duckworth.

Mercille, J. (2014) 'Ireland under austerity', *CounterPunch,* www.counterpunch. org/2014/04/03/ireland-under-austerity-2/.

NCWI (National Women's Council of Ireland) (2010) *Submission to Budget, 2011,* Dublin, NCWI.

NESC (National Economic and Social Council) (2005) *The Developmental Welfare State,* Dublin, NESC.

Nussbaum, M.C. (2011) *Creating Capabilities: The Human Development Approach,* Cambridge, MA, Harvard University Press.

OECD (Organisation for Economic Co-operation and Development) (2014) *Society at a Glance, 2014: OECD Social Indicators,* OECD Publishing.

O'Toole, F. (2009) *Ship of Fools: How Stupidity and Corruption Sank the Celtic Tiger,* London, Faber and Faber.

O'Toole, F. (2012) *Up the Republic,* London, Faber and Faber.Plato (2007) *The Republic,* London, Penguin Classics.

Powell, F.W. (1992) *The Politics of Irish Social Policy 1600–1990,* New York, Edwin Mellen Press.

Rush, M. (2007) 'The politics of care', in Fanning, B. and Rush, M. (eds) *Care and Social Change in the Irish Welfare Economy,* Dublin, UCD Press.

Scheff, T. (1988) 'Shame and conformity: the defense-emotion system', *American Sociological Review,* 53, 395–406.

Sen, A. (2005) 'Human rights and capabilities', *Journal of Human Development,* 6(2), 151–66.

TASC (Think-tank for Action on Social Change) (2009) *The Solidarity Factor: Public Responses to Economic Inequality in Ireland,* Dublin, TASC.

Webb, S. (2006) *Social Work in a Risk Society,* Basingstoke, Palgrave Macmillan.

Wilkinson, R. and Pickett, K. (2009) *The Spirit Level: Why More Equal Societies Always Do Better,* London, Penguin.

4

Child Welfare and Protection in Ireland: Déjà Vu All Over Again

Helen Buckley and Kenneth Burns

Introduction

This chapter demonstrates how social work with children and families has advanced from a rudimentary set of activities prior to the 1970s into the current system of what could loosely be described as family-focused child protection. It describes how it evolved along a somewhat ambiguous trajectory through the 1980s and 90s, attempting to adopt a policy orientation based on user consultation, consensus and family participation, which could intervene early and proportionately with children who were vulnerable or at risk. It illustrates how, in the wake of scandals and revelations of poor practice, it inevitably reverted to a narrower and more strictly defined service that operated high thresholds for intervention. The chapter goes on to show how the aspirations articulated in early seminal policy documents and reports are once again optimistically reflected in the plans for a new structure under the Child and Family Agency Act 2013. While it acknowledges the positive opportunities underpinning the new template for service delivery, the chapter identifies some historical reasons for caution. It also identifies new challenges that stem from global trends and pose a threat to the effectiveness of the new structure.

The chapter concludes by reviewing the opportunities and threats to the profession of social work within the new arrangements, arguing that the prospects of more diverse, welfare-oriented ways of working that are underpinned by children's rights may be hindered or limited by a combination of austerity and a failure by all relevant stakeholders to accept child protection as a universal responsibility.

51

Social work and the development of the child protection system in Ireland, 1970–2013

The beginnings of child and family social work in Ireland can be traced back to the early 1970s. Although not specifically mentioned in the Health Act 1970, social work was identified as one element of the personal social services, for which the health boards would take responsibility. What was then, and for many years afterwards, known as 'community care social work' initially undertook a generic casework role, providing services to children and families, but also to individuals in the community, including the elderly and disabled. Its gradual evolution into an exclusively child protection and welfare service began in 1974 with the assignment of responsibility for childcare services to the minister for health. A fairly significant shift took place over the following decade, which contributed to the shape of modern child protection social work. This was the change in focus during the 1970s and 80s from institutional to community-based solutions for children at risk (O'Sullivan, 2009). Health board social workers began to take over from religious and philanthropic organizations, adopting the duties formerly held by lady inspectors and children's officers in the health authorities (Skehill, 2004). The establishment of a social work team in the Eastern Health Board in 1977, known as the Fostering Resource Group, was a significant step in reshaping children's out-of-home care from residential to foster care.

During the 1970s, child abuse had been largely constructed in terms of physical injury, generally inflicted by parents on their children. This depiction had been reflected in the earliest procedures produced for health board staff and other children's services, where the lead responsibility was assigned to medical staff, and the main sites for the detection and initial response to such 'non-accidental injury' were identified as surgeries, clinics and hospital emergency departments (O'Sullivan, 2009). The senior community care social worker was to have an important role in responding to reported child abuse, but its nature and extent was to be determined by the (medical) director of community care who had the overall coordinating authority (Department of Health, 1980a). In the meantime, the Task Force on Child Care Services (Department of Health, 1980b) had been set up by the minister in 1975 to develop a blueprint for childcare services and reported in 1980. Having envisaged a 'Child Care Authority' as the statutory body responsible for children's service, the report outlined a clear role for the statutory social worker in terms of identifying and assessing 'difficulties … affecting children's well-being and development' (p. 115) and providing appropriate intervention. The report made reference to the 'insufficient emphasis' that had been given to social work with children in their own homes and noted that most professionally qualified social workers at the time were 'concentrated in child placement services concerned with children subsequent to their removal from home and in specialized services provided by or in association with medical services' to the detriment of community-based social work services (Department of Health, 1980b, pp. 115–16).

This prototype for childcare services, some, though not all, of which was adopted by the Department of Health, provided an opportunity for social work to lay claim to an area of work that was fast gaining prominence. As Skehill (2004) has argued, the incursion into child protection work was not, as some might have perceived, undertaken unwillingly by social workers at the time. Her historical account of the development of childcare social work challenges the notion that statutory responsibility was foisted on the discipline. Skehill (2004, p. 124) describes how, from the mid-20th century onwards, social workers 'were desperately seeking to find legitimate space to occupy within the professional sphere of social service provision', having formerly found it difficult to achieve a separate identity within the largely health-focused multidisciplinary team. As Skehill (2004, p. 121) observed, social work gladly colonized the 'site of expertise' that was emerging in response to new legislation and a growing awareness of the incidence and prevalence of child harm. Once established in community care, social work made a bid for independence in its campaign for the establishment of the 'Fourth Programme' (Langford and Cullen, 1981), which would give the personal social services, including child and family work, autonomy from the other three medically dominated programmes being operated by the health boards. This movement came to naught at that time, but as we will show, the idea of a stand-alone agency emerged again some 25 years later.

The 1980s and early 1990s saw acceleration in the regulation of child protection, much of which contributed to the characterization of the social work role. New legislation went through various incarnations, culminating in the Child Care Act, which was enacted in 1991 and implemented at what Gilligan (1993, p. 366) described as a 'genteel pace' over the following years. Earlier versions of the law had been criticized by a large group of NGOs as well as the Irish Association of Social Workers (IASW), who pointed out the failure of the draft legislation to establish the paramount rights of children. The Child Care Act 1991 reflected a number of the United Nations Convention on the Rights of the Child tenets, clarifying the statutory role, duties and responsibilities of the state to 'take such steps as it considers requisite to identify children who are not receiving adequate care and protection and coordinate information from all relevant sources relating to children it its area' (Section 3(2)(a)). The implications were clear; health board practitioners were statutorily obliged to intervene early to prevent harm to children and were to do so in collaboration with a range of services.

In the meantime, what were then called the 1987 'child abuse guidelines' significantly widened the classification of child harm. The term 'child abuse' now encompassed 'physical injuries, severe neglect and sexual or emotional abuse' (Department of Health, 1987, p. 7). While still allocating overall responsibility for child protection to the medical director of community care, the guidelines clearly identified the community care social worker as a primary agent in the investigation and management of cases. The document also, for the first time, identified expectations in respect of different services such as schools and child psychiatry departments as well as other medical services, thus placing social work in a key position in the multidisciplinary network. Although the 1987 guidelines identified 'severe neglect' as a form of child abuse, this particular type of child harm got no further mention in the document, nor in the appendices, which gave explicit guidance on how to identify physical abuse and child sexual abuse. During the 1980s, awareness about the extent and impact of child sexual abuse began to exert an influence on child protection social work. McKeown and Gilligan (1991) claim that Irish social workers were leaders in bringing a high profile to the issue; for example, the IASW held a seminar on 'incest' in 1983. As professional awareness grew, the proportion of child sexual abuse reports made to health board social work departments rose by 54% between 1984 and 1987 (McGrath, 1996).

The publication of the report on the *Kilkenny Incest Investigation* (McGuinness, 1993; see also McGuinness, 2012) created what is largely regarded as a watershed in the development of child protection services, including, but not confined to, social work (Ferguson, 1996; Buckley and O'Nolan, 2013). This high-profile child abuse inquiry was critical of some elements of social work and professional practice, and interagency cooperation. However, the review team contextualized their comments within a more systemic perspective, which highlighted the inadequacies of the system and the need for a cultural shift in attitudes towards the abuse of women and children, and children's rights. The report raised awareness and reflected an already growing consciousness in Ireland of social problems such as gender-based violence (Kelly et al., 1993), child sexual abuse (Cooney and Torode, 1989), tensions between social workers and An Garda Síochána (Buckley, 1993), and children's rights (Department of Health, 1980b). In response to the report, the government pledged significant investment to resource the operation of the Child Care Act 1991 and, within a relatively short period, the number of staff employed in child protection services had expanded in number and nature, with social care workers and family support workers joining the statutory social work teams.

By the time the Child Care Act 1991 was fully implemented at the end of 1996, a number of parallel and competing perspectives were continuing to shape the delivery of child and family social work services. Concern about the direction being taken by the child protection system was affirmed by research conducted in the South Eastern Health Board area (Buckley et al.,

1997) and a study conducted in the Eastern Health Board region during the same year (Eastern Health Board/Impact Review Group, 1997). These two reports used empirical evidence to show that the majority of financial resources and social work time in community care were being expended in the investigation of reports, with inadequate attention to, or investment in, early intervention services. This trend was considered to undermine the philosophical basis of the Child Care Act 1991, which was to promote the welfare of children. It also reflected a universal concern, particularly evidenced in the UK (Department of Health, 1995) and the US (Waldfogel, 1998) about the forensic focus being adopted by child protection systems and the need for a refocusing towards a supportive and preventive response to children and families in need.

A debate on the merits or otherwise of legalizing the reporting of suspected child abuse, which was conducted in 1996, raised similar concerns. This issue, generally regarded as a 'political football' (McGrath, 1998), arose each time a child abuse scandal was publicized, and as later sections will show, the government finally capitulated to its introduction in 2011. It was argued at the time that social work services would be overwhelmed with referrals if failure to report was criminalized, and the government of the day decided instead to introduce measures to strengthen the child protection system. The abolition of the director of community care post finally put an end to the medical domination of child protection social work, which now became accountable to a general administrative manager. Furthermore, a new post of child care manager was created, with social workers occupying many of these senior management roles. There was considerable emphasis on the need for social work to operate collaboratively with other services, and a protocol on joint notification and investigation between health boards and Gardaí was published by the Department of Health (1995) and later elaborated on in *Children First: National Guidelines for the Protection and Welfare of Children* (Department of Health and Children, 1999). This move had been preceded by mutual unease from both services, each of which was seen to operate from differing perspectives (Horgan, 1996).

Another concept that was gaining traction around the start of the new millennium was 'inclusiveness'. This stemmed from a combination of advocacy, research and a general recognition of the changing population of social work clientele who now included many more ethnic groups including refugees and families seeking asylum (Torode et al., 2001). The impact of gender on child protection practice and the effect of domestic violence on children (Kelly, 1996; Buckley, 1998) were becoming increasingly recognized, and the particular vulnerability of children with disabilities (Kennedy and Kelly, 1992) began to be highlighted. This new awareness led to an increased focus on anti-discriminatory practice, and consciousness of the perspective of service users and their exclusion from participation in child protection processes became more prominent at this time (Department of Health (UK), 1995; Ferguson and O'Reilly, 2001). Research had also highlighted the low level of direct communication with children whose situations were largely constructed in accounts provided by carers or professionals (Buckley, 2002, 2003). An action research project commissioned by the Southern Health Board in the early 1990s (Gilligan and Chapman, 1997) provided a national template for constructive attendance of parents at case conferences, and when *Children First* was published in 1999, it largely adopted this framework, which emphasized the importance of parental participation at all stages of child protection work. The need for direct contact with children and consideration of their views was also stipulated, and the guidance exhorted professionals against prejudice and discrimination in any child protection activity (Department of Health and Children, 1999).

The inclusion of the word 'welfare' in the title of the 1999 *Children First* guidance signalled the establishment of family support and early intervention as fundamental elements of child protection work. Subsequent investment throughout the early 2000s in Springboard (see McKeown et al., 2001) and other community-based projects broadened the children's service landscape considerably and social workers played a prominent role in these services. However, many of these services were targeted at specific geographical areas of need and were not universal family support and preventive services. While social workers had, at this point, been designated by the CEOs of the health boards as the principal statutory agents, the number of stakeholders in the child protection network now included other disciplines whose role was to work directly with families in their homes and in the community, responding to their identified welfare and parenting needs and building supports in the community to boost social capital.

Despite the insertion of these preventive elements into the child welfare system, the more investigative aspect of child protection social work continued to dominate practice. Annual statistics published by the Health Service Executive (HSE) implied that the greater part of social work activity was spent screening and investigating reports made to it, with high attrition rates between initial referral and closure of cases and little coordination of early intervention and preventive activities (HSE, 2009). Over the decade, statistics showed a clear trend whereby welfare concerns and reports of child neglect comprised two-thirds of the total number of reports received, the majority of which were screened out quickly or only received a short-term supportive response. The *Agenda for Children's Services* (Office of the Minister for Children, 2007) sought to rectify this by laying out a blueprint for an evidence-based model of service delivery that would prioritize the support of children and families in their own communities. The introduction of differential or alternative response models in a small number of areas (Canavan and Landy, 2011; Yalloway et al., 2012) represented further efforts to provide proportionate and more immediate responses and integrate social work with family support services to a greater degree.

However, despite the aspiration to develop a community-based, preventive, participative and inclusive approach to child welfare, the publication of a number of high-profile inquiry reports, including the Ryan Report (2009) and the Roscommon Report (Gibbons et al., 2010), followed by reports on clerical sexual abuse, kept political attention on the 'front door' of the statutory social work service, with less attention paid to either early intervention or long-term solutions. Since the beginning of Ireland's economic crisis, social work has been the only profession exempt from the public sector recruitment embargo, and there was a clear government intention to retain investigative social work as the main centre of child protection and welfare. Managerialist strategies were introduced in an effort to render frontline practice more consistent and thereby more measurable. These methods included the categorization of social work interventions in the form of standardized business processes (see, for example, HSE, 2009) and the introduction of tighter controls over the activities of community-based agencies and funded services to align them with the child protection social work service. The Health Information and Quality Authority (HIQA, 2012) issued standards for statutory child protection social work departments and teams are now inspected against a range of performance benchmarks and indicators. In 2011, the government signalled its intention to make reporting of suspected child abuse a legislative requirement and followed this, first, with the Children First (Heads of) Bill 2012 and later with the Children First Bill 2014.

In the interim, the review of children's services in 2011 had indicated serious weaknesses in early childcare and a lack of coherence, particularly in respect of mental health, access to healthcare and school retention (Harvey, 2011). Annual 'report cards' issued by the Children's Rights Alliance (2013, p. 1) also cited 'consistent shortcomings and the lack of real progress in the areas of poverty, health and discrimination'. Child poverty rates[1] in Ireland grew from 18% in 2008 to 28.6% in 2012, placing Ireland in one of the lowest performing countries (UNICEF, 2014). Deficits in the areas of poverty, health and discrimination have been reiterated in annual reports from the Office of the Ombudsman for Children, particularly in respect of access to education and therapeutic interventions (Ombudsman for Children, 2012; Burns and Lynch, 2012). Together, these indicators may demonstrate that child protection and welfare is once more becoming narrowly defined, with culpability for child-related problems divided between the social work profession and parents themselves, with little regard for the structural context in which difficulties arise.

Over 30 years after the publication of the report from the Task Force on Child Care Services, despite significant investment, a vastly increased knowledge base and some tangible efforts at reform, social work with children and families is still struggling to meet its aims of intervening early and maintaining children in the community. However, the establishment of a single agency for child protection and welfare, which espouses partnership and interagency working (Tusla, Child and Family Agency, 2013a), provides new opportunities. These will be examined later, but first we will shift the focus of this chapter from the child protection system to the children and families whose needs it is intended to serve. Available data will illustrate the challenges posed to the change and reform process and the agency's ability to provide an adequate response.

Childhood and child abuse data in Ireland

Ireland has the largest numbers of children in the EU as a percentage of the country's total population. In the last census, out of a total population of 4.59 million, 1.15 million people were under 18 years of age (25% of the population) (CSO, 2012). Historically, data on outcomes for children in Ireland has been inadequate, but a strong series of initiatives such as *Growing Up in Ireland: National Longitudinal Study of Children* (Economic and Social Research Institute/Trinity College Dublin, 2015) and the annual *State of the Nation's Children Reports* (Department of Children and Youth Affairs, 2006–12) have sought to address knowledge gaps. However, data on children at risk and children in the care of the state continues to be deficient, with limited and sometimes inconsistent data between areas (Buckley, 2008; Burns and MacCarthy, 2012). In particular, data on child abuse and child welfare reports (referrals), social work caseloads and data in relation to childcare court proceedings has been limited and unavailable for certain years. Similar to other countries (see Gilbert et al., 2011), Ireland has witnessed a steady growth in referrals. Between 2006 and 2012 (the most recent year for which published data is available), the numbers of reports made to statutory social work departments effectively doubled (HSE, 2013a). This doubling of child protection reports has not been matched by a corresponding increase in the workforce. The Ryan implementation report (Office of the Minister for Children and Youth Affairs, 2009) promised an extra 200 posts, later increased to 270 posts. Conflicting accounts provided by the IASW, the labour union and the department on the actual realization of these posts, together with acknowledged delays in recruitment, have made it difficult to calculate the precise size of the workforce at present.[2] 'Frontline' child protection social workers are primarily female and early career, which means that regular maternity leave is an inevitability (Burns and Christie, 2013). Overall, it is clear that regardless of the extra investment, the capacity of the child protection system to cope with the increase in reports is unavoidably strained, a fact reflected in the reports produced by the Independent

Child Death Review Group (Shannon and Gibbons, 2012) and the National Review Panel, which examines child deaths (HSE, 2012, 2013b).

The pattern of referrals to the statutory child welfare and protection services has remained consistent with previous years, whereby just over half of reports were ultimately designated as 'welfare' and just under half classified as 'child protection' (Tusla, Child and Family Agency, 2014). The dearth of information on the nature of child welfare and protection concerns provides little insight into the needs of the children in contact with the system. The provision of services in response to welfare reports is not analysed; it is given to understand that the children and families concerned are linked with community-based family support services and/or short-term statutory social work services, although the nature and longevity of interventions are not documented, nor is any detailed information provided on the accessibility and availability of family support services.

The information provided on the processing of child protection reports in 2014 provides equally scant information on the nature of the child harm reported to the system. According to the *National Performance Activity Report*, published in late 2014, 57% of reports initially designated as 'child protection' were considered to require initial assessment, and 50% of those referrals were closed with no further action (Tusla, Child and Family Agency, 2014), but it is not known whether these families were left with unmet needs, just that they fell below the threshold for child protection action. Irish datasets do not record social demographic information with the referral data. In September 2014, it was confirmed in Dail Eireann that 9,000 child protection cases were awaiting allocation of social workers (Oireachtas Joint Committee on Health and Children, 2014). The statistics indicate a continuation of the trend that began to be of concern in the 1990s, whereby most social work time appears to be invested in investigation at the expense of intervention. This may mean a high level of screening out or it might mean that families are worked with, or referred to appropriate services where positive outcomes are achieved. However, the data does not elaborate on the nature of interventions, nor does it provide a picture of the pathway of reports through the assessment and intervention process, and the available data indicates that high thresholds continue to operate.

We are aware from other sources that many more children suffer adversity in Ireland than appear to be reflected in the official child protection and welfare statistics. For example, large numbers of children are negatively impacted by issues such as parental substance abuse (Buckley et al., 2006; Alcohol Action Ireland, 2009; National Advisory Committee on Drugs, 2011; Hope, 2011) and domestic violence (Buckley et al., 2007; Safe Ireland, 2014). On the other hand, there is also evidence of improving outcomes for children and their welfare in Ireland (see Department of Children and Youth Affairs, 2006–12). It could be concluded that opportunities to make a difference to these children's lives are being missed because of the narrow orientation of the referral and intake social work system. Our review of the available data points towards the necessity for an updated study similar to those conducted in the late 1990s (Buckley et al., 1997; Ferguson and O'Reilly, 2001), which examined the nature, scope and pathways of referrals and interventions in child protection teams. In the meantime, it is vital that the problem of inadequate data collection and reporting is addressed; real reform will only be effected if it is based on accurate information about what is required, what is available and what gaps exist.

New agency, new rights, new systems: From child protection to a comprehensive prevention and family support response?

The establishment in January 2014 of the new Child and Family Agency, known as Tusla, a conjunction of the Irish words for new (tús) and day (lá), represents an attempt by the government to ring-fence and raise the profile of child protection (see Child and Family Agency Act 2013). The main impetus for moving the (primarily social work) services away from health services was, as the minister for children put it: 'to emancipate our child protection and welfare services from the monolith of the health services where for too long in the past they were lost and rudderless' (Department of Children and Youth Affairs, 2013a). A Regulatory Impact Analysis (Department of Children and Youth Affairs, 2013b, p. 4) prepared in respect of the legislation identified 'leadership, enhanced accountability and more efficient interdisciplinary and interagency working' as features of the reform. In her launch speech, the minister promised that Tusla would 'pull together and give single coherent direction to all of the strands of service for our families most in need in a way that has never happened in this country before' (Fitzgerald, 2014, p. 1). She also acknowledged that existing problems in the system will not be fixed 'overnight'; this note of caution provides some room for optimism that serious reflection will be applied to the shape services should adopt.

The new agency structure does provide a number of opportunities to redress some of the inexorable difficulties outlined in the previous section. The model of service delivery aspired to closely resembles that which was envisioned in the report from the Task Force on Child Care Services of the early 1980s. The fact that the aspirations never came to fruition was acknowledged by the minister for children and youth affairs in her launch speech, with the observation that: 'The system failed because it was never designed to work' (Department of Children and Youth Affairs, 2013c, p. 1).

However, the aphorism (variously attributed to Narcotics Anonymous and Albert Einstein among others) that 'insanity is repeating the same mistakes and expecting different results' could be tentatively applied to some of the ambitions of the new venture unless some serious reflection is applied as to why the hoped-for model of service delivery failed before.

One of the major weaknesses manifest in previous attempts to provide early intervention and prevention was the lack of coherence around family support, evidenced by the absence of any attempt to quantify either its operation or its outcomes. Its profile was vague, and it had fallen into the meaningless and all-inclusive 'warm and fuzzy' sphere that had been cautioned against by Pinkerton (2000, p. 207). The more recent formalization of community-based, non-statutory services represents a hopeful step. The establishment of local area pathways (Tusla, Child and Family Agency, 2013b) to implement the differential response model should stimulate and strengthen the community and voluntary organizations' contribution to the service provision mix. However, some significant threats need to be addressed.

The first threat is the assumption that this model of service delivery can be achieved on a virtually cost-neutral basis.[3] The impact of the crisis in international financial and banking systems and the ensuing period of austerity and retrenchment of public services in Ireland (see Kirby, 2011; Kirby and Murphy, 2011) raises questions as to whether the change management process will be adequately resourced and whether there will be sufficient staffing to meet the increasing demand for services for all the children and families in need of support. Inadequate funding has been identified as a risk factor in the implementation of the differential response approach in the US (Waldfogel, 1998). Another threat is the belief that differential response or alternative response approaches will work consistently or are universally understood. A special issue of *Research on Social Work Practice* published in September 2013 has demonstrated the diversity of differential response approaches applied in the US and the lack of uniformity in assessment and decision-making protocols, which can risk a return to the bias and misjudgement that gave rise to reform in the first place. Hughes et al. (2013) argue for a standardization of tools to ensure a consistent response.

However, the third threat lies in this very standardization. Featherstone et al. (2012) have warned that standardization in the UK was far from successful and care needs to be taken to learn from, rather than repeat, such mistakes. Family support, as envisaged by Pinkerton (2000), needs to challenge traditional welfare policies and accommodate the changing nature of families and their needs. This could be extended to differing communities and their needs. There is a danger that the homogenization of services will stifle pockets of initiative and expertise that have arisen in particular environments and may be best suited to meet local challenges. The new model may pose a risk to the therapeutic and supportive identities of some of the existing voluntary and community organizations, particularly if pressure leads to some quasi-statutory functions being delegated to them. With the publication of the Children First Bill 2014, Ireland is coming nearer to the adoption of a mandatory reporting model for professionals and community and voluntary sector organizations in receipt of state funding (Department of Children and Youth Affairs, 2013d), which may present a further risk to the identity of community and voluntary organizations. As Garrett (2013, p. 36) argues, the sort of initiatives described in this chapter may be thwarted and lead to failure, because of what he describes as 'economic imperatives and the overriding commitment to intensified neoliberation'.

A further challenge to the goal of 'one cohesive support system' (Tusla, Child and Family Agency, 2013b, p. 1) will be the potential failure to bring all children's services together in one agency and it remains to be seen if different services can find a way to implement the new goals and policy from within different structures. Many jurisdictions, jaded from criticism of their child protection services, particularly the lack of shared responsibility and collaboration between services, have concluded that the most constructive and coherent approach to working with vulnerable and at risk children is through what is termed a 'public health model'. This is defined as 'a concept with currency in many disciplines including health, education and welfare' (Hunter, 2011, p. 1) and has been incorporated into the National Framework for Protecting Australia's Children (Council of Australian Governments, 2009). It is similar to the popular Hardiker et al. (1991) model in terms of the different levels of intervention, but its difference is that it takes a holistic perspective and draws its benchmarks from a range of children and young people's services, including health, disability, mental health, youth justice and education, and encompasses a variety of interventions from speech and language to housing and other environmental issues (Woodman and Gilbert, 2013).

Another variant on this theme is what is often called the 'whole of government approach'. Although the Irish government has claimed this orientation for children and family services in its recently published national policy framework, *Better Outcomes, Brighter Futures: The National Policy Framework for Children and Young People 2014-2020* (Department of Children and Youth Affairs, 2014), it is more commonly applied to strategies where the responsibility of government departments to resource and operate child protection activities is named in childcare legislation (see, for example, the Keep Them Safe programme operated by the New South Wales Government (2009) in Australia) and mechanisms are put in place to build the capacity of adult services to be child centred, such as the Australian federally funded project *Protecting and Nurturing Children: Building Capacity, Building Bridges* (Australian Centre for Child Protection, 2014).

The inability to get disciplines and agencies to work together has been at the root of child protection system failure since its beginnings in the 1970s. Research, along with many child abuse inquiries in Ireland and elsewhere, has demonstrated the multifaceted tensions and failures of communication between social workers and other disciplines and agencies in Ireland (Duggan and Corrigan, 2009; National Review Panel, 2011–14). The difficulties stem not just from the physical separation of services but from a combination of complex dynamics, including differing goals and perspectives, diverse funding arrangements, and arguments about responsibility for the 'dirty work' of child protection, which is seen to belong to social work (Butler, 1996; Buckley, 2003). A recent doctoral study (Buckley, 2014), which ascertained the views of professionals in schools, youth services, hospitals, addiction and other health and justice services on the potential impact of the forthcoming mandatory reporting legislation, revealed a low level of interest, ownership and awareness of child protection issues among staff in these areas. This was attributed partly to deficiencies in basic grade and post-qualifying training, particularly among teachers and health professionals, but also to a culture that relegated responsibility to social work departments.

A positive opportunity for Tusla and social work will be the embracing of a children's rights ethos across the whole service to shift Ireland from a family-centric model to one where children's as well as parental rights are operationalized. While Ireland is a full signatory to the UN Convention on the Rights of the Child (UN, 1989), the implementation of a children's rights ethos throughout children's services and Irish society has yet to be realized. For example, the Ombudsman for Children (2012, p. 8) has stated that 'the core principles of best interests and respect for the views of the child are not being respected systematically in Ireland'. The attempted shift away from a legalistic and investigative approach, which is characteristic of a child protection system, towards a child-focused, early intervention and needs assessment model (see Gilbert et al., 2011) should be bolstered by the full implementation of the new Article 42A (Children) of the Irish Constitution. The new amendment:

- recognizes that children are rights holders in their own right

- allows for children in long-term care to be adopted

- affirms that all children are equal, irrespective of the marital status of their parents

- states that, in all proceedings, 'the best interest of the child principle shall be the paramount consideration', and provision should be made in law to ensure that children's views 'shall be ascertained and given due weight having regard to the age and maturity of the child' (Government of Ireland, 2012, p. 8).

These changes will underpin the future of child and family social work in Ireland. The final section briefly considers the implications of these changes for the future of social work in Ireland and questions how Tusla and the government will ensure that the new service delivery model is implemented for the benefit of children and their families.

Conclusion: the future of social work in child and family services in Ireland

The changes examined in this chapter open up opportunities for social work with children and families in Ireland over the next decade. However, while there is much to be optimistic about, it has been our contention that there is an element of déjà vu about the plan, which closely resembles the blueprint for services first envisaged more than 30 years ago in the Task Force on Child Care Services report recommendations. We have contended that economic constraints and cutbacks to the community and voluntary sector will impede progression towards a model that provides early intervention in a meaningful way. We have also highlighted the necessity for greater integration and sharing of responsibility for child protection, adopting a more ecological approach that encompasses such sectors as health, mental health, housing and education in the delivery of child welfare and protection services. We have drawn attention to understrength social work teams that are struggling to deal with a doubling of new reports between 2006 and 2012. Finally, we have cautioned that newly imposed administrative pressures may have a stifling effect on statutory and nongovernmental services. Of course, it is not certain that managerialism will define the new agency, but its pervasiveness in child welfare bureaucracies across the world suggests the need for some caution.

While the planned changes have been made fully manifest, it is less clear what this will mean for social work, how active the profession was in contributing to the redesign of the system, and how social workers feel about these changes. A truly integrated child protection service would provide interesting opportunities for social workers to operate in diverse ways with different service user groups. Some social workers may choose to move to non-statutory settings to undertake more preventive and supportive roles with children and families that may be more congruent with their understanding of the profession. It will be important for social workers within the new agency to adopt a critical, questioning stance towards it. These social workers will be part of Tusla, but should foster a unique professional identity that seeks to:

- promote social integration and community and interpersonal relationships

- be critical of government policies and structures that are oppressive reject individual, personal-blaming approaches in favour of ecological and structural understandings of social and interpersonal issues.

The increasing workload of statutory child protection workers will make it more difficult for staff to contribute to the profession's development and collectively seek to progress social policy and legislative change agendas. However, such work remains a core focus of the profession and practitioners will need to find ways, for example through the media and various professional and advocacy organizations as well as pressure groups, to contribute to these aspects of professional social work.

Finally, we reiterate our contention that the confinement of responsibility for child protection and the provision of services to the Child and Family Agency, in a context where referral rates continue to rise, will relegate social workers in the agency to a tertiary role, applying high thresholds and responding in a narrow and forensic manner to concerns about vulnerable children. Their workload may become defined in terms of serious abuse and neglect cases, with the concomitant hazards that this high-risk, high-skill work suggests in terms of staff retention and job satisfaction (see Burns, 2011, 2012). If this is allowed to happen, the problem will come full circle, with the social work profession carrying a disproportionate level of responsibility and criticism for future shortcomings in children and family services.

Note

1. UNICEF (2014, p. 9) calculated child poverty changes between 2008 and 2012 by using a 'fixed reference point, anchored to the relative poverty line in 2008, as a benchmark against which to assess the absolute change in child poverty over time', rather than using a relative poverty line each year.
2. This absence of data is not helped by the agency's reluctance, thus far, to publish a breakdown of its posts, revealing the numbers of social workers in frontline child protection posts.
3. However, the agency did receive an investment in April 2015 of €8 million from Atlantic Philanthropies to fund a three-year prevention and early intervention programme. Although welcome, it raises a question as to whether the government is sufficiently resourcing the agency to fulfill its remit and whether such an investment is sufficient.

References

Alcohol Action Ireland (2009) *Keeping it in the Family Survey, 2009*, Dublin, Alcohol Action Ireland.

Australian Centre for Child Protection (2014) *Protection and Nurturing Children: Building Capacity, Building Bridges,* http://w3.unisa.edu.au/childprotection/projects/bcbb/, accessed 20 February 2014.

Buckley, H. (1993) 'Joint approach to child abuse', *Garda Review,* 21(1), 14–15.

Buckley, H. (1998) 'Filtering out fathers: the gendered nature of social work in child protection, *Irish Social Worker,* 16(3), 7–11.

Buckley, H. (2002) *Child Protection and Welfare: Innovations and Interventions,* Dublin, Institute of Public Administration.

Buckley, H. (2003) *Child Protection Work: Beyond the Rhetoric,* London, Jessica Kingsley.

Buckley, H. (2008) 'Heading for collision? Managerialism, social science, and the Irish child protection system', in Burns, K. and Lynch, D. (eds) *Child Protection and Welfare Social Work: Contemporary Themes and Practice Perspectives,* Dublin, A & A Farmar.

Buckley, H. and O'Nolan, C. (2013) *An Examination of Recommendations from Inquiries into Events in Families and their Interactions with State Services, and their Impact on Policy and Practice,* Dublin, Department of Children and Youth Affairs.

Buckley, H., Holt, S. and Whelan, S. (2007) 'Listen to me! Children's experience of domestic violence', *Child Abuse Review,* 16(5), 283–95.

Buckley, H., Horwath, J. and Whelan, S. (2006) *Framework for the Assessment of Vulnerable Children and their Families,* Dublin, Children's Research Centre, Trinity College.

Buckley, H., Skehill, C. and O'Sullivan, E. (1997) *Child Protection Practices in Ireland: A Case Study,* Dublin, Oak Tree Press.

Buckley, R. (2014) Child Abuse Reporting in Ireland and the Socio-legal Implications of Introducing a Mandatory Reporting Law, PhD thesis, Trinity College Dublin.

Burns, K. (2011) '"Career preference", "transients" and "converts": a study of social workers' retention in child protection and welfare', *British Journal of Social Work,* 41(3), 520–38.

Burns, K. (2012) *Strengthening the Retention of Child Protection Workers: Career Preferences, Exchange Relationships and Employment Mobility,* Bremen, EHV Academic.

Burns, K. and Christie, A. (2013) 'Employment mobility or turnover? An analysis of child welfare and protection employee retention', *Children and Youth Services Review,* 35(2), 340–6.

Burns, K. and Lynch, D. (2012) 'Politics, democracy and protecting children', in Lynch, D. and Burns, K. (eds) *Children's Rights and Child Protection: Critical Times, Critical Issues in Ireland,* Manchester, Manchester University Press.

Burns, K. and MacCarthy, J. (2012) 'An impossible task? Implementing the recommendations of child abuse inquiry reports in a context of high workloads in child protection and welfare', *Irish Journal of Applied Social Studies,* 12(1), 4–17.

Butler, S. (1996) 'Child protection or professional self-preservation by the baby nurses? Public health nurses and child protection in Ireland', *Social Science and Medicine* 43, 303–14.

Canavan, J. and Landy, F. (2011) *North Dublin Differential Response Model: Early Implementation Report,* http://childandfamilyresearch.ie/sites/www.childandfamily research.ie/files/north_dublin_drm_early_implementation_report_june_2011_0. pdf, accessed 28 February 2014.

Children's Rights Alliance (2013) *Report Card 2013: Is Government Keeping its Promises to Children?*, www.childrensrights.ie/sites/default/files/submissions_reports/files/ReportCard2013.pdf, accessed 9 December 2013.

Cooney, T. and Torode, R. (1989) *Irish Council for Civil Liberties Working Party on Child Sexual Abuse Report*, Dublin, ICCL.

Council of Australian Government (2009) 'Protecting children is everyone's business: National Framework for Protecting Australia's Children 2009–2020', www.fahcsia. gov.au/sa/families/pubs/framework_protecting_children/page s/default/aspx, accessed 28 February 2014.

CSO (Central Statistics Office) (2012) *This is Ireland: Highlights from Census 2011, Part 1*, Dublin, Stationery Office.

Department of Children and Youth Affairs (2006–12) *The State of the Nation's Children Reports 2006-2012*, www.dcya.gov.ie/viewdoc.asp?fn=%2Fdocuments%2FResearch %2FStateoftheNationReport.htm, accessed 28 February 2014.

Department of Children and Youth Affairs (2013a) 'Press Release on Child and Family Agency Bill 2013', www.dcya.gov.ie/viewdoc.asp?fn=/documents/press/17072013Press.htm, accessed 13 October 2013.

Department of Children and Youth Affairs (2013b) *Child and Family Agency Bill 2012: Regulatory Impact Analysis, 2013*, www.dcya.gov.ie/documents/chidfamily supportagency/RIA_CFA.pdf, accessed 28 February 2014.

Department of Children and Youth Affairs (2013c) 'Government investing in important reforms' press statement, 15 October, www.dcya.gov.ie/viewdoc.asp?DocID=2999, accessed 20 February 2014.

Department of Children and Youth Affairs (2013d) *Children First Legislation*, www.dcya.gov.ie/viewdoc.asp?fn=%2Fdocuments%2FChildren_First%2FChildrenFirstLegislation.htm, accessed 15 December 2014.

Department of Children and Youth Affairs (2014) *Better Outcomes, Brighter Futures: The National Policy Framework for Children and Young People 2014-2020*, www.dcya. gov.ie/documents/cypp_framework/BetterOutcomesBetterFutureReport.pdf, accessed 14 May 2014.

Department of Health (1980a) *Non-Accidental Injury to Children: Guidelines on Procedures for the Identification, Investigation and Management of Non-Accidental Injury to Children*, Dublin, Department of Health.

Department of Health (1980b) *Task Force on Child Care Services: Final Report*, Dublin, Stationery Office.

Department of Health (1987) *Guidelines on Procedures for the Identification, Investigation and Management of Child Abuse*, Dublin, Department of Health.

Department of Health (1995) *Notification of Suspected Cases of Child Abuse between Health Boards and Gardai*, Dublin, Stationery Office.

Department of Health (UK) (1995) *Messages from Research*, London, HMSO.

Department of Health and Children (1999) *Children First: National Guidelines for the Protection and Welfare of Children*, Dublin, Stationery Office.

Duggan, C. and Corrigan, C. (2009) *An Analysis of Research Literature on Inter-agency Cooperation in Children's Services*, Dublin, Children Acts Advisory Board.

Economic and Social Research Institute/Trinity College Dublin (2015) *Growing Up in Ireland: Overview*, www.growingup.ie/index.php?id=9, accessed 15 December 2014.

Eastern Health Board/Impact (1997) *Report of the Eastern Health Board/Impact Review Group on Child Care and Family Support Services*, Dublin, Eastern Health Board.

Featherstone, B., White, S. and Wastell, D. (2012) 'Ireland's opportunity to learn from England's difficulties? Auditing uncertainty in child protection', *Irish Journal of Applied Social Studies*, 12(1), 49–62.

Ferguson, H. (1996) 'Protecting Irish children in time: child abuse as a social problem and the development of the child protection system in the Republic of Ireland', *Administration*, 44(2), 5–36.

Ferguson, H. and O'Reilly, M. (2001) *Keeping Children Safe: Child Abuse, Child Protection and the Promotion of Welfare*, Dublin, A & A Farmar.

Fitzgerald, F. (2014) An Taoiseach and Minster for Children and Youth Affairs officially launch Ireland's new Child and Family Agency, www.dcya.gov.ie/viewdoc.asp?DocID=3087, accessed 22 February 2014.

Garrett, P.M. (2013) 'Beyond the community of person to be accorded "respect"? Messages from the past for social work in the Republic of Ireland', in Carey, M. and Green, L. (eds) *Practical Social Work Ethics: Complex Dilemmas within Applied Social Care*, Farnham, Ashgate.

Gibbons, N., Harrison, P., Lunny, L. and O'Neill, G. (2010) *Roscommon Child Care Case: Report of the Inquiry Team to the Health Service Executive*, Dublin, HSE.

Gilbert, N., Parton, N. and Skivenes, M. (eds) (2011) *Child Protection Systems: International Trends and Orientations*, Oxford, Oxford University Press.

Gilligan, R. (1993) 'The Child Care Act 1991: an examination of its scope and resource implications', *Administration*, 40, 345–70.

Gilligan, R. and Chapman, R. (1997) *Developing Good Practice in the Conduct of Child Protection Case Conferences: An Action Research Project*, Cork, Southern Health Board.

Government of Ireland (2012) *Thirty-First Amendment of the Constitution (Children) Bill 2012*, www.oireachtas.ie/viewdoc.asp?DocID=21772&&CatID=59, accessed 5 February 2014.

Hardiker, P., Exton, K. and Barker, M. (1991) *Policies and Practices in Preventive Child Care*, Aldershot, Avebury.

Harvey, B. (2011) *A Way Forward for Delivering Children's Services*, www.barnardos.ie/assets/files/Advocacy/Brian%20Harvey%20Mar%202011%20_2_.pdf, accessed 9 December 2013.

HIQA (Health Information and Quality Authority) (2012) *National Standards for the Protection and Welfare of Children. For Health Service Executive Children and Family Services*, Cork, HIQA.

Hope, A. (2011) *Hidden Realities: Children's Exposure to Risks from Parental Drinking in Ireland*, Letterkenny, North Western Alcohol Forum Ltd.

Horgan, D. (1996) 'Inter-agency co-operation: team work and child protection', *Irish Social Worker*, 1(4), 4–6.

HSE (Health Service Executive) (2009) *HSE Child Welfare and Protection Social Work Departments Business Processes: Report of the NCCIS Business Process Standardisation Project October 2009*, Dublin, HSE.

HSE (2012) *National Review Panel Annual Report 2011*, Dublin, HSE.

HSE (2013a) *Review of Adequacy for HSE Children and Families Services 2011*, Dublin, HSE.

HSE (2013b) *National Review Panel Annual Report 2012*, Dublin, HSE.

Hughes, R.C., Rycus, J., Saunders-Adams, S.M. et al. (2013) 'Issues in differential response', *Research on Social Work Practice*, 23(5), 493–520.

Hunter, C. (2011) *Defining the Public Health Model for the Child Welfare Services Context*, Child Family Community Australia, www.aifs.gov.au/nch/pubs/sheets/rs11/rs11. pdf, accessed 28 February 2014.

Kelly, L. (1996) 'When women protection is the best kind of child protection', *Administration*, 44(2), 118–33.

Kelly, L., Regan, L. and Burton, S. (1993) 'Beyond victim to survivor; the implications of knowledge about children's resistance and avoidance strategies', in Ferguson, H., Gilligan, R. and Torode, R. (eds) *Surviving Childhood Adversity*, Dublin, Social Studies Press, TCD.

Kennedy, M. and Kelly, L. (1992) 'Inclusion not exclusion', *Child Abuse Review*, 1(3), 147–9.

Kirby, P. (2011) *When Banks Cannibalise a State: Analysing Ireland's Financial Crisis*, www.realinstitutoelcano.org/wps/portal/rielcano_eng/Content?WCM_GLOBAL_ CONTEXT=/elcano/Elcano_in/Zonas_in/ARI178-2010, accessed 5 February 2014.

Kirby, P. and Murphy, M. (2011) *Towards a Second Republic: Irish Politics after the Celtic Tiger*, Dublin, Pluto Press.

Langford, S. and Cullen, M. (1981) Towards a Fourth Programme for the Social Services, internal unpublished Eastern Health Board Document.

McGrath, K. (1996) 'Intervening in child sexual abuse in Ireland: towards victim centred policies and practices', *Administration*, 44(2), 57–72.

McGrath, K. (1998) 'Mandatory reporting: Will it remain a political football?', *Irish Social Worker*, 16(4), 2–4.

McGuinness, C. (1993) *Kilkenny Incest Investigation: Report Presented to Mr. Brendan Howlin T.D. Minister for Health*, Dublin, Stationery Office.

McGuinness, C. (2012) 'It is a long way from Kilkenny to here: reflections on legal and policy developments before and since the publication of the Kilkenny Incest Investigation', in Lynch, D. and Burns, K. (eds) *Children's Rights and Child Protection: Critical Times, Critical Issues in Ireland*, Manchester, Manchester University Press.

McKeown, K. and Gilligan, R. (1991) 'Child sexual abuse in the Eastern Health Board region of Ireland in 1988: an analysis of 512 confirmed cases', *Economic and Social Review*, 22, 101–34.

McKeown, K., Haase, T. and Pratschke, J. (2001) *Springboard Promoting Family Well-Being Through Family Support Services*, Dublin, Department of Health and Children.

National Advisory Committee on Drugs (2011) *Parental Substance Misuse: Addressing its Impact on Children*, Dublin, Stationery Office.

National Review Panel (2011–14) *National Review Panel Reports*, www.tusla.ie/ publications/national-review-panel-reports, accessed 15 December 2014.

New South Wales Government (2009) *Keep Them Safe: A Shared Approach to Child Wellbeing, 2009-2014*, www.dcya.gov.ie/viewdoc.asp?DocID=2999, accessed 20 February 2014.

Office of the Minister for Children (2007) *The Agenda for Children's Service: A Policy Handbook*, Dublin, Stationery Office.

Office of the Minister for Children and Youth Affairs (2009) *Report of the Commission to Inquire into Child Abuse, 2009: Implementation Plan*, Dublin, Department of Health and Children.

Oireachtas Joint Committee on Health and Children (2014) *Update on Child and Family Services: Child and Family Agency,* www.kildarestreet.com/committees/?id=2014-09-25a.287, accessed 16 January 2015.

Ombudsman for Children (2012) *Ombudsman for Children Annual Report 2011*, Dublin, Ombudsman for Children's Office.

O'Sullivan, E. (2009) 'Residential child welfare in Ireland, 1965-2008: an outline of policy, legislation and practice: a paper prepared for the Commission to Inquire into Child Abuse', www.childabusecommission.com/rpt/04-04.php, accessed 27 February 2014.

Pinkerton, J. (2000) 'Emerging agendas for family support', in Canavan, J., Dolan, P. and Pinkerton, J. (eds) *Family Support: Direction and Diversity*, London, Jessica Kingsley.

Research on Social Work Practice (2013) Special issue on differential response, 23(5).

Ryan, S. (2009) *Commission to Inquire into Child Abuse Report* (vols i–v), Dublin, Stationery Office.

Safe Ireland (2014) *Safe Ireland Domestic Violence Services National Statistics 2013,* www.safeireland.ie/2014/launch-of-2013-annual-statistics, accessed 10 March 2015.

Shannon, G. and Gibbons, N. (2012) *Report of the Independent Child Death Review Group,* Dublin, Government Publications.

Skehill, C. (2004) *The Nature of Social Work in Ireland,* New York, Edwin Mellen.

Torode, R.T., Walsh, T. and Woods, M. (2001) *Working with Refugees and Asylum-Seekers: A Social Work Resource Book*, Dublin, Department of Social Studies.

Tusla, Child and Family Agency (2013a) *Suite of Policy and Guidance Documents for the Child and Family Agency*, www.childandfamilyresearch.ie/publications/policy-practice, accessed 5 February 2014.

Tusla, Child and Family Agency (2013b) *Guidance for the Implementation of an Area Based Approach to Prevention, Partnership and Family Support,* www.childandfami-lyresearch.ie/publications/policy-practice, accessed 5 February 2014.

Tusla, Child and Family Agency (2014) *Quarter 3 2014: National Performance Activity Report,* www.tusla.ie/uploads/content/National_Performance_Activity_Report_Quarter_3_2014_Final_(2).pdf, accessed 16 January 2015.

UN (United Nations) (1989) *Convention on the Rights of the Child*, Geneva, UN.

UNICEF (2014) *Innocenti Report Card 12: Children of the Recession: The Impact of the Economic Crisis on Child Well-Being in Rich Countries*, www.unicef-irc.org/publications/series/16.

Waldfogel, J. (1998) *The Future of Child Protection*, Cambridge, MA, Harvard University Press.

Woodman, J. and Gilbert, R. (2013) 'Child maltreatment: moving towards a public health approach', in BMA Board of Science, *Growing up in the UK: Ensuring a Healthy Future for Children.*

Yalloway, M., Hardagen, M. and MacNab, E. (2012) 'Making "new connections": the development of a differential response to child protection and welfare', in Lynch, D. and Burns, K. (eds) *Children's Rights and Child Protection: Critical Times, Critical Issues in Ireland*, Manchester, Manchester University Press.

5
Adoption in Ireland: Exploring the Changing Context

Simone McCaughren and Muireann Ní Raghallaigh

Introduction

Internationally, adoption has been, and continues to be, a matter of great controversy. Social work professionals play a pivotal role in adoption practice. Therefore, it is essential that they not only have an understanding of the key issues at play, but also use their expertise as frontline workers to highlight and address these issues. This chapter outlines some of these issues from an Irish perspective and discusses their relevance to social work practice. As well as outlining some of the legal developments, the chapter discusses the practice of open adoption, identity and belonging, and the ethical challenges that need to be considered within this field of practice. Both domestic and international adoption are discussed. The chapter explores the fast-changing context of adoption, at national and global levels, and identifies that changes are increasingly being shaped by the experiences of those directly affected by adoption. So, there is an onus on social workers to reflect on and re-evaluate their role. In order to do so, it is essential that professionals develop their understanding of the past, particularly in relation to mistakes that have been made.

A brief overview of Ireland's adoption history

In Ireland, up until the 1980s (and perhaps even later), there was huge public shame associated with having a child outside wedlock. O'Hare et al. (1983, p. 12) stated that attitudes to unmarried mothers 'have been harsh and have had the effect of isolating these women from their communities'. This was largely due to the strong influence of the Roman Catholic Church. Women who became pregnant outside marriage were viewed with disdain and their children had to endure the stigma of illegitimacy. However, this ideology did not provide women with an alternative – there was little social support for women to single-handedly care for their children. With few other options at their disposal, these women became outcasts and were forced to live in mother and baby homes – mostly run by religious orders – where their pregnancies were hidden from society. Many of these homes became known as places of retribution where mothers had to earn their keep through hard labour. In recent years, the conditions endured by many women living in mother and baby homes have been highlighted (see, for example, O'Sullivan and O'Donnell, 2012; Department of Children and Youth Affairs, 2014a). In addition, attention has been drawn to the high number of infant deaths within these homes (Department of Children and Youth Affairs, 2014a). For example, from archival research, one journalist discovered that the infant death rate in one Cork mother and baby home soared to almost 70% in the early 1940s (O'Fatharta, 2014).

For those 'illegitimate' children who did survive, in many respects their fate rested with the nuns. The dominant view at the time was that birth mothers had acted immorally and had therefore forfeited social and legal legitimacy. The religious orders took on responsibility for decision making and mothers were 'strongly encouraged to give up their children' (Maguire, 2002, p. 389). Often, the mothers were not consulted, with nuns deliberately sidelining them regarding the plans for their children (Milotte, 2012). A large number of children were removed from their mothers and placed with families overseas, particularly America, where, according to Milotte (2012, p. 12), Ireland became a 'happy hunting ground' for people who wanted to adopt a child.

It has been argued that the 'disposal' of 'illegitimate' children relieved the Irish state of the financial burden of caring for babies and children (Maguire, 2002). Increasingly, the legitimacy of these adoptions has been questioned. Many were not properly documented and this has made it extremely difficult, if not impossible, for now adult adoptees to trace their biological mothers. Although domestic adoption became legal in Ireland in 1952, it is believed that the practice of sending children overseas, particularly to the US, continued for some time after (Milotte, 1997). The Commission of Investigation into Mother and Baby Homes and Certain Related Matters, which commenced its work in 2015, will cover forced adoptions.

Finally, it is evident that while Ireland has a long history as a 'sending country', it now finds itself receiving a number of internationally adopted children each year. Thus, it is facing a range of contemporary challenges posed by the move to international adoption, the difficult legacy of the past, and changing family structures. These challenges will now be discussed.

Adoption in a changing landscape

Adoption in Ireland is governed by the Adoption Authority of Ireland (AAI, formerly the Adoption Board). It is an independent quasi-judicial statutory body appointed by government and was established as a central authority under the Adoption Act 2010. It has a number of functions, including making or refusing adoption orders and registering and supervising the work of accredited bodies (Shannon, 2011). There are four types of domestic adoption: domestic infant adoption, stepfamily adoption, extended/relative adoption, and long-term foster care leading to adoption.

Adoption in the current Irish context must be viewed against the backdrop of a society that is now more diverse. Single parenthood has become more socially acceptable and there are a number of new and accepted family structures. Drawing on Central Statistics Office figures, the AAI indicates that in 1973, 1,402 children were placed for domestic adoption, which accounts for 64.7% of non-marital births. Forty years later, in 2013, the corresponding figure was 116 (0.47% of non-marital births). In addition, of these 116 domestic adoptions, 86 were stepfamily adoptions (AAI, 2014a), thus suggesting that only 30 were non-family adoptions.[1]

Reform of adoption law

On 24 April 2015, the Irish Supreme Court confirmed that a new provision on children's rights should be inserted into the Irish Constitution under the Thirty-First Amendment of the Constitution (Children) Act 2015, which was signed into law on 28 April 2015. The amendment will mean that children of married parents will be increasingly eligible for adoption. It will also allow for the adoption of children who are in long-term foster care after a specific period of time. Up until the amendment of the Constitution, the position was that children in long-term foster care were only eligible for adoption in limited circumstances. Significantly, the new amendment sets out that provision will be made, by law, for children to have a voice in adoption proceedings affecting them. It is anticipated that this legislation will open the way for more children to be domestically adopted.

Ireland has not traditionally used the foster care system as a pathway into adoption. The statistics show that in October 2013, there were 6,486 children in care, with just over 90% placed in foster care (Department of Children and Youth Affairs, 2014b). In 2013, the number of children placed for adoption from long-term fostering was 17 (statistics provided by the AAI to the authors).

As previously stated, in 2013 there were 86 'stepfamily adoptions' (AAI, 2014a). This term is often used where a new spouse wishes to apply to adopt the child of their new husband/wife. This was another area of adoption in need of reform that was addressed in the Children and Family Relationship Act 2015. Up until now, in a situation where a biological single mother wished for her new partner to become the adoptive parent of the child, the birth mother had to relinquish her legal rights to the child. She and her new partner had to undergo an adoption assessment to establish their suitability and eligibility to be adoptive parents. In effect, this meant that the child's original birth certificate became defunct and the child was issued with a new adoption birth certificate, which included the name of the child's birth mother and legal father. This has now been addressed in the new Act, which allows for new forms of guardianship.

Currently, in Ireland, same-sex couples cannot marry but can formalize their relationship under the Civil Partnership and Certain Rights and Obligations of Co-habitants Act 2010. In May 2015, the Irish government will hold a Marriage Referendum. Under the Children and Family Relationships Act 2015, the categories of applicants who may be deemed eligible and suitable to adopt has been extended to include civil partners and couples living together for over three years. While this is a positive step forward, it has been argued that it does not provide all children with the same protections as children born into a heterosexual married relationship. The Marriage Referendum, if passed, will address this.

It is worth noting that up until the aforementioned changes, an anomaly existed in the case of intercountry adoption where a single person, regardless of their sexual orientation, could apply to adopt. This meant that a same-sex couple could undergo a joint assessment, but only one person in the relationship could become the legal guardian of the child. This had serious implications for the rights of the child (see Parkes and McCaughren, 2013).

A move from open to closed adoption

There are some areas of adoption practice that have reflected wider societal changes, such as open adoption. For more than a decade now, Ireland has moved away from the traditional closed model of adoption, and embraced a much more open approach to domestic adoption. This is due to a combination of reasons, including:

- research and literature that explored the negative psychological impact of closed adoptions emerging in the 1980s (Sorosky et al., 1984)

- a call for legal reform by adoption rights groups to address the issue of records being sealed perpetually

- recognition by professionals that traditional closed adoptions were out of sync with a fast-changing modern society.

Open adoption can be defined in general terms as an adoption whereby the adoptive parents and child maintain some level of contact with the birth mother and/or father and sometimes other birth family members after an adoption order has been made. The level of contact can vary enormously, with each open adoption being unique to each family (McCaughren, 2010). Some families want total anonymity and therefore rely on the adoption agency to forward correspondence and arrange face-to-face meetings at a neutral venue. Other families are comfortable in exchanging identifying details and manage their contact independent of the adoption agency. Families can correspond with one another in a variety of ways, including letter writing, text messaging, telephone calls, emails and face-to-face meetings.

In the Irish context, open adoption agreements are drawn up with support from the respective social workers for the adoptive family and birth family. Indeed, social workers play a central role in mediating and facilitating open adoptions. However, the agreements are based on goodwill and are not recognized in Irish law. There are many debates as to whether open adoptions should continue to be based on goodwill agreements or whether the law has a role to play (Parkes and McCaughren, 2013). Indeed, there are currently moves to legislate for open adoption with the introduction of the Open Adoption Bill 2014. Open adoption not only recognizes the importance of children having access to accurate and personal information regarding their biological backgrounds, it also acknowledges the significance and impact of the lifelong decision the birth mother is making. Contemporary domestic adoption practice not only provides counselling support for the birth mother, but includes her in choosing the adoptive family with whom she wishes to place her child. The birth mother can read detailed profiles of prospective adoptive couples and can also meet them prior to making any permanent adoption decision. Thus, domestic adoption practice has moved away from the model where birth mothers were completely disempowered in the process.

As indicated, Ireland has a long history as a 'sending country', yet now finds itself receiving a number of internationally adopted children each year.

However, the openness now associated with domestic adoption in Ireland does not, in the main, apply to intercountry adoptions. In their study of intercountry adoption in the Irish context, Greene et al. (2007) found that just 7% of adoptive parents had maintained some kind of contact with birth parents. Indeed, in the Australian context, Cuthbert et al. (2010, p. 427) argue that the move to increased openness in domestic adoption has been an 'unacknowledged driver of intercountry adoption for many Australian families', and that its increased use cannot be explained simply as a response to the lack of 'supply' of Australian babies available for adoption. Other research has found that parents often choose closed adoption so as to avoid the emotional turmoil considered to be associated with more open arrangements (Zhang and Lee, 2010). This may result in some families choosing intercountry adoption where the complexity of negotiating relationships with the birth family is less likely to come into play.

Yet, while open adoption is most commonly associated with domestic adoption, it is not unheard of in intercountry adoption. Although no Irish research has focused specifically on this area, the evidence from the Greene et al. (2007) study suggests that a minority of Irish parents maintained a level of contact with birth families. There are a number of factors that make open adoption in intercountry adoption difficult, including geographical distance, language barriers and poor record keeping in institutions (Scherman, 2012). Although valuable research is being undertaken by Scherman to explore open adoption in intercountry adoption, it has been acknowledged that it is a practice still in its infancy.

Information and tracing

While openness is a key principle governing any domestic adoptions that now occur in Ireland, as discussed above, this was not the case in the past. Instead, the very essence of those adoptions was built on secrecy. Thus, the issue of information and tracing is an area of contemporary adoption policy that remains highly sensitive and controversial. Despite the introduction of adoption legislation in 2010, the issue of information and tracing was once more ignored. Therefore, Irish law in relation to information and tracing remains as it did in 1952 when adoption was first legislated for in Ireland. As such, the law is outdated by international comparison, as a number of other jurisdictions have been successful in securing legislative reform.[2] Currently, in the Irish legal context, the confidentiality and anonymity that were 'guaranteed' to birth mothers at the time of the adoption take precedence over an adoptee's wish to obtain information pertaining to their birth. However, it is important to point out that there are many birth mothers who strongly deny that they were ever given any promises of confidentiality. At a recent international adoption conference, Philomena Lee showed delegates a copy of the form she signed, which stated that: 'I further undertake never to attempt to see, interfere with, or make any claims to the said child at any time in the future.'[3] The questions that have been asked by adoption reform advocates (Adoption Rights Alliance et al., 2014) are: 'Is there evidence to support such claims of confidentiality? And if not, why not?'

Thus social work practice finds itself having to operate within the strict limitations of the law, which has resulted in a blanket ban on the disclosure of any meaningful or identifying information. In fact, adoptees have no right in law to non-identifying information, but in practice, adoption agencies will provide adopted persons with information from their adoption file that is non-identifying. Social workers will go through the file and put together information for the adoptee, such as the name they were given at birth (since it was common practice for children's original names to be changed once they were adopted), the birth mother's first name, her physical description, medical information, and any other information pertaining to the birth mother's background. However, the quantity and quality of the information on file varies considerably. In the Irish context, adopted persons do not have an automatic right to access their original birth certificate on reaching the age of maturity, as is the case in some other jurisdictions. While an adopted person can apply to the AAI for the release of their original birth certificate, it is completely discretionary and only released in exceptional circumstances. The rationale is that the original birth certificate contains the name of the birth mother and her address at the time of birth and, therefore, an adopted person could potentially identify birth mothers who, in some cases, were given a promise by the state that their anonymity would be protected. Under current law, the only way in which this archaic practice can be circumvented is if the birth mother agrees for identifying information to be released or has herself requested contact.

The withholding of identifying information is, no doubt, a complex and emotive one for all involved. At the centre of this debate is the issue of balancing the rights of the individuals in the adoption triangle (the adopted person, the birth mother and adoptive parents) that have been directly affected by adoption. The closed system suppressed adoptees' natural curiosity, with little or no information shared in relation to their genetic backgrounds. Many adopted people believe that they have a basic human right to personal information. Others believe that birth mothers were provided with the anonymity they needed in order to reintegrate into a society that was, at the time, unaccepting and unsupportive of single motherhood. Some birth mothers have spoken out about the lifelong suffering they've endured having to bury their adoption secret, with many only revealing it later in life and others never doing so. There are some birth mothers who do not want contact with their children. Thus, the Irish government finds itself in a serious predicament and has, to date, been unable to find a solution that meets everyone's needs. O'Brien (2013, p. 114) argues that despite the complexities, 'search and reunion is a topic that needs decisive action and resolution'.

Against the backdrop of stringent laws preventing the release of identifying information, the advent of the internet and social media has also introduced new challenges for contemporary adoptions. Today, information is easily accessible and this has led to new opportunities as well as risks for those who initiate tracing birth relatives (see Fursland, 2010; O'Brien, 2013; McCaughren and Lovett, 2014) without the support of social workers. In an era of austerity and continuous cuts to resources, people face long waiting times, while birth mothers are getting older. In addition, because social work has encountered some reputational damage due to its association with the traditional closed model of adoption, many adopted persons and birth mothers choose to circumvent their placing agency when searching for information relating to their adoption. Thus, many adoptees and birth mothers have started to initiate their own searches, in their own homes and in private. At the heart of these searches are questions of identity and belonging.

The significance of identity

In the field of adoption – whether domestic or intercountry – identity is a key theme. The importance of having a coherent and integrated identity has long been recognized as a significant part of individual development and central to long-term psychosocial wellbeing. Indeed, O'Brien (2013) suggests that knowledge of who you are is a basic human right. For the adopted person, their sense of identity – of who they are, so to speak – is crucially linked with their adoptive status. The issues can range from basic factual information regarding the names of a person's birth parents and birth siblings to more complex questions about the reasons for adoption. While these issues are relevant for most adopted people, they may be more complex in the context of intercountry adoption, and particularly where individuals are adopted by a family of a different race or ethnicity, something that is frequent in the current Irish context.

One's sense of identity becomes particularly important during adolescence and early adulthood, when young people begin to seek answers to the question 'who am I'?, in a way that is meaningful and involves seeking continuity between the past, the present and the future (Erikson, 1968). When a person's identity develops, their sense of self as an individual person comes to the fore, as does their sense of belonging (Feast, 2009). While the question 'who am I?' can be difficult for anyone to answer, for the adopted person it is likely to be more complex, particularly if information is not readily available. Feast (2009, p. 440) suggests that adopted people may have many unanswered questions and may 'live with the feeling that there are missing pieces'. As discussed above, the previous closed system of adoption in Ireland, and elsewhere, deliberately encouraged the complete severing of ties between the adoptee and the birth family. In this context, adopted persons have argued that knowledge of their biological roots is fundamental in allowing them to form a narrative of their lives. It is vital for the development of their sense of identity. Likewise, many birth mothers have spoken about the dehumanizing and disempowering nature of the traditional adoption system, a system that left a lifelong legacy of pain and suffering (Kelly, 2005). Indeed, for these women, their identities as mothers were largely ignored when they were prevented from having any knowledge about what happened to their children following relinquishment.

Thus, it is evident that members of the adoption triangle have broken the silence and have, to some extent, contributed to a reformulation of contemporary adoption practice, in favour of a more open approach that better recognizes the importance of identity. This is at least the case in relation to domestic adoption. In relation to intercountry adoption, the general identity issues regarding adoptive status are relevant but other identity issues are also at play. As discussed above, few intercountry adoptions that take place in the Irish context are open adoptions. So, in the current context, those who are adopted from outside Ireland are less likely to have accurate or detailed information about their birth parents. Where they do have this information, it is likely to be non-identifying information that does not allow for contact to be maintained. In their study of intercountry adoption outcomes in the Irish context, Greene et al. (2007) found that adoptive parents had very little information about the children's birth families or their life before adoption. The authors found that the story provided by parents to their adopted children 'often seems to become ritualized and is frequently repeated' and that sometimes the story 'seems to be a little romanticized' (Greene et al., 2007, p. 344). In addition to these issues about a lack of information, those who are adopted from other countries may have to contend with the added challenges of being ethnically different from their adopted parents, thus raising questions about ethnic identity and belonging as well as the possibility of prejudice and racism. The Irish study by Greene et al. (2007, p. 345) found that 'a worrying number' of the children reported incidences of racist or prejudicial remarks and attitudes. Scherman (2010, p. 134) argues that in intercountry adoption, parents 'have the role of fostering in their children an ethnic awareness and pride in the birth culture'. While playing such a role has been shown to support the successful identity development of the child and their overall adjustment (Scherman, 2010), it is by no means easy. Indeed, Greene et al. (2007, p. 346) found that across all age groups, the knowledge that the children had in relation to their birth countries was 'typically fragmented and often stereotyped'. It is relevant to note that recent foster care research has suggested that there can be divergence between the views of carers and the views of ethnic minority young people in relation to culture, with the carers believing the young people are 'integrated' and not recognizing that the young people want to know more about their culture of origin (Ní Raghallaigh and Sirriyeh, 2014). This suggests the importance of regular open and age-appropriate discussions with children in order to best facilitate the identity development process.

While paying attention to birth culture, researchers suggest that it is crucial that adoptive parents ensure that their children adapt to the dominant culture. As Westhues and Cohen (1998, p. 49) point out in the Canadian context:

> Always remembering that your roots are in another cultural reality, but acknowledging that you are now a part of a new culture, would satisfy the child's right to remain connected with their history, but without making them feel that they do not fully belong here … with their adoptive families.

It has been argued that it is unlikely that the intercountry adopted person will develop a truly bicultural identity – especially if they were adopted at a very young age – but it is important that they have the opportunity to incorporate their two cultures into their sense of self (Scherman, 2010). Social work practitioners need to be equipped with the knowledge and skills to provide the appropriate post-placement support in this regard and not just in the immediate aftermath of the adoption. Indeed, support in relation to identity is likely to be more necessary as the child grows older and begins asking questions about their culture of origin and their ethnicity. A social worker needs to be available to offer guidance and resources to adoptive parents who are faced with these questions. In addition, trends indicate that children available for intercountry adoption will now be older, perhaps having spent longer periods of time in institutions. The needs of such children will be different and identity issues will merge with issues of deinstitutionalization. Thus, these children and their adoptive families will require more tailored support services and professional intervention.

Ethical considerations

Adoption cannot be viewed as an 'unproblematic social good' (Cuthbert et al., 2010, p. 433). Indeed, it could be suggested that it is, in fact, a *'problematic social good'*. Adoption serves multiple extremely positive functions, such as finding parents for orphaned or abandoned children and children for parents who are childless. It can be argued that the wellbeing of a child who previously lived in an institution in a developing country is enhanced through being adopted by Irish parents who have been appropriately assessed and trained and who receive adequate post-placement support. Certainly, while recognizing that orphanages and residential homes vary hugely in their quality, international research evidence suggests that adoption is a better way of promoting child development compared to institutional care (Johnson, 2002; van IJzendoorn and Juffer, 2006; Groza et al., 2011). As Jones (2010, p. 364) argues, while 'intercountry adoption is not an ideal *sustainable* solution for children, it remains at present a better option for many children than being raised in their birth country in orphanages'. Indeed, drawing on a plethora of research evidence, Selman (2009, p. 291) contends that most children adopted from overseas 'do well'. In addition, the adoptive parents, who may be unable to have their own children, now have the child for whom they longed. In such a case, the 'social good' of adoption may seem entirely unproblematic.

However, such an analysis is contested as overly simplistic and reflects the questionable portrayal of adoption as 'a relatively straightforward union of children in need and loving parents' (Kirton, 2013, p. 104). With regard to intercountry adoption specifically, Roby et al. (2013, p. 296) suggest that this form of adoption 'involves multiple layers of structurally based disparities, creating fertile ground for seeds of social injustice'. A range of ethical questions are posed. For example:

- Is it acceptable that individuals and couples 'end up' turning to intercountry adoption when other methods of having a family have failed or when domestic adoption is not possible?

- Are the attitudes of prospective adoptive parents towards birth parents based on principles of equality and rights or do they hold questionable beliefs that, as Roby et al. (2013, p. 4) suggest, 'poor people are less deserving of raising their children' or that those at 'the bottom rung of society will not feel the pain of separation as much as others'?

- Is it ethical that, through their relative wealth, adoptive parents can obtain children from impoverished nations using sums of money that, arguably, if given to the children's birth parents would allow the children to remain with them?

Freundlich (2000, p. 53) highlights the 'strong relationship between the limited social and economic power of women in developing countries and the practice of international adoption'. She refers to what many see as the 'ongoing exploitation of poor women as "breeders" for affluent families in Western countries' (p. 52). Indeed, it could be argued that this equally applied in the case of children who were adopted *from* Ireland in the past. Issues of equity and injustice can be at the heart of intercountry adoption (O'Brien, 2009), despite the social work profession's commitment to social justice principles and the good intentions of adoptive parents. As Jones (2010, p. 360) notes, Madonna, celebrity singer, songwriter and actress, was criticized by the public 'for removing a child, who was not an orphan, from his birth culture and community, rather than supporting the child within his community'. In addition, in many situations, children are placed for intercountry adoption having been born outside wedlock. As such, does the adoption of these children help to perpetuate harmful cultural beliefs about unmarried mothers by offering 'solutions' to the 'problem' of babies who are born outside marriage?

Indeed, as we have noted, such 'solutions' were used in the Irish context in the not-so-distant past and are now considered as having been a gross infringement of the rights of the birth mothers involved, and contributing to a life of negative emotional and psychological consequences. Bos's (2007) account of relinquishment and adoption from the perspective of unmarried mothers in South India raises serious questions about the extent to which babies are relinquished voluntarily. Her research found that counsellors often coached unmarried mothers towards a particular outcome – that of relinquishment – for a number of reasons, including the desire to satisfy prospective adoptive parents. Other authors have discussed the worrying practice of 'rehoming', whereby adoptive parents attempt to find new homes for their adopted children when problems arise (Twohey, 2013). Some have raised concerns about the risk of child trafficking occurring in the context of intercountry adoption (Smolin, 2004; Selman, 2009). In 1993, the Hague Convention on the Protection of Children and Co-Operation in Respect of Intercountry Adoption (the Hague Adoption Convention) was introduced to provide a regulatory framework that would eliminate the possibilities of child trafficking and baby-selling (McCaughren and Parkes, 2012, p. 3). However, some believe that the Hague Adoption Convention has not gone far enough in ensuring the best interests of children involved in intercountry adoption (Ryan, 2006; McCaughren and Parkes, 2012).

It is clear that there are myriad complex and emotive ethical issues associated with intercountry adoption. Domestic adoption is also a fraught area, particularly in the context where a child in the care of the state is placed for adoption without the consent of the birth parents (as happens regularly in the UK and the US and is now likely to happen more frequently in Ireland). While adoption has the capacity to offer a child a sense of permanency, it raises ethical questions about the rights of birth parents, the capacity of social workers or other professionals to make such onerous decisions, and the capacity of parents to recover from adversity. Children in many of these situations are likely to be older and may come from more complex backgrounds, suggesting that social workers may need to provide additional post-placement support. Also, in circumstances where birth parents have not consented to the adoption, openness is likely to be particularly challenging, leading to additional ethical dilemmas.

In both intercountry and domestic adoption, there is a danger that children can be used as 'fodder in some ideological argument' (O'Brien, 2009, p. 2) against adoption, or that unethical practices will be allowed to continue on the basis of simplistic arguments in relation to individual 'orphans' or 'abandoned' children. As such, given the social work profession's commitment to ethical practice and social justice principles, it is essential that social workers grapple with these complex dilemmas and encourage prospective adopters to do likewise. The ethical dilemmas of adoption pose some serious challenges for practitioners and there is a real need to engage in further research and dialogue regarding what constitutes best practice.

The future of adoption

There is no doubt that the practice of domestic and intercountry adoption is currently undergoing a period of significant transition. In relation to intercountry adoption, since Ireland's ratification of the Hague Adoption Convention in November 2010, prospective adopters can only adopt from countries that are also signatories to the Hague Adoption Convention or countries that have entered into an agreement with the AAI based on Hague principles. This has limited the pool of countries available to prospective adopters. The Hague Adoption Convention has also resulted in countries of origin having to review their child protection frameworks, with many countries focusing on maintaining children in-country. There are now fewer children being adopted internationally and the profile of children being adopted has also changed. As was previously alluded to, children are now older, having spent longer periods of time in institutions. This can mean that the profile of children being adopted presents adoptive parents with even more challenges in terms of their overall health and medical needs. Although prospective adoptive parents attend a preparatory course before their adoption assessment, there is very little formal support provided for adoptive parents once the adoption has taken place. Resources are weighted towards the pre-adoption stage, with few resources available for post-adoption work. While, in the context of austerity, it is difficult to increase resources, it has been noted that if the best interests of the child are to be given due consideration, then ongoing post-adoption support should be seen as a priority (McCaughren and Sherlock, 2008). Although Article 9C of the Hague Adoption Convention requires that every central authority 'promote the development of adoption counselling and post-adoption services in their States', Ireland has yet to see the introduction of initiatives that will provide structured support services for internationally adopted children and their families.

Given the recent legislative reforms, priority must now be given to addressing the legislation relating to information and tracing, and the only way that a meaningful change can occur is by tackling legislation that is now 62 years old. A commitment must also be made to birth mothers in acknowledging the state's role in facilitating what have now become known as 'forced adoptions'. In moving forward, the state must accept the reputational damage that has been done to adoption practice and put the necessary supports in place to establish an adoption service that is in line with international best practice.

Since the amendment to the Irish Constitution, Ireland will have to reassess its approach to the practice of adoption and fostering. The insertion of Article 42A into the Constitution means that children in long-term fostering will be eligible for adoption. This means that permanency will have to be given genuine consideration as part of a child's long-term care plan. From a child welfare point of view, every effort should be made to ensure that children do not drift into care. However, the concern to avoid drift must be balanced against the fact that 'fostering provides a safe haven and allows the professionals to work, for as long as it takes, on the best outcomes for the child' (Rees, 2013). It is, therefore, important that fostering does not become regarded as a 'second rate solution' and become 'some kind of automatic conveyor belt towards adoption' (Rees, 2013). Indeed, as Kirton (2013, p. 103) warns, it would be simplistic to assume that higher levels of adoption of children from care are equivalent to 'better performance'. Currently, social work practice in the fields of adoption and fostering is generally carried out by different teams. Will a more integrated service be needed in the future? This might, for example, involve social workers using a model of dual assessment, or what Kirton (2013) terms 'concurrency', where prospective parents are assessed as foster carers and adopters.

Conclusion

Adoption is an area of practice that is changing fast and is increasingly influenced by the experiences of those directly affected by adoption. Social workers have played a significant role in this area of work. However, if they are to make a contribution to practice that reflects their social justice value base, they need to bring a questioning lens to their work and reflect on their role, re-evaluating practices that may not be in line with their code of ethics. This may mean challenging policy in this area. Given that adoption policy and practice are on the cusp of change, there is now a real opportunity to develop evidence-based practice that is not only child centred, but also makes a genuine commitment to addressing the needs of all the stakeholders in the process. At the heart of this, there must be a move towards practice that genuinely reflects the ethical obligations of social work.

Notes

1. However, other statistics provided by the AAI indicate that there were 29 non-family domestic adoptions in 2013 (AAI, 2014b). This discrepancy is unclear. A detailed breakdown of the figures is not always available for non-family domestic adoptions.

2. In 1975, adopted people became entitled to obtain their original birth certificates on reaching 18 years. In New Zealand, the Adult Information Act allows the adopted person and birth parents to access their records, which were previously closed.

3. Philomena Lee is the subject of the film *Philomena*, in which she is played by Judi Dench as a mother on a quest to find her son, who she had given up for adoption some 50 years earlier. Philomena spoke at a two-day international conference Redefining Adoption in a New Era: Opportunities and Challenges for Law and Social Work hosted by the School of Applied Social Studies and the School of Law, UCC in September 2014.

References

AAI (Adoption Authority of Ireland) (2014a) *The Adoption Authority of Ireland Annual Report 2013*, www.aai.gov.ie/attachments/article/32/Annual_Report_2013. pdf.

AAI (2014b) *Notice: 2013 Annual Statistics, AAI Statistics Jan-Dec 2013*, www.aai.gov. ie/attachments/article/32/Notice%20-%202013%20Annual%20Stats%20website. pdf, accessed 8 January 2015.

Adoption Rights Alliance, Parkes, A. and McCaughren, S. (2014) 'Time to reform adoption laws has arrived', *Irish Examiner*, 5 November, www.irishexaminer.com/ viewpoints/analysis/time-to-reform-adoption-laws-has-arrived-296344.html, accessed 8 January 2015.

Bos, P. (2007) *Once a Mother: Relinquishment and Adoption from the Perspective of Unmarried Mothers in South India*, Amsterdam, Ipskamp.

Cuthbert, D., Spark, C. and Murphy, K. (2010) '"That was then, but this is now": historical perspectives on intercountry adoption and domestic child adoption in Australian public policy', *Journal of Historical Sociology*, 23(3), 427–52.

Department of Children and Youth Affairs (2014a) *Report of the Inter-departmental Group on Mother and Baby Homes*, www.dcya.gov.ie/documents/publications/2014 0716InterdepartReportMothBabyHomes.pdf, accessed 8 January 2015.

Department of Children and Youth Affairs (2014b) *Foster Care*, www.dcya.gov.ie/ docs/Foster_Care/2591.htm, accessed 8 April 2014.

Erikson, E.H. (1968) *Identity: Youth and Crisis*, New York, Norton.

Feast, J. (2009) 'Identity and continuity: adults' access to and need for information about their history and origins', in Schofield, G. and Simmonds, J. (eds) *The Child Placement Handbook: Research, Policy and Practice*, London: British Association for Adoption and Fostering.

Freundlich, M. (2000) *Adoption and Ethics: The Role of Race, Culture and National Origin in Adoption*, Washington DC, Child Welfare League of America.

Fursland, E. (2010) *Facing up to Facebook: A Survival Guide for Adoptive Families*, London, British Association for Adoption and Fostering.

Greene, S., Kelly, R., Nixon, E. et al. (2007) *A Study of Intercountry Adoption Outcomes in Ireland*, Dublin, Children's Research Centre/Adoption Board.

Groza, V.K., McCreery Bunkers, K. and Gamer, G.N. (2011) 'Ideal components and current characteristics of alternative care options for children outside of parental care in low-resource countries', *Monographs of the Society for Research in Child Development*, 76(4), 163–89.

Johnson, D.E. (2002) 'Adoption and the effect on children's development', *Early Human Development*, 68, 39–54.

Jones, S. (2010) 'The ethics of intercountry adoption: why it matters to healthcare providers and bioethicists', *Bioethics*, 24(7), 358–64.

Kelly, R. (2005) *Motherhood Silenced: The Experience of Natural Mothers on Adoption Reunion*, Dublin, Liffey Press.

Kirton, D. (2013) '"Kinship by design" in England: reconfiguring adoption from Blair to the coalition', *Child and Family Social Work*, 18, 97–106.

McCaughren, S. (2010) A Study of Open Adoption in Ireland through the Narrative of Adoptive Parents, unpublished PhD thesis submitted to the School of Applied Social Studies, University College Cork.

McCaughren, S. and Lovett, J. (2014) 'Domestic adoption in Ireland: a shifting paradigm?', *Adoption & Fostering Quarterly Journal*, 38, 238–54.

McCaughren, S. and Parkes, A. (2012) 'Ireland and the global landscape of adoption: the Adoption Act 2010 – a missed opportunity', *Irish Journal of Family Law*, 1, 3–10.

McCaughren, S. and Sherlock, C. (2008) 'Inter-country adoption in Ireland: law, children's rights and contemporary social work practice', *Ethics and Social Welfare*, 2(2), 133–49.

Maguire, M.J. (2002) 'Foreign adoptions and the evolution of Irish adoption policy', *Journal of Social History*, 36(2), 387–404.

Milotte, M. (1997) *Banished Babies: The Secret History of Ireland's Baby Export Business*, Dublin, New Island.

Milotte, M. (2012) *Banished Babies: The Secret History of Ireland's Baby Export Business*, 2nd rev. edn, Dublin, New Island.

Ní Raghallaigh, M. and Sirriyeh, A. (2014) 'The negotiation of culture in foster care placements for separated refugee and asylum seeking young people in Ireland and England', *Childhood*, doi: 10.1177/0907568213519137.

O'Brien, V. (2009) 'The potential of Ireland's Hague Convention legislation to resolve ethical dilemmas in inter-country adoptions', *Irish Social Worker*, summer, 13–19.

O'Brien, V. (2013) 'Social networking, adoption and search and reunion', *Irish Social Worker*, summer, 24–32.

O'Fatharta, C. (2014) 68% of babies in Bessborough home died, *Irish Examiner*, 25 August 2014.

O'Hare, A., Dromey, M., O'Connor, A. et al. (1983) *Mother Alone? A Study of Women Who Gave Birth outside Marriage*, Dublin, Federation of Services for Unmarried Parents and their Children.

O'Sullivan, E. and O'Donnell, I. (eds) (2012) *Coercive Confinement in Ireland: Patients, Prisoners and Penitents*, Manchester, Manchester University Press.

Parkes, A. and McCaughren, S. (2013) 'Viewing adoption through a children's rights lens: looking to the future of adoption law and practice in Ireland', *Irish Journal of Family Law*, 16(4), 99–111.

Rees, J. (2013) 'We need to value foster care, not fixate on adoption', *Guardian Professional*, 16 April, www.theguardian.com/social-care-network/2013/apr/16/value-foster-care-adoption, accessed 5 March 2014.

Roby, J.L., Rotabi, K. and Bunkers, K.M. (2013) 'Social justice and intercountry adoptions: the role of the US social work community', *Social Work*, 58(4), 295–303.

Ryan, E.J. (2006) 'For the best interests of the children: why the Hague Convention in intercountry adoption needs to go farther, as evidenced by implementation in Romania and the United States', *Boston College International and Comparative Review*, 29(2), 353–63.

Scherman, R.M. (2010) 'Openness in intercountry adoption in New Zealand', in Gibbons, J.L. and Rotabi, K.S. (eds) *Intercountry Adoption: Policies, Practices, and Outcomes*, Farnham, Ashgate.

Scherman, R.M. (2012) 'A theoretical look at biculturalism in intercountry adoption', *Journal of Ethnic and Cultural Diversity in Social Work*, 19, 127–42.

Selman, P. (2009) 'The rise and fall of intercountry adoption in the 21st century', *International Social Work*, 52(5), 575–94.

Shannon, G. (2011) *Adoption Law*, Dublin, Roundhall.

Smolin, D. (2004) 'Intercountry adoption as child trafficking', *Valparaiso Law Review*, 39(2), 281–325.

Sorosky, A.D., Baron, A. and Pannor, R. (1984) *The Adoption Triangle: Sealed or Open Records, How They Affect Adoptees, Birth Parents and Adoptive Parents*, Garden City, NY, Anchor Books.

Twohey, M. (2013) 'Americans use the Internet to abandon children adopted from overseas', *Reuters Investigates*, 9 September, www.reuters.com/investigates/adoption/#article/part1, accessed 2 April 2014.

Van IJzendoorn, M.H. and Juffer, F. (2006) 'The Emanuel Miller Memorial Lecture 2006: Adoption as intervention: meta-analytic evidence for massive catch-up and plasticity in physical, socio-emotional, and cognitive development', *Journal of Child Psychology and Psychiatry*, 47(12), 1118–245.

Westhues, A. and Cohen, J. (1998) 'Ethnic and racial identity of internationally adopted adolescents and young adults: some issues in relation to children's rights', *Adoption Quarterly*, 1(4), 33–55.

Zhang, Y. and Lee, G.R. (2010) 'Intercountry versus transracial adoption: analysis of adoptive parents' motivation and preferences in adoption', *Journal of Family Issues*, 32(1), 75–98.

6

Fostering the Future:
A Change Agenda in the
Provision of Alternative Care

Valerie O'Brien and Mairie Cregan

Introduction

Alternative care is defined as the placement of children within state care
and refers to family-based care (foster and kinship care) and residential care.
This chapter explores aspects of the alternative care system, primarily foster care, which is the principle form of care for looked after children in
Ireland. First, the chapter provides a historical overview and offers a context for the contemporary picture. It then relates the perspectives of key
participants – children, biological families and carers. Here, we focus on two
specific aspects of the care experience, namely education and leaving care.
Finally, the chapter considers selected policy and legal issues, including the
concept of permanence, recruitment and retention of carers, kinship care,
meeting the needs of diverse populations, and the future of the social work
role arising from changes in the wider domains.

Overview of children in care

Historically, the number of children in state care in Ireland was higher in
the years prior to the establishment of professional social work services. The
figures reduced in the 1970s and 80s, only to peak again in recent times.
At the time of the Kennedy Report in 1970, the industrial and reformatory school system was a regime with enormous scope; 130,000 children
had been admitted to the system between 1869 and 1969 (Ferguson, 2007).
While the practice of 'boarding out' children with families was a feature

from the early years of the 20th century, the numbers involved remained small. A policy shift in favour of family-based alternative care was heralded by the Kennedy Report (1970) and the Task Force on Child Care Services Report (1980).

In more recent years, the number of children in alternative care in Ireland increased from 5,307 in 2007 to 6,160 in 2011. This is one part of a significant general increase in activity levels in the child welfare and protection system arising from the greatly increased number of referrals being received over these same years (see Table 6.1). According to a report submitted to the UN Convention on the Rights of the Child (Department of Children and Youth Affairs, 2013a, p. 82), a rise in the population and a growing awareness of the impact of long-term neglect, as well as the impact of the economic downturn on vulnerable parents, contributed to the increase in the care population. The majority of children in state care (91%) were living with foster families and the remaining 9% were living in residential care units or other types of placements. Of the 91% of children, 31% were living with relatives (formal kinship placements) and 60% were living with non-related foster carers.

While there is an increase in overall numbers, the level of children in alternative care in Ireland at 54.6 per 10,000 of population remains lower than the rate in the UK, Wales and Australia (see Table 6.2). Thoburn's (2010) comparative work on rates of children in alternative care places Ireland at mid-point, when the lower rates in countries such as Denmark and Japan are included. An analysis and explanation of these differences requires a major study; however, poverty and social isolation have always been significant features of the profile of children in the care system, and these issues,

Table 6.1 Activity in Irish child welfare and protection system, 2006–11

Year	Child welfare referrals	Child protection referrals	Total number of children in care system	Total number admitted to care per year
2006	11,579	9,461	5,247	1,845
2007	12,715	10,453	5,307	2,134
2008	12,932	11,736	5,345	2,013
2009	14,875	12,013	5,674	2,372
2010	16,452	12,825	5,965	2,291
2011	15,808	15,818	6,160	2,218

Sources: Data from HSE, 2012; Department of Children and Youth Affairs, 2013b

Table 6.2 Children in care: international comparative rates for populations 0–17 years

	Children in care, 2011	Children in care, 2012	Annual change	Population 0–17 years	Rate per 10,000 pop.
Ireland (Dec 2012)	6,160	6,332	+ 2.8%	1,160,000	54.6
Northern Ireland (Mar 2012)	2,511	2,644	+ 5.3%	n/a	61.2
England (Mar 2012)	65,520	67,050	+ 2.3%	n/a	59
Australia (June 2012)	37,648	39,621	+ 5.2%	n/a	77
Wales (Mar 2012)	5,419	5,726	+ 5.7%	n/a	92
Scotland (July 2012)	16,231	16,248	+ 0.1%	1,036,409	157

Source: HSE, 2012, p. 52

coupled with the impact of growing inequalities and marginalization of communities, have contributed to the increase of children currently in care in Ireland (Cregan, 2014).

The historical evolution of alternative care services in this country continues to be an issue of some controversy and debate. Legacy issues arising from the treatment of children and their families by the child welfare system have been a recurring theme for the past 15–20 years and have had a major influence on the current structure of the care system. The work of Raftery and O'Suillivan (1999) and Raftery's powerful 1997 TV documentary, *States of Fear*, regarding the treatment of children in state care, were pivotal to this awareness. The subsequent investigations into the abuse of children within institutional settings (Ryan, 2009) and by members of the Catholic Church (Murphy, 2009), as well as into the deaths of children within the care system (Shannon and Gibbons, 2012), resulted in public outrage and a debate on Ireland's failure to protect vulnerable children in recent years. Thus, the issues of child abuse and children's rights have occupied a position high on the political agenda (O'Brien, 2012a). Two major features of this evolution provide a context within which to understand the legacy from previous decades of institutional care with which professional social work childcare services has had to contend.

First, the role of social work was slow to develop in Ireland compared to other Western countries (Skehill, 1999). Major developments are traced back to the Health Act 1970, and, since that time, social work has been central in child welfare and protection and the provision of alternative care. The social work role was strengthened with the Child Care Act 1991, the Child Care Regulations 1995, and the alternative care standards developed in 2003. The service delivery model currently in use is generally referred to as a 'two-worker model', with one social worker having responsibility for the child and the birth family and the second providing support to and supervising the foster home.

Second, the policy of preferring family-based care (foster care), first set out in the 1954 Boarding Out Regulations, was also slow to develop in Ireland. However, the reassertion of the policy in the Task Force on Child Care Services (1980) has been successful (Considine and Dukelow, 2009) and Ireland now has the distinction of sharing a lead position with Australia in the provision of such care (Thoburn, 2010). Social workers have been pivotal in delivering this achievement. There is evidence of a widespread commitment to the idea that foster care is the 'only really good care for children' (Horgan, 2002, p, 35), but social workers continue to advocate the need for a continuum of care facilities and arrangements, including residential care, to meet the wide range of children's needs (IASW, 2011).

Ireland's current child welfare system is now seen as sharing many trends with systems in other jurisdictions (Buckley and Nolan, 2013). There has been a growing emphasis within policy and practice on partnership, solution-focused and family-centred practices and a commitment to family support. Where care is needed, there is recognition that children can have complex needs that warrant a range of responses and that kinship place-ment is a preferred choice if possible (O'Brien, 2012b). Paradoxically, it is suggested that the childcare system is becoming more risk averse in response to investigations and is seeking certainty and outcome prediction. Today, it is characterized by growing managerialism, legalism and reliance on tighter procedural approaches (Featherstone et al., 2012).

In 2009, a policy decision was made to separate services for children and families from general health services, where it had been located since 1970. Part of the rationale for this change was to ensure that the focus on children and families would remain a priority as, under the old system, there was evidence that other health-related crises frequently dominated children's issues. Preparations for a stand-alone Child and Family Agency, known as Tusla, underway since 2009 (HSE, 2009; Department of Children and Youth Affairs, 2012), finally became operational in January 2014. There has been some welcome for this change, especially for the aim of providing consistent and standardized child welfare services across the country. However, there is concern that safeguards against the negative features associated with overly procedure-driven systems identified elsewhere (IASW, 2011; Munro, 2011) have not been incorporated sufficiently into the new Irish system processes.

Issues from stakeholders' perspectives

Here, the most pertinent issues as identified by different stakeholders – the children themselves, birth parents, carers and social workers – are mapped out and incorporated in the discussion.

Children's perspective

The principle of giving voice to children and adopting a 'whole child' approach is central to Irish policy (Department of Health and Children, 2000). Since 2000, a number of developments have occurred to drive forward this policy initiative. The setting up of a National Children's Strategy Implementation Group in 2006, the publication of *Agenda for Children's Service* (Department of Health and Children, 2007), *Better Outcomes, Brighter Futures* (Department of Children and Youth Affairs, 2014) and the support for the organization Empowering Young People in Care (EPIC, 2011, 2013) is evidence of a major commitment to children and young people.

The decision in 2011 to appoint a minister for children and young people, with a separate government department, can be seen as the strongest political commitment to prioritize child wellbeing in Irish society. In the context of the changes in Ireland's economic fortunes since 2008, this decision is significant. Core questions remain about how the political wish to prioritize children's welfare has been implemented and what the profession of social work has been able to achieve since.

A series of outcomes, set out by the responsible government department, provide a new benchmark against which outcomes for children in care can now be examined. However, McAuley and Rose (2010) urge social workers to be cautious, as they argue that too great a focus on outcomes, at the expense of process, may militate against real progress for children. While outcomes for children in care are, and should be, held as core measures, the experiences of the system by children and young persons are also seen as key indicators. A consultation process with 211 children in state care regarding what they consider as important aspects of the care system adds significantly to the available research (McEvoy and Smith, 2011). The strength of this report is that children from across the spectrum of care, as well as children in different age cohorts, were interviewed. The children's views are abundantly clear and, from a social work perspective, contain important messages.

Social work interventions and workers' ability to build good relationships with children were generally welcomed by children under 12 years of age. This positivity was not followed through in respect of the older cohort of children, who called for more manageable social work caseloads to fulfil their wish that social workers had more time to engage with them. Calls were made for better assessments and vetting of social workers and foster carers, as well as a re-examination of the childcare review process to enable them to participate more fully in decisions that affected their lives. This Irish research reiterates the high levels of adversity facing children in the care system, especially when they reach the age to leave it (Daly, 2012). When this is combined with the issues identified by the Child Death Review (Shannon and Gibbons, 2012), the challenges facing social work remain of enormous proportions. A number of these issues are examined in this chapter and are dovetailed with a discussion of service delivery issues.

Birth parents

The voices of birth parents who are engaged in the alternative care system in Ireland are heard less, compared to other stakeholders. The work of Coulter (2013) in reporting judicial childcare proceedings offers some insights. The limited extent to which the parental perspective, experience and 'voice' is heard has been recognized internationally (Smeeton and Boxall, 2011). However, the relative silence of the parental voice and experience of the care system in Ireland is noteworthy, given the repeated claim that birth parents and family needs are prioritized over children's needs by Irish society. This claim was one of the arguments cited to support a referendum to underpin children's rights in the Constitution in 2013. So what processes give rise to this marginalization of birth parents' voices and are there particular social work interventions that may be useful?

It is at the point when children enter care that the birth parents' situation becomes more difficult, especially if longer term care is indicated. For those cases where reunification is deemed possible, it is likely that much work will be carried out towards achieving this outcome. Birth parents of children where the care plan is for more long-term/permanent care are engaged primarily by the social worker who also carries responsibility for the child in care. It is at this stage that birth parents' interests may begin to suffer. The social worker is charged with a great number of tasks, especially in relation to meeting the child's needs, and thus may have limited time to focus on the needs of birth parents. The social worker's main focus with parents is frequently to ensure attendance at reviews and facilitate access when the parents are willing and able to cooperate. The underlying issues and challenges experienced by the parents and associated with the child's entry into care remain largely outside consideration.

The stigma and disqualification from parenthood that occurs with having children removed by the care system can amplify parents' underlying difficulties and this can often lead to a downward spiral. The anger, frustration and powerlessness of parents engaging with the care system can militate against meaningful contact (Deignan, 2009). Given the importance of contact with parents for the child and vice versa, maintaining meaningful contact with parents and families remains an issue.

There is a clear need for more 'wrap-around' services for parents to counteract what can be a bewildering, onerous and negative experience, and which could enhance their understanding and ability to manage at a time of crisis. Providing parents with support and advocacy in their own right may, in turn, effect change for the other participants in the system, most importantly for the child. Advocacy and support services can ensure a level of stability for birth parents, even though the care plan may not change significantly

Foster carers

The demographic features of the 3,783 foster and kinship carers (Department of Children and Youth Affairs, 2013b) is largely unknown but 'snapshots' are provided by Meyler (2002), Daly and Gilligan (2005) and Irwin (2009). The profile of kinship carers is an even more unknown quantity (O'Brien, 2002, 2012b; Munro and Gilligan, 2013). The precise profiles, challenges and opportunities faced by carers are therefore hard to describe. It is known, however, that the tasks involved in caring for children in care can be enormous (Department of Health and Children, 2001). A high level of skill and capacity and a willingness to be innovative, creative, energetic and yet grounded are needed to find ways to deal with the challenges of the caring role. The foster carer role is complex. The work can sometimes engender huge conflict while, at other times, it provides great rewards and personal satisfaction (Irwin, 2009). Carers provide for the child on a day-to-day basis, while striving to address the challenges that children in care face. They act as advocates when the need arises and work to sustain relationships between children and their birth parents and other family members. At the same time as carrying out fostering tasks, they juggle the demands associated variously with their own work, relationships with family and the community aspects of their lives. In order to meet the children's needs, personal sacrifice is often the carer's default position (Kennedy, 2002; Cregan, 2002).

The provision of supports to enable carers to do the job is critical (Department of Health and Children, 2001; HSE, 2010). The allocation of a social worker and payment of a weekly allowance in respect of the child are two central supports provided by the state. Unlike other countries, fostering agencies in Ireland have limited provision to make variable payments to carers, but the levels of financial reimbursement provided are seen as high when compared to social protection rates paid to other families in respect of children. This point is frequently raised by birth parents who lose custody of their children.

An ongoing shortfall between the numbers of carers and the children in care, as well as a shortage of designated social workers to provide support to both, has been a repeated finding in Health Information and Quality Authority (HIQA) inspection reports of foster care services.

Key issues within the care experience

While many issues are pertinent to a discussion of alternative care, the place of education and the aftercare experience are seen as two issues of such importance that they warrant particular consideration in this chapter.

Education and children in care

The relationship between educational achievement and enhanced economic life chances is well established in modern economies. Thus, the trends in respect of educational outcomes for children in care are crucial. Internationally, there is evidence that school performance and educational completion rates of children in alternative care are inferior compared to their peers (Fernandez, 2008). However, more research is needed in respect of class differences and inequality factors that impact educational outcomes across peer groups. Studies of children that succeed educationally while in alternative care are needed to enable the factors involved to be identified and incorporated into future systems. This is crucial, as an important comparative study shows that the rate of educational participation of young people leaving care is estimated as five times lower than the national average across five European countries – Hungary, England, Sweden, Spain and Denmark (Jackson and Cameron, 2010).

In Ireland, only a small number of studies have explored the educational experiences of children in care. Daly and Gilligan (2005) explored the experiences of 13- to 14-year-olds, Darmody et al. (2013) examined the care experience and the educational context, and Kelleher et al. (2000) and Daly (2012) considered educational influence in respect of young people's aftercare experiences. In Kelleher's study, only 10% of the young people who had left care took the Leaving Certificate examination, while 60% of the respondents had left school aged 15 or under. In Daly's (2012) more recent work, 37% of the 65 respondents (in foster and/or residential care) had sat the Leaving Certificate examination. Twelve months after leaving the care system, one-fifth (37%) were engaged in further education, with multiple accommodation moves associated with the cessation of education or training (Daly, 2012). This is in contrast to the general population of 19-year-olds in Ireland, of whom 77% of females and 66% of males were in full-time education during 2010–11 (CSO, 2012). The absence of specific data to indicate children's educational outcomes is part of a wider gap in outcome data for children in care. We await more robust longitudinal data on outcomes for children in care as a subset of the general population from the Growing Up in Ireland project. Meanwhile, social workers have an important role to play as they carry responsibility for the child's care plan, and advocating for the enhancement of children's educational outcomes should be a priority. This is crucial in light of a level of evidence that social workers pay more attention to other aspects of children's lives, rather than their education (McEvoy and Smith, 2011; Darmody et al., 2013).

Aftercare and transitions to adulthood for young people in care

The transition from care to 'independence' presents significant challenge to young people, and social workers have been to the fore in calling for greater action in this area (IASW, 2011). Officially, young people leave formal care when they reach the age of 18, although there is discretion to extend formal care where young people are in full-time education. This provides for the agency to continue to pay an allowance to the carers and assist with other approved expenses. Under this arrangement, 1,110 young people were supported in 2013, compared to 847 in 2009 (Department of Children and Youth Affairs, 2013a, p. 87). For many young people who progress to college, continuing to live with their foster family provides a significant level of security.

Overall, the vulnerabilities faced by young people transitioning from care can lead to an increased risk of homelessness and the risk increases for those leaving residential care (Kelleher et al., 2000; Daly, 2012). Internationally, accommodation instability and homelessness have been identified as issues of particular concern (Hojer and Sjöblom, 2009) as this can set off a cycle of other events. Mayock et al.'s Irish study captured a young person's experience: 'You just don't turn into an adult straight away overnight ... I think they should give you more time' (2008, p. 139).

Healthcare risks are also higher for young people leaving care, again with those leaving residential care showing particular vulnerability (McNicholas et al., 2011). Studies show higher than average rates of illegal drug use, teenage pregnancy and mental health issues (Daly, 2012). Karen, an 18-year-old in Daly's study, encapsulates the difficulties when she states:

> Yesterday, I was having an extremely bad day … I had nobody to talk to … I tried phoning one of my [support] worker's colleagues and she didn't ring, and I was thinking 'Please, just even a five minute conversation to calm me down,' y'know and it wasn't there. I just think, you don't get as much support when you turn 18. It's a lot harder. (Daly, 2012, p. 67)

While the vulnerabilities of young people leaving care have been widely recognized for many years by social workers, it wasn't until 2011 that a national 'aftercare' policy was established. This policy development, while welcome, has been implemented slowly. The discretionary nature of aftercare proposed in the 2011 policy highlights the need for legislative change to enable young people and their carers to be supported until the age of 21 or until they complete their education. This is an area of advocacy that should remain a priority for social workers, given the levels of vulnerability and other factors involved.

Future issues

Here, selected policy and legal issues, including the concept of permanence, recruitment and retention of carers, kinship care, meeting the needs of diverse populations as well as the future of the social work role arising from changes in the wider domains, are considered.

'Permanence', historical practices and adoption

The length of time children spend in care, the multiple placements experienced by some, the use of 'permanence' as a concept underpinning care planning, and the place of long-term care and adoption in providing stability for children in care are issues that will challenge social workers in respect of decision making in the future. A level of clarity regarding what may be involved is important. Table 6.3 shows that the majority of children in care between 2006 and 2011 spent between one and five years in care, with 35.2% of the total number of children spending more than five years in care.

Children are rarely adopted from the Irish care system. An Adoption Bill 2012, published as part of the Children's Referendum campaign, contains proposals to permit children to be adopted if they are with foster carers for three years or more. The limited position of adoption in the care system was linked in the Children's Referendum campaign to the 'lack of voice

Table 6.3 Period of time children spent in care, 2006–11

	Amount of time in care		
	<1 year	1–5 years	More than 5 years
2006	27%	39.4%	33.6%
2007	25.2%	37.4%	37.4%
2008	23.1%	40.1%	36.2%
2009	27.5%	39.4%	33.1%
2010	25.3%	39%	35.7%
2011	23.1%	43.3%	33.5%

Source: HSE, 2012, p. 62

for children' and 'the protection of the family based on marriage' in the Irish Constitution. Prior to this proposal, adopting children of marriage or without parental consent could only occur in the rarest of circumstances (Adoption Act 1988). The use of this 1988 legislation by professionals, including social workers, has been limited (AAI, 2011). The specific definition of 'abandonment', which the 1988 law is based on, has been a factor in this.

However, it is contended that an understanding of the potential place of adoption in the alternative care system needs more detailed analysis. It is argued that the linkages between oppressive past practices and the specifics of the legislative proposal will need to be taken into account in any future legislative debate (O'Brien, 2013).

The legacy of the past continues to evoke a level of societal unease and shame, especially in relation to forced adoptions. While there is an obvious need to safeguard children's placements to offer them stability and security, adoption should only be seen as one option. There is a need to continue to explore why so few foster carers have taken advantage of the legislative provision enacted in 2005 for them to become 'special' guardians for children in their care for more than five years. Is this to do with limiting the provision to pay an allowance for those carers who opt to adopt children in their care? Is there a link between declining numbers of children available via intercountry adoption and renewed interest in adoption for children of marriage and expanding legislative provision for terminating parental rights? Finally, there is a need to consider seriously the circumstances in which children themselves should have the right to choose adoption over long-term foster care, and whether social workers should advocate for this to happen or whether legal advocates should be involved.

Recruitment and retention of foster carers

The international trend in respect of the challenges of recruiting and retaining foster carers (Colton et al., 2008) is very much evident in Ireland. Arising from fostering recruitment shortfalls, a private fostering sector has emerged since 2005 to fill the gap in supplying foster placements through the HSE system. Limited data is available regarding the specifics of market share, but two factors in particular may influence the future direction and pace of this development. First, private agencies face the same problems of recruiting in areas where placement demand is highest. Thus, many placements purchased by the statutory services involve moving children a great distance from their family and community networks. The impact in the medium and long term, especially in terms of identity formation and maintaining sibling and parental bonds, should not be underestimated.

Second, the commitment to family-based care in Ireland may be compromised if more active measures are not put in place to address the challenge of recruiting sufficient foster carers. The role of existing foster carers in the successful recruitment of new foster carers, as well as the need to provide realistic information and target specific groups in the population and in the location where the need is highest are well recognized internationally (Colton et al., 2008). While this factor has been recognized in Ireland (HSE, 2010), there is a need for a more strategic approach incorporating social media, marketing strategies and creative ways to incorporate foster carers into the recruitment process.

Internationally, there is evidence to suggest that foster carers leave caring and thus retention issues arise because they are unsupported in the task. For some, it may be associated with a life cycle stage. There is a need for more research to understand the specifics of the fostering/family life cycle, compared to the more 'normative' family life cycle. Furthermore, the relationship between motivation to foster, recruitment, support and retention, while complex, needs to be better understood. Finally, there is an urgent need to ensure that there is a cohort of foster carers to meet the care needs of a growing number of children in care, otherwise the past success of providing family-based care to Irish children in care is threatened. This is not a policy or practice development that social workers would favour.

Kinship care

Through tapping into kinship care, the Irish care system has been able to deliver the policy commitment of providing a family-based experience for children in need of care (O'Brien, 2012a). While there is some useful information regarding general trends in respect of kinship care in Ireland (O'Brien,

2012b, 2012c; Munro and Gilligan, 2013), a gap remains in terms of an up-to-date profile of kin carers, family and children. It is also unknown how many other children are living with relatives through informal care arrangements, which may be organized by family members, either in conjunction with child welfare services or privately. There is an urgent need to research this further. It is especially important to establish the extent to which an extended family has the resources to provide care for children and to explore the relationship between family and the state in respect of children who need care and protection (O'Brien, 2012c, 2013), taking into account new diverse family forms and the realities of transnational parenting, as outlined in Chapter 2. The issue of recruitment and assessment of the kinship home remains a challenge to the growth and development of kinship care. A model developed for the Irish context (O'Brien, 2014) redefines kinship care assessment to be part of a larger case management system and moves assessment from a narrow 'home study' perspective to an appraisal of the information available about the network of evolving relationships in the family.

The model builds on a number of international initiatives. However, to date, the Irish childcare system has been slow to adopt the changes required to incorporate the model in the system. Instead, the existing foster care case management system has been utilized, although a level of adaptations has occurred to take account of the differences in the kinship relational field. Whatever case management model is used, it needs to take into account fully the profile of kinship carers, the policy and value positions regarding the role and expectations of the extended family in caring for children, and the pathways between formal and informal kinship care, including the resourcing and supervision requirements.

Meeting the needs of diverse populations: ethnic and cultural minorities and the care system

The change in Ireland's ethnic profile has direct implications for child welfare but there is no official data available on the rates of placement for children, or the number of carers, from ethnic minorities. This gap is increasingly difficult to justify. Most importantly, in the absence of data, it is not possible to establish if disproportionality is a feature of the care system. This is defined as children from certain racial/ethnic groups entering into the care system at different rates than other racial/ethnic groups. Kirk and Griffith (2008) suggest that this may occur due to discriminatory practices in society and within the child welfare agencies' processes. International research (Earner, 2007) suggests that ethnic minority families have been negatively stereotyped by the child welfare system and this may contribute to the overrepresentation of these groups in child protection and welfare cases.

Coulter's (2013) presentation of Irish data shows some worrying trends, whereby there were high rates of children from certain ethnic minority groups entering care. She found that children of African origin were 20 times more likely than an Irish child to be the subject of court childcare proceedings. She suggests that, for ethnic minority parents in Ireland, parental mental illness/intellectual disability and parental absence were the two main reasons for children going into care. While the data on the rate at which children from ethnic minorities are entering care is limited, urgent action is needed to monitor and address this potential trend. Irish practice and policy should be able to learn from the vast experiences of other jurisdictions that have worked with more diverse populations for long periods.

Social workers are to the fore in Ireland in working with unaccompanied minors and are involved in advocating for change through their professional association and conducting research (Ní Raghallaigh, 2013). The position of separated children has improved, having been removed from largely unsupervised hostels and they are now being placed more with carers. However, a level of concern remains, in terms of the adequacy of social work and fostering services, in particular the return of separated children into the direct provision system when they reach 18, which is an ongoing issue. There are difficulties in matching children with carers from within their own communities due to the shortage of such placements (Ní Raghallaigh, 2013).

Future service delivery

Evidence that the model of preferred service delivery has been under increasing pressure in economically straitened times in trying to deliver targets set out in the regulatory frameworks and standards has been established through HIQA inspection reports. The gaps in service delivery to children and carers have led to criticism in the public domain and concerns within the social work profession itself. Has the time come to critically examine if the 'one-size-fits-all' approach still fits? To what extent is there a need to revisit the models of service delivery, as well as the regulatory standards and inspection frameworks? While such an invitation requires multiple stakeholders to engage with the idea, social workers could, in the meantime, take the lead in putting forward proposals to roll out a series of demonstration projects aimed at addressing many of the issues raised in this chapter. Social work needs to be alert to the possibilities and constraints of alternative care remaining as a single disciplinary responsibility. No doubt change at this level will have an impact on social work's professional identity. Such considerations may provide opportunities to the profession to widen its scope. The profession should, perhaps, choose to take the initiative to lead such developments, while recognizing that such a change process will bring significant challenges.

Conclusion

In conclusion, this chapter provides an overview of demographic features of the Irish foster care system. It locates the system within its historical context and demonstrates how it has been influenced and shaped by the UK model. The challenges resulting from a limited research base and information management systems, the shifting and decreasing role of residential care in a context of an increasing rate of family foster placements, and the emergence, use and particular challenges of kinship care are discussed. The use of permanency in care planning and, in particular, how the recent insertion of children's rights into the Constitution may change the position of adoption within the alternative care system are explored. The specific needs of a number of parties are highlighted and include young people leaving care, birth parents whose rights are relinquished by the courts, and the changing requirements of foster carers. Finally, some implications for the social work profession in respect of the emerging issues are discussed, presenting social workers with new challenges and changes to which the profession can and will adapt.

Note

We wish to acknowledge the input of Professor Robbie Gilligan (Trinity College Dublin) into the earlier structure of this chapter.

References

AAI (Adoption Authority of Ireland) (2011) *Annual Report 2011*, Dublin, AAI.

Buckley, H. and O'Nolan, C. (2013) *An Examination of Recommendations from Inquiries into Events in Families and their Interactions with State Services, and their Impact on Policy and Practice*, Dublin, Department of Children and Youth Affairs.

Colton, M., Roberts, S. and Williams, M. (2008) 'The recruitment and retention of family foster-carers: an international and cross-cultural analysis', *British Journal of Social Work*, 38(5), 865–85.

Considine, M. and Dukelow, F. (2009) *Irish Social Policy: A Critical Introduction*, Dublin, Gill & Macmillan.

Coulter, C. (2013) *Interim Report: Child Care Law Reporting Project*, www.childlawproject.ie/wpcontent/uploads/2013/11/correctedinterimreport.pdf, accessed 25 March 2014.

Cregan, M. (2002) 'Learning to cry out loud', *Irish Journal of Applied Social Studies*, 3(1), 96–102.

Cregan, M. (2014) Going Forward – Looking Back, paper presented to International Foster Care Organisation, European Conference, Waterford.

CSO (Central Statistics Office) (2012) *Statistical Yearbook of Ireland 2012*, Dublin, Stationery Office.

Daly, F. (2012) *My Voice Has to be Heard: Research on Outcomes for Young People Leaving Care in North Dublin*, Dublin, EPIC.

Daly, F. and Gilligan, R. (2005) *Lives in Foster Care: The Educational and Social Support Experiences of Young people aged 13 to 14 Years in Long-term Foster Care*, Dublin, Children's Research Centre.

Darmody, M., McMahon, L., Banks, J. and Gilligan, R. (2013) *Education of Children in Care in Ireland: An Exploratory Study*, Dublin, Children's Research Centre.

Deignan, A. (2009) 'Look, I realise what's going on': a study of young adult's experiences of contact provision while in care and the implications for social work practice, unpublished MSocSc thesis, University College Dublin.

Department of Children and Youth Affairs (2012) *Report of the Task Force on the Child and Family Support Agency*, Dublin, Government Publications.

Department of Children and Youth Affairs (2013a) *Ireland's Consolidated 3rd and 4th Report to the UN Convention on the Rights of Children*, Dublin, DCYA.

Department of Children and Youth Affairs (2013b) *Statistical Annex: Consolidated 3rd and 4th Report to the UN Convention on the Rights of Children*, Dublin, DCYA.

Department of Children and Youth Affairs (2014) *Better Outcomes, Brighter Futures: The National Policy Framework for Children and Young People 2014–2020*, Dublin, Government Publications.

Department of Health and Children (2000) *The National Children's Strategy: Our Children, Their Lives*, Dublin, Stationery Office.

Department of Health and Children (2001) *Report of the Working Group on Foster Care: A Child Centred Partnership*, Dublin, Government Publications.

Department of Health and Children (2007) *The Agenda for Children's Services: A Policy Handbook*, Dublin, Government Publications.

Earner, I. (2007) 'Immigrant families and public child welfare: barriers to services and approach for change', *Child Welfare*, 86(4), 63–91.

EPIC (Empowering Young People in Care) (2011) *Summary of EPIC Research into Outcomes for Young People Leaving Care in North Dublin*, Dublin, EPIC.

EPIC (2013) *EPIC Annual Report 2013*, Dublin, EPIC.

Featherstone, B., White, S. and Wastell, D. (2012) 'Ireland's opportunity to learn from England's difficulties? Auditing uncertainty in child protection', *Irish Journal of Applied Social Studies*, 12(1), 49–62.

Ferguson, H. (2007) 'Abused and looked after children as "moral dirt": child abuse and institutional care in historical perspective', *Journal of Social Policy*, 36(1), 123–39.

Fernandez, E. (2008) 'Unravelling emotional, behavioral and educational outcomes in a longitudinal study of children in foster care', *British Journal of Social Work*, 38(7), 1283–301.

Hojer, I. and Sjöblom, Y. (2009) 'Young people leaving care in Sweden', *Child and Family Social Work*, 15(1), 118–27.

Horgan, R. (2002) 'Foster care in Ireland: historical and current contexts', *Irish Journal of Applied Social Studies*, 3(1), 30–50.

HSE (Health Service Executive) (2009) *Report of the NCCIS Business Process Standardisation Project*, Dublin, HSE.

HSE (2010) *Foster Care Audit*, Dublin, HSE.

HSE (2012) *Review of Adequacy of Services for Children and Families 2011*, Dublin, HSE.

IASW (Irish Association of Social Workers) (2011) *A Call for Change Discussion Document: Children and Families Social Workers Make their Voices Heard 2011*, www. aai.gov.ie/attachments/article/32/Annual%20Report%202012.pdf, accessed 10 April 2014.

Irwin, B. (2009) *The Voice of Foster Carers*, Dublin, Irish Foster Care Association.

Jackson, S. and Cameron, C. (2010) *Final Report of the YiPPEE Project: Young People from a Public Care Background: Pathways to Further and Higher Education in Five European Countries*, London, Institute of Education.

Kelleher, P., Kelleher, C. and Corbett, M. (2000) *Left Out on Their Own: Young People Leaving Care in Ireland*, Dublin, Oak Tree.

Kennedy, J. (2002) 'Believing in fostering', *Irish Journal of Applied Social Studies*, 3(1), 103–7.

Kennedy Report (1970) *Reformatory and Industrial Schools System Report*, Dublin, Stationery Office.

Kirk, R.S. and Griffith, D.P. (2008) 'Impact of intensive family preservation services on disproportionality of out of home placement of children of color in one state's child welfare system', *Child Welfare*, 87(5), 87–105.

McAuley, C. and Rose, W. (eds) (2010) *Child Well-Being: Understanding Children's Lives*, London, Jessica Kingsley.

McEvoy, O. and Smith, M. (2011) *Listen to Our Voices! Hearing Children and Young People Living in the Care of the State. Report of a Consultation Process*, Dublin, Government Publications.

McNicholas, F., O'Connor, N., Bandyopadhyay, G. et al. (2011) 'Looked after children in Dublin and their mental health needs', *Irish Medical Journal*, 104(4), 105–8.

Mayock, P., Corr, M.L. and O'Sullivan, E. (2008) *Young People's Homeless Pathways*, Dublin, The Homeless Agency.

Meyler, M. (2002) *Counting on Foster Care*, Dublin, Northern Area Health Board.

Munro, E. (2011) *The Munro Review of Child Protection, Interim Report: The Child's Journey*, London, Department of Education.

Munro, E. and Gilligan, R. (2013) 'The "dance" of kinship care in England and Ireland: navigating a course between regulation and relationships', *Psychosocial Interventions*, 22(3), 185–92.

Murphy, Y. (2009) *The Commission's Report into the Catholic Diocese of Cloyne*, Dublin, Government Publications.

Ní Raghallaigh, M. (2013) *Foster Care and Supported Lodgings for Separated Asylum Seeking Young People in Ireland: The Views of Young People, Carers and Stakeholders*, Dublin, Barnardos.

O'Brien, V. (2002) 'Children and relative care', in Nic Ghiolla Phadraig, M. and Quin, S. (eds) *Children in Irish Society*, vol. 2, Cork, Oak Tree.

O'Brien, V. (2012a) 'The place of family group conferencing in child welfare in the Republic of Ireland', in Clarijs, R. and Malmberg, T. (eds) *The Quiet Revolution: Aggrandising People Power by Family Group Conference*, Amsterdam, SWP.

O'Brien, V. (2012b) 'The challenges and benefits of kinship care', *Child Care in Practice*, 18(2), 127–46.

O'Brien, V. (2012c) 'Kinship care: enhanced support needed', in *Voices of the Forgotten: 30 Years of the International Foster Care Organization*, Dublin, University College Dublin.

O'Brien, V. (2013) Children in Care and Permanency, paper presented to IASW conference, http://hdl.handle.net/10197/5123.

O'Brien, V. (2014) 'Responding to the call: a conceptual model for kinship care assessment', *Child and Family Social Work*, 19(3), 355–66.

Raftery, M. and O'Sullivan, E. (1999) *Suffer the Little Children*, Dublin, New Island Books.

Ryan Report (2009) *The Commission to Inquire into Child Abuse*, Dublin, Government Publications.

Shannon, G. and Gibbons, N. (2012) *Report of the Independent Child Death Review*, Dublin, DCYA.

Skehill, C. (1999) *The Nature of Social Work in Ireland*, New York, Edwin Mellen.

Smeeton, J. and Boxall, K. (2011) 'Birth parents perceptions of professional practice in child care and adoption proceedings: implications for practice', *Child and Family Social Work*, 12(4), 444–53.

Task Force on Child Care Services (1980) *Final Report*, Dublin, Government Publications.

Thoburn, J. (2010) 'International perspectives on foster care', in Fernandez, E. and Barth, R.P. (eds) *How Does Foster Care Work? International Evidence on Outcomes*, London, Jessica Kingsley.

7

Responding to Family Violence: New Challenges and Perspectives

Declan Coogan and Stephanie Holt

Introduction

The past 30 years have witnessed remarkable developments in the awareness of and responses to domestic violence and abuse in Ireland, in tandem with legislative reform, policy development and the emergence of practice initiatives (Cosc, 2010). Similar developments are mirrored throughout the European Union and indeed internationally (Brown and Alexander, 2007; European Union Agency for Fundamental Rights, 2014). In Ireland, our understanding of what constitutes domestic violence has been broadened to reflect changing social norms and the diverse ways in which people live their lives together – policy and practice initiatives also recognize domestic violence as forms of violence distinct from married heterosexual couples with children, such as elder abuse, violence within gay and lesbian relationships, and violence between cohabiting couples (Cosc, 2010). Launched by the government in early 2010, the *National Strategy on the Prevention of Domestic, Sexual and Gender-based Violence 2010–2014* recognizes the complexity of violence in intimate relationships and in the family by the deliberate use of the terms 'domestic violence' and/or 'domestic abuse' interchangeably, which 'highlights the fact that the problem is not restricted to physical violence but involves also psychological, verbal, sexual, financial and emotional abuse' (Cosc, 2010, p. 20).

While there is growing international consensus on how to measure the extent of domestic violence, it is also important to note that rates of disclosure do not reflect true prevalence rates, the scale of the problem is likely to be far greater than statistics indicate, and prevalence figures represent the tip of the iceberg (Watson and Parsons, 2005; European Union Agency for Fundamental Rights, 2014). There are three primary sources of prevalence data for domestic abuse in the Republic of Ireland:

1.   The national survey of women conducted by Kelleher and O'Connor (1995) found that 18% of the 679 participating women indicated that they had experienced violence by a current or former male partner.

2.   The second Irish survey to generate prevalence data on domestic abuse was conducted in 2003 (Watson and Parsons, 2005). This larger crime survey of 3,077 adults included men and women, and established that 15% of female respondents and 6% of male respondents experienced severe abusive behaviour of a physical, sexual or emotional nature from a partner at some point in their lives.

3.   *The SAVI Report: Sexual Abuse and Violence in Ireland*, produced by McGee et al. (2002), is based on a population survey of 3,000 adults and provides information on the prevalence of sexual violence for men and women in Ireland. It specifically highlighted that 42% of women and 28% of men reported some form of sexual abuse or assault in their lifetime, with nearly 30% of women and 25% of men reporting varying levels of sexual abuse in childhood.

While acknowledging that the different methodologies employed in these three Irish studies render comparisons or conclusions about trends difficult, it does seem that the prevalence of domestic abuse among women did not change significantly from 1995 to 2005 during which time these surveys were completed (Horgan et al., 2008). Rooted in the Irish women's liberation movement, which started in the 1970s, it is only in the past four decades that the enormity of the impact and consequences of domestic abuse has begun to be realized and translated into policy, law reform and service provision in the Republic of Ireland. Cosc, the National Office for the Prevention of Domestic, Sexual and Gender-based Violence, was established in June 2007 with the key responsibility to ensure the delivery of a well-coordinated 'whole of government' response to domestic, sexual and gender-based violence. Safe Ireland coordinates the activities of approximately 40 agencies that provide refuge, support and advocacy services for women and children experiencing domestic violence, while the government spends approximately €650,000 per annum funding a number of organizations to provide domestic violence perpetrator programmes across Ireland.

Research on social work practice in cases involving domestic violence in Ireland and internationally has consistently highlighted the many issues and concerns social work encounters in dealing with this complex and multifaceted phenomena (Holt, 2003; Humphreys and Absler, 2011). Social workers and social care workers in Ireland are further challenged by questions that have been largely ignored in domestic violence discourses so far, which tend to be limited to the dynamics and prevention of adult-initiated violence. Situated in the context of the UN Universal Declaration of Human Rights (1948) and the UN Convention on the Rights of the Child (UNCRC, 1989), this chapter focuses on two largely neglected issues of concern regarding children, parents and violence. We begin with the complex issue of post-separation contact for children with their fathers where there has been a prior history of domestic violence perpetrated by the father against the mother. In doing so, we are, first, responding to the demands from children and young people to be consulted, listened to and taken seriously, by seeking a greater insight into their views, feelings and understanding of contact with their father (Holt, 2011a). In adopting this focus, we are simultaneously highlighting the struggle children, parents and professionals face in reconciling the needs of the child regarding the paternal relationship, and the potentially deleterious impact that the absence of parental contact *and* ongoing and perhaps unwanted contact with an abusive father can have on the developing child.

We then call attention to an emerging problem of responding to the various forms of emotional and/or physical abuse carried out by children under the age of 18 against their parents, known as 'child to parent violence' (CPV) or parent abuse. Parents living with CPV seem to live lives surrounded with a veil of silence, with embarrassment, shame and fear (Tew and Nixon, 2010; Holt A., 2013), making it difficult for a parent to initiate a conversation about CPV. The invisibility of CPV in domestic violence official guidance and policy in Ireland and the UK further hinders the resolution of this complex problem (Coogan, 2011; Condry and Miles, 2012). We aim to provide the student and the practitioner with some useful starting points, while indicating some of the pitfalls of 'commonsense' approaches to understanding CPV. We also outline some the first steps that can be taken to enhance family members' rights to dignity, safety and wellbeing at home. We propose that social work and social care practitioners are well positioned to respond effectively to family violence and outline some evidence-supported responses to the problem of violence within the family.

Ascertaining the views and wishes of the child in post-separation contact

The lens of research and practice interest has, in recent years, expanded to include a consideration of the scope and consequences of children's exposure to domestic abuse, resulting in a depth of empirical knowledge about its prevalence, and the impact this experience has on its youngest victims (Buckley et al., 2007). This increased awareness of children's needs and their heightened visibility and prominence in the context of domestic abuse is reflective of the core ethos of the UNCRC. A substantive theme within the UNCRC concerns children's participatory rights, including the freedom to have a say in matters affecting their lives. This reflects a commitment to honour the principle of 'listening to the voice of the child', as demanded by the *National Children's Strategy* (Department of Health and Children, 2000), by recognizing and accepting children as active, sentient social actors in the unfolding story of their ongoing development in family life.

In tandem with this developing empirical knowledge base is a growing interest in and awareness of the role of fathers in family life and child development (Lamb, 2013). Children with highly involved fathers are understood to demonstrate increased cognitive abilities and empathy, less stereotyped beliefs, and a greater internal locus of control (Lamb, 2004). Therefore, the absence of fathers is considered harmful for children, as many aspects of the fathering role subsequently remain unfulfilled (Lamb, 2004). In the context of domestic abuse, experts impose a caveat on the construction of the role of the father as critical for healthy child development, as many aspects of the fathering role are compromised for domestically abusive fathers (Bancroft and Silverman, 2002). While research evidence regarding the fathering of non-resident domestically abusive men remains scant, the comprehensive range of literature that examines the implications of separation and divorce for children's wellbeing broadly supports the view, and is drawn on to underpin the prevailing discourse in the majority of jurisdictions, which is that outcomes for children are better when they can maintain relationships with both parents. The dominance of this discourse is such that Kaganas and Day Sclater (2004) surmise that it has passed into the realms of 'incontestable truth'.

Rhoades (2002) comments on this new discourse or reconstruction of post-separation parenthood, established in many jurisdictions through legislative reforms, that endorses the concept of shared parenting as the 'ideal custodial arrangement for children' (Kurki-Suonio, 2000, pp. 183–4). Furthermore, Kaganas and Day Sclater (2004) argue that there is not just one, but often a range of competing discourses against which separating and divorcing parents are required to position themselves and their children. Those competing discourses include the dominant welfare discourse and the human rights discourse, which, according to Kaganas and Day Sclater (2004), conceptualize the issues in fundamentally different ways. For example, under the dominant welfare discourse, divorce (and parental separation) is perceived to be damaging for children and society (Neale and Smart, 1999). Children are conceptualized as particularly vulnerable and therefore need their parents to 'manage' their divorce properly, engage in cooperative parenting, and be committed to continued non-resident parent–child relationships. The 'best interests of the child' are equated with protecting children from exposure to, and involvement in, this process and in promoting post-separation contact. The human rights discourse similarly underscores the right of the child and the non-resident parent to continued contact, but also recognizes the child's right to be part of the process where decisions are being made about their lives (Piper, 1999). Opinion diverges, however, within that discourse regarding the agency of children and whether their best interests are served by affording them the right to participate or by protecting them from the perceived harm that participation in adult affairs would incur (Kjorholt, 2002). This tension is also encapsulated in the rights versus welfare debate centred on a particular concern that rights to participation risk overburdening children with responsibility and thus potentially jeopardizes their right to protection while denying them their 'childhood' (Morrow, 1999).

An inherent tension therefore prevails regarding how the best interests of the child are constructed within and across these discourses. This tension centres on the question of how far we are prepared to go in according children the authority to pursue active yet appropriately child-centred involvement: Should the phenomenon of the 'best interests of the child' be constructed by adults or informed by children? This tension becomes most acute when we acknowledge the ongoing presence of domestic abuse in post-separation contact arrangements, highlighting children's vulnerability arising from their father's *presence* not his absence (Holt S., 2011b, 2013; Murphy and Holt, 2014). Concurring with this, Jaffe and Crooks (2004) assert that the presence of domestic abuse demands a paradigm shift from the drive towards post-separation joint custody and the 'friendly parent' construct, on the basis that the playing field is not level and the non-resident parent is not necessarily friendly.

The outcome of these debates and tensions is that the current construction of post-separation family life supports the ongoing and often unmonitored involvement of domestically abusive men in children's lives, based on the belief that post-separation contact serves children's rights and is in their best interests (Lamb, 2012). Two prevailing assumptions have underpinned this belief (Roche, 1999; Holt, 2011b); first, the automatic assumption that post-separation contact is in the child's best interests, and, second, that participation in the decision-making process regarding post-separation contact arrangements is harmful for children.

Constructing post-separation parenting: in 'the best interest of the child'

The construction of post-separation parenting, within which children are conceptualized as vulnerable and in need of co-parenting, has led to what Smart and Neale (1999) describe as a concerted effort to socially engineer the domain of family life by reconstructing the essence of post-divorce family life. Collier's (2006) observation of the repositioning of fatherhood within that process of social engineering, which reconstructs the idea of the 'good father' in post-separation arrangements, is also reflected in Irish research (Holt, 2011b). Previously constructed as problematic because of the child's exposure to the abuse of their mother, research highlights a combination of disappearing and disregarded histories of domestic and child abuse overshadowed by a potent perception of the child's need for continued paternal involvement (Hester, 2011; Holt, 2011b). Even where a father has been abusive to his child, research finds that the absence of the father in the child's life is considered by the relevant professionals involved to be more harmful than the experience of his abuse (Holt, 2011b). Collier (2001, p. 521) concludes that the evolving debate on familial roles and family life has relied to a great extent on an 'optimistic' model of fatherhood that assumes men share equally in the work and life of the family. This resonates to some degree with Collier's (2006) assertion that the professional assessment of an abusive father's capacity to parent is often concluded without any discussion or agreement on what constitutes 'good enough' parenting, or, as Harrison (2006) posits, little evidence of 'safe parenting'. Domestic abuse is consistently considered an adult affair, a feature of the adult relationship that is no longer a child welfare concern as separation has effectively defused this concern. While research has consistently highlighted the risks associated with post-separation contact for women and children with a domestically abusive man (Holt S., 2013), post-separation contact is nonetheless considered the 'preferred' vehicle for continued father involvement. Mothers and children who resist or object to the contact arrangements are reconstructed respectively as malicious and brainwashed, and as the history of domestic abuse disappears, so too does the child's right to be heard.

Participation or protection? Constructing children within the contact debate

Pryor and Rodger's (2001) identification of three separate areas to the debate provides a useful point of reflection in this chapter. These concern, first, children's competence to participate, second, their construction as either 'beings' or 'becomings' (Hogan, 2005) and, third, children's interest in or willingness to participate.

First, on the issue of competence, the question is raised as to whether children can articulate an understanding of what is happening in their family, why their parents are separated, and what their wishes are in relation to contact with their father. Participants as young as five in research have clearly demonstrated that they can articulate, through a variety of means employed to engage them, age-appropriate understandings of what was happening in their family and could provide coherent and rational reasoning to support their position on contact with their father (Holt, 2011a; Kilkelly and Savage, 2012). Research also finds that when participating children and young people express unhappiness with their current arrangements for contact, and can provide consistent reasoning for this, this did not necessarily mean they wanted an end to contact – in fact very few do. Rather, they express a deep yearning for a different kind of relationship with their father, a meaningful relationship that can exist independently of their parents' relationship. They also express a need to be informed in an inclusive manner of what was happening to their family, and varying levels of desire to have a choice to participate in that debate. Overwhelmingly, the articulate, insightful data drawn from children's participation in the research process concurs with Butler et al.'s (2002, p. 99) view that 'they are also the most reliable witness of their own experience' and confirms their competency to understand and manage their post-separation lives.

Powerful assumptions about competence and welfare can, however, militate against a child ever being heard, particularly if the child's views run contrary to those universally held assumptions about what is considered to be in their best interests. As such, many children are ordered to engage in contact because a prevailing professional view presumes it is good for them and indeed is their right. The strength of this prevailing view, combined with fluid notions of age and maturity (Kilkelly, 2008), includes children's views when they want contact but overrides them if they don't (James et al., 1998). The imposition by the UNCRC of restrictions on participation based on age and maturity grounds has been criticized for rendering such participation at the discretion of adults and vulnerable to the powerful assumptions and constructions of children, childhood and the family (Smith et al., 2003). Holt (2011a) found no evidence, however, of the systematic application of age and maturity indices to participation; rather, a potent blanket exclusion of children of any age participating in the process and a subsequent denial of real participatory rights. The absence of real participation was justified by legal personnel in this research on competency and welfare grounds (Roche,1999).

Pryor and Rodger's (2001) second question relates to the manner in which children are understood or constructed: Are children viewed as experts on, and indeed in, their own lives (Christensen and Prout, 2005) or constructed as incomplete and in a process of 'becoming' rather than 'being' (Hogan, 2005)? This second question illustrates the debate that has become polarized on the issue of whether children should have rights equal to those of adults or be protected by adults. Dominant constructions are found to interpret, understand and process the child's voice in questionable and one could say inaccurate ways (Piper, 2000; Kilkelly and Savage, 2012). It can also run counter to what children want and what is in their best interests (Smart et al., 2001; Smart, 2002).

Despite clear rhetorical commitment to the concept of children's rights, as evidenced by the international and domestic embracing of the UNCRC, research on post-separation contact highlights a rather conservative approach to protecting rather than empowering children (Mantle et al., 2007). Kaganas and Day Sclater's (2004) observation that how children are understood or constructed in terms of their capacity or their vulnerability determines how they are responded to resonates loudly from a review of the research. A clear commitment to a protectionist or welfare agenda (Mantle et al., 2007) is grounded in the belief that such involvement makes 'unreasonable demands on their maturity' (Pryor and Rodgers, 2001, p. 112), manifesting itself in considerable ambivalence and concern expressed about the appropriateness of children's involvement in this domain.

Neale (2002) condemns this orientation for critically limiting children's participation, positioning them as subordinate to adults, vulnerable and in need of protection, and rendering their right to speak at the discretion of adults' judgement. Research engaging with children as young as four years of age has challenged the use of age as an barometer of competence, demonstrating children's competence to discourse on aspects of family life providing age-appropriate measures are employed (Sturgess et al., 2001; Murphy and Holt, 2014). This, of course, challenges the adults involved, be they researchers or health and social care practitioners, to adapt their position to the children's capacity instead of using the children's capacity to engage in adult debate as the indicator of competence (Thomas and O'Kane, 2000).

The third question posed concerns whether or not children actually want to participate in the decision-making process. It also addresses their need for choice in that endeavour: the choice to participate and to exercise some control over the manner that participation might take. While the first part of this question is contingent to a large degree on the prevailing adult consensus, as discussed above, the latter half of this question is entirely reliant on the structures in place to realize child participation. Kilkelly (2008, p. 14) asserts that unprecedented legislative developments and a 'relatively extensive policy base' have led to administrative and political structures that can, in theory anyway, begin to place children's rights at the heart of the debate. At a more micro-level, however, Kilkelly's (2008) criticism of the structures and mechanisms to enforce those rights renders children largely invisible in the decision-making process. Where they were consulted, research has highlighted that the overwhelming experience of those children was that their views were neither listened to nor taken seriously (Holt, 2011a). The findings concur with Laing (2006), who observes that claims to proceed in the child's best interests cannot be valid where the child's view is not sought, not heard or not considered.

Domestic violence, child to parent violence (CPV) and human rights

Child to parent violence (CPV) also challenges us to find ways to elicit and take seriously the usually hidden views of parents living with this form of family violence. While there are many similarities between domestic violence and CPV, there are also significant differences. Similarities in both of these forms of intrafamilial violence include, for example, the types of abusive behaviour used, the survivor's experiences of self-blame and shame, and the fact that women/mothers are the most frequent targets of abuse. We shall consider the differences between these types of family violence later in this chapter.

The Universal Declaration of Human Rights (1948) states that everyone has the right to life, liberty and security of person (Article 3) and that no one should be subjected to torture or to cruel, inhuman or degrading treatment or punishment (Article 5). Domestic violence and CPV are infringements of these rights, as illustrated by the following quotes from two mothers in the Hunter et al. (2010, p. 268) study of antisocial behaviour and the risk of homelessness in the UK:

> He was like a bloke at 13, shouting at me, made me go to bits and you know, I mean, I couldn't deal with it.

> I was having a lot of trouble with my children and like my son was hitting me – and mental abuse.

Although CPV is a feature of daily life for some families and is an issue with which practitioners are all too familiar, it has yet to feature in policy and practice guidance in Ireland. In recent years, more parents are challenging practitioners with questions about how best to address CPV (Coogan and Lauster, 2014). Yet the *National Strategy on the Prevention of Domestic, Sexual and Gender-based Violence 2010–2014* (Cosc, 2010) does not explicitly identify CPV or recognize the harsh realities of such experiences. This makes CPV largely invisible, leading to minimal guidance or training for practitioners about how best to respond to this type of violence. Although individual practitioners and teams throughout Ireland are responding innovatively to CPV, there is no specific statutory service taking responsibility for coordinating or providing interventions or research nationally in response to CPV.

What is CPV?

CPV can be defined as a harmful act carried out by a child with the intention to cause physical, psychological, or financial pain or to exert power and control over a parent (Calvette et al., 2013). The term 'child to parent violence' includes a wide range of abusive behaviours, including acts of physical violence and controlling tactics, such as psychological and financial abuse, and clarifies that it is the parent (or a person acting in the role of a parent, such as a step-parent or foster carer, for example) who is the target of the abusive behaviour by the child under the age of 18. We also adopt a self-defining approach to a definition of CPV, that is, a child or adolescent's behaviour should be considered violent and abusive if family members feel controlled, intimidated or threatened by it, and if they feel they must adapt their own behaviour because of threats or use of abuse or violence (Paterson et al., 2002; Wilcox, 2012, p. 278).

The differences between domestic violence and CPV

Apart from the ethical and legal duties of parents to provide housing, education and welfare for their children, it is not legally possible to seek safety, barring or protection orders for children under the age of 18. Another important difference is that CPV involves a reversal of power that challenges the ways in which we usually understand abuse and power within families.

Violence within the family usually involves attacks on less powerful individuals (children and/or partners) by more powerful individuals. But CPV involves attacks on parents, usually regarded among social work and social care practitioners as more powerful individuals, by the usually less powerful child or adolescent (Agnew and Huguley, 1989). The reversal of conventional power dynamics within families where CPV takes place can make this problem even more difficult to detect and understand (Tew and Nixon, 2010).

Social work and social care practitioners are also presented with a challenge to make a further paradigm shift when thinking about CPV by looking beyond seeing an individual as being either a 'victim' or 'perpetrator'. Children and family services tend to be based on the assumption that children are victims and need support (Tew and Nixon, 2010). This makes it difficult for practitioners to acknowledge that a child can be *both* a victim and perpetrator of violence. Children who use violence towards their parents are likely to be regarded by practitioners more as victims than as perpetrators because the aggressive behaviour of children is often understood as being 'caused' by parents due to either some deficits in their parenting ability or as a consequence of the parents' failure to protect the child from experiencing or witnessing abuse in the family of origin (Gallagher, 2004;

Tew and Nixon, 2010). But *understanding* why an individual might use violence does not mean *accepting* the use of violence. Taking violence seriously requires practitioners to provide support to those who have lived through abuse in the past, while still challenging them and holding them to account for their abusive behaviour in the present.

How prevalent is CPV?

The policy silence on CPV is partly because research into CPV is still in its early stages of development (Holt A., 2013). The few incidents of CPV that are reported, for example to juvenile justice services, are likely to reflect only a small minority of cases, given the difficulties a parent may have in reporting their own child to the police (Ibabe et al., 2013). This makes it difficult for us to develop a clear picture about how many incidents of CPV take place, when and where it occurs, and the ways in which social work and social care practitioners respond to this problem.

The lack of information about CPV across Europe led to the development of the Responding to Child to Parent Violence (RCPV) project, co-financed by the Daphne fund of the EU. Involving a partnership between practitioners and academics in England, Ireland, Spain, Sweden and Bulgaria over two years (2013–15), the project developed a deeper understanding of CPV in these countries. The RCPV project also increased awareness about CPV, and implemented and researched two intervention programmes, including the Non Violent Resistance Programme, which will be described later in this chapter. (More information about the RCPV project is available at www.rcpv.eu.)

Although there are significant gaps in our knowledge about CPV, there seems to be clear evidence that CPV occurs across a variety of family circumstances and socioeconomic backgrounds and is not confined to single-parent, underprivileged and multi-stressed families. For example, in their review of the CPV literature, Walsh and Krienert (2009) found that 18% of two-parent and 29% of one-parent families in the US experience CPV. Within a European context, between 2004 and 2011, the number of requests from parents in Portugal for assistance with violence perpetrated by children has dramatically increased (Patuleia and Alberto, 2014). From Spain, Calvete et al. (2013) report that the number of complaints recorded by the Public Prosecutor's Office by parents against their children increased from 1,627 in 2006 to 5,377 in 2011; this represents a significant increase and has led to the enactment of legislation that provides for an order restraining an adolescent, similar to measures applied in cases of domestic violence in Spain. Reviews of the literature on CPV also suggest that, similar to patterns that occur in domestic violence, mothers are more likely than fathers to be targets of CPV (Holt A., 2013), although some fathers experience CPV (Pagani et al., 2009).

Cycle of violence theory: Does domestic violence lead to CPV?

The cycle of violence theory regards children as replicating the abusive behaviour of the parent who shares the same gender as the child; the theory presumes that boys will react to domestic violence by acting out, using violence and other externalized behaviours, while girls will react in a passive, submissive and internalized manner (Baker, 2012). The cycle of violence theory about domestic violence has been influential in courts in the US and the UK (Wilcox, 2012). The appeal and power of such a commonsense explanation for CPV may be due to generally accepted gender norms where men are regarded as being violent by nature, women as naturally caring and passive victims, and violence is passed down through generations from father to son (Baker, 2012). In the absence of alternative explanations for CPV, the cycle of violence theory could become the dominant way of understanding CPV (Baker, 2012). But Holt and Retford (2012) and Baker (2012) urge us to avoid accepting childhood experiences of domestic violence and abuse as a 'one-size-fits-all' explanation for the emergence of CPV.

One important problem with such assumptions is that they are based on the belief that the way a person behaves is determined by the behaviour of their adult role models, suggesting that all men are inclined to violence simply because they are male and that all men accept and enact hegemonic masculinity. But there are complex reasons why children react to domestic violence in the ways they do, which are not based on perceived gender norms (Baker, 2012). Although undoubtedly some do, not all young people who experience domestic abuse at home have violent and abusive relationships as they develop into adults (Rogers, 2009). If we adopt an oversimplistic view of childhood and make general predictions about the behaviour of all children who experience domestic abuse, we forget that each child is a distinct individual and that each child who lives with domestic abuse and violence at home experiences and responds to it differently.

Understanding CPV: an interactional perspective

How, then, can social work or social care practitioners begin to understand the emergence of CPV in families? Omer and Weinblatt (2008) suggest that one characteristic shared by families with children who use violence at home are escalation cycles that lead to violent and controlling behaviour. In some families, a cycle of escalation and coercion between parent and child may develop, in which increasing levels of aggression become part of a conflict pattern between the child and the parent leading to incidents of CPV (Omer, 2011). One of the advantages of this perspective is that parents can be asked in a non-blaming way about habits of interaction that can lead to violence. It also makes room for the practitioner and parents to work together in changing such patterns by identifying new skills to break cycles of escalation. Starting from this interactional perspective, social work and social care practitioners can assist parents to develop new skills by adopting evidence-influenced models such as the Non Violent Resistance (NVR) Programme (Omer, 2004; Weinblatt and Omer, 2008).

Adapting the NVR Programme for social work and social care practice

Based on the work of Haim Omer and his colleagues in Tel Aviv, Israel, the Non Violent Resistance (NVR) Programme has shown promising results and seems to offer parents a useful way to respond to CPV without resorting to harsh or punitive methods themselves (Weinblatt and Omer, 2008). An integrated systemic, short-term and strengths-based approach, the programme aims to assist parents in the development of a new awareness of their own role in (de)escalation cycles, new parenting skills and a support network in their responses to CPV. An additional advantage of the programme is that it does not require the direct involvement of the child. This offers hope to parents even when the child refuses to engage with practitioners or parents in resolving the problem of CPV.

A detailed description of the implementation of the NVR Programme lies outside the remit of this chapter, but we will briefly summarize the initial steps a practitioner could take when responding to CPV.

Following an initial assessment of the nature and extent of the abusive behaviour, the practitioner can share with parents some of what we have already described in this chapter about CPV, its prevalence and its occurrence in a wide range of family circumstances. The practitioner can then suggest that one way to understand CPV is to consider the escalating patterns or habits of aggression that can lead to the problem. Perhaps when the child was younger, for example, the parents and the child developed a habit of shouting and screaming at each other. Now that the child is older, taller and physically stronger, perhaps this pattern of interaction leads to threats or acts of physical harm, damage to property and persistent and hurtful name-calling.

Adopting a strengths-based approach that also looks for exceptions to problem behaviour (de Jong and Berg, 2002), the practitioner can ask the parents about times when the problem is not as severe and when the parents and child can interact with each other, without abuse or harm taking place. The practitioner can also begin to talk with parents about committing themselves to non-violent behaviour in their relationship with their child (including avoiding hurtful or humiliating language). Many parents find it useful to 'press the pause' button as a way of breaking escalation cycles. This entails parents resisting provocation and avoiding responding immediately to a crisis or outburst. Instead, parents decide to remain calm and inform the child that the unacceptable behaviour would be dealt with later when they and the child are calm. The principle of parental self-control and delayed responses to provocative behaviour is a cornerstone of the evidence-based Parents Plus Programme and the NVR Programme (see Sharry and Fitzpatrick, 2004; Omer, 2011).

Towards the end of the first conversation about CPV, parents can be invited to consider implementing the short-term NVR Programme, supported with NVR-focused meetings with the social work and/or social care practitioner. The parents could also be encouraged to commit to resisting violence (no physical or verbal aggression) in their responses to the child, regardless of the provocation.

As they begin to address the use of violence at home, it is best to advise parents that the problem of CPV may intensify before it is resolved, as their child may resist changes to patterns of interaction with which they had become familiar. The NVR Programme (Omer, 2004) is not the only response but it is one response to the problem of CPV. It responds to the immediate protection and safety needs and rights of family members, while empowering parents to develop the skills and support network necessary to bring an end to violence. (A more complete description of the NVR Programme is available in Omer, 2004; Weinblatt and Omer, 2008; Coogan and Lauster, 2014.)

Conclusion: promote the rights of parents and children to participation, protection and safety

Critical reflection on practice with children and families challenges us to make a significant paradigm shift when confronted by the complexities of family violence. We are challenged to prioritize the construction of fathers as 'risk' in the context of post-separation father–child contact and to reflect on how abusive men can be 'good enough' fathers to their children. We are also invited to consider the voice of the child in post-separation domestic abuse contact cases: How are their 'best interests' determined? Are children considered competent and integral to the discussion? If so, how is that determined and reflected in their participation in the process; if not, on what grounds is their incompetency determined and their welfare secured? We are also invited to critically reflect on the dynamics of power and the use of abuse within families so that we recognize CPV and avoid mistaken beliefs about the 'causes' of this form of family violence.

It is our view that in their commitment to working in partnership with families and enhancing the rights of children and families to protection, social work and social care practitioners are well placed to challenge conventional thinking. Although the cumulative impact of cutbacks in an age of austerity undermines the possibilities for effective practice, especially the building of strong partnerships with families (Featherstone et al., 2012), perhaps the establishment in Ireland in 2014 of Tusla, the new Child and Family Agency, could support innovative responses to violence within the home. Lessons learned from domestic violence prevention and intervention have much to offer in terms of effective public awareness raising, developing community supports, and providing training on the dynamics involved in violence in the home and on asking safely about experiences of violence. Developing respectful and safe practices can elicit hidden experiences of violence. Social work and social care practitioners can start with a broader understanding of family violence that includes the voice of the child in domestic violence and the voice of the parent in CPV as they continue to support the family relationship, protection and safety needs and rights of all family members, parents and children.

References

Agnew, R. and Huguley, S. (1989) 'Adolescent violence towards parents', *Journal of Marriage and the Family*, 51(3), 699–711.

Baker, H. (2012) 'Problematising the relationship between teenage boys and parent abuse: constructions of masculinity and violence', *Social Policy and Society*, 11(2), 265–76.

Bancroft, L. and Silverman, J.G. (2002) *The Batterer as Parent: Addressing the Impact of Domestic Violence on Family Dynamics*, New York, Sage.

Brown, T. and Alexander, R. (2007) *Child Abuse and Family Law: Understanding the Issues Facing Human Service and Legal Professionals*, Crows Nest, NSW, Allen & Unwin.

Buckley, H., Holt, S. and Whelan, S. (2007) 'Listen to me! Children's experiences of domestic violence', *Child Abuse Review*, 16(5), 296–310.

Butler, I., Scanlan, L., Douglas, G. and Murch, M. (2002) 'Children's involvement in the parents' divorce: implications for practice', *Children & Society*, 16(2), 89–102.

Calvete, E., Orue, I. and Gamez-Guadix, M. (2013) 'Child to parent violence: emotional and behavioural predictors', *Journal of Interpersonal Violence*, 28(4), 755–72.

Christensen, P. and Prout, A. (2005) 'Anthropological and sociological perspectives on the study of children', in Greene, S. and Hogan, D. (eds) *Researching Children's Experiences: Approaches and Method*, London, Sage.

Collier, R. (2001) 'A hard time to be a father?: Reassessing the relationship between law, policy, and family (practices)', *Journal of Law & Society*, 28(4), 520–45.

Collier, R. (2006) '"The outlaw fathers fight back": fathers' rights groups and the politics of family law reform – reflections on the UK experience', in Collier, R. and Sheldon, S. (eds) *Fathers' Rights Activism and Law Reform in Comparative Perspective*, Oxford, Hart.

Condry, R. and Miles, C. (2012) 'Adolescent to parent violence and youth justice in England and Wales', *Social Policy and Society*, 11(2), 241–50.

Coogan, D. (2011) 'Child to parent violence: challenging perspectives on family violence', *Child Care in Practice*, 17(4), 347–58.

Coogan, D. and Lauster, E. (2014) *The Non Violent Resistance Handbook for Practitioners: Responding to Child to Parent Violence in Practice*, Galway, RCPV Project/UNESCO Child and Family Research Centre.

Cosc (2010) *National Strategy on the Prevention of Domestic, Sexual and Gender-based Violence 2010–2014*, National Office for the Prevention of Domestic, Sexual and Gender-based Violence, Dublin, Government Publications Office.

De Jong, P. and Berg, I.K. (2002) *Interviewing for Solutions*. Pacific Grove, CA, Brooks/Cole.

Department of Health and Children (2000) *National Children's Strategy: Our Children, Their Lives*, Dublin, Stationery Office.

European Union Agency for Fundamental Rights (2014) *Violence against Women: An EU-wide Survey*, Luxembourg, FRA.

Featherstone, B., Broadhurst, K. and Holt, K. (2012) 'Thinking systemically – thinking politically: building strong partnerships with children and families in the context of rising inequality', *British Journal of Social Work*, 42(4), 618–33.

Gallagher, E. (2004) 'Youth who victimise their parents', *Australian & New Zealand Journal of Family Therapy*, 25(2), 94–105.

Gallagher, E. (2008) Children's Violence to Parents: A Critical Literature Review, unpublished MA thesis, Monash University.

Harrison, C. (2006) 'Damned if you do and damned if you don't: the contradictions between private and public law', in Humphreys, C. and Stanley, N. (eds) *Domestic Violence and Child Protection: Directions for Good Practice*, London, Jessica Kingsley.

Hester, M. (2011) 'The three-planet model: towards and understanding of contradictions in approaches to women and children's safety in contexts of domestic violence', *British Journal of Social Work*, 41(5), 837–53.

Hogan, D. (2005) 'Researching the child in developmental psychology', in Greene, S. and Hogan, D. (eds) *Researching Children's Experiences: Approaches and Methods*, London, Sage.

Holt, A. (2013) *Adolescent to Parent Abuse: Current Understandings in Research, Policy and Practice*, Bristol, Policy.

Holt, A. and Retford, S. (2012) 'Practitioner accounts of responding to parent abuse: a case study in ad hoc delivery, perverse outcomes and a policy silence', *Child and Family Social Work*, 18(3), 365–74.

Holt, S. (2003) 'Child protection social work and men's abuse of women: an Irish study', *Child and Family Social Work*, 18(1), 53–65.

Holt, S. (2011a) 'Domestic abuse and child contact: positioning children in the decision-making process', *Journal of Child Care in Practice*, 17(4), 327–46.

Holt, S. (2011b) 'A case of laying down the law: post-separation child contact and domestic abuse', *Irish Journal of Family Law*, 14(4), 87–97.

Holt, S. (2013) 'Post-separation fathering and domestic abuse: challenges and contradictions', *Child Abuse Review*, doi: 10.1002/car.2264.

Horgan, J., Muhlau, P., McCormack, P. and Roder, A. (2008) *Attitudes to Domestic Abuse in Ireland: Report of a Survey on Perceptions and Beliefs of Domestic Abuse among the General Population of Ireland*, Dublin, Department of Justice, Equality and Law Reform.

Humphreys, C. and Absler, D. (2011) 'History repeating: child protection responses to domestic violence', *Child and Family Social Work*, 16(4), 464–73.

Hunter, C., Nixon, J. and Parr, S. (2010) 'Mother abuse: A matter of youth justice, child welfare or domestic violence?', *Journal of Law and Society*, 37(2), 264–84.

Ibabe, I., Jaureguizar, J. and Bentler, P.M. (2013) 'Risk factors for child to parent violence', *Journal of Family Violence*, 28(5), 523–34.

Jaffe, P.G. and Crooks, C.V. (2004) 'Partner violence and child custody cases', *Violence Against Women*, 10(8), 917–34.

James, A., Jenks, C. and Prout, A. (1998) *Theorizing Childhood*, Cambridge, Polity.

Kaganas, F. and Day Sclater, S. (2004) 'Contact disputes: narrative constructions of "good" parents', *Feminist Legal Studies*, 12(1), 1–27.

Kelleher, P. and O'Connor, M. (1995) *Making the Links: Towards an Integrated Strategy for the Elimination of Violence against Women in Intimate Relationships with Men*, Dublin, Women's Aid.

Kilkelly, U. (2008) *Children's Rights in Ireland: Law, Policy and Practice*, Dublin, Tottel.

Kilkelly, U. and Savage, E. (2012) 'Legal and ethical dimensions of communicating with children and their families', in Lambert, V., Long, T. and Kelleher, D. (eds) *Communication Skills for Children's Nurses*, Buckingham, Open University Press.

Kjorholt, A.T. (2002) 'Small is powerful: discourses on "children and participation" in Norway', *Childhood*, 9(1), 63–82.

Kurki-Suonio, K. (2000) 'Joint custody as an interpretation of the best interests of the child in critical and comparative perspective', *International Journal of Law, Policy and the Family*, 14(3), 183–205.

Laing, K. (2006) 'Doing the right thing: cohabiting parents, separation and child contact', *International Journal of Law, Policy and the Family*, 20(2), 169–80.

Lamb, M.E. (ed.) (2004) *The Role of the Father in Child Development*, Chichester, Wiley.

Lamb, M.E. (2012) 'Critical analysis of research on parenting plans and children's well-being', in Kuehnle, K. and Drodz, L. (eds) *Parenting Plan Evaluations: Applied Research for the Family Court*, Oxford, Oxford University Press.

Lamb, M.E. (2013) *The Father's Role: Cross Cultural Perspectives*, Hillsdale, NJ, Lawrence Erlbaum.

McGee, H.R., Garavan, R., de Barra, G.M. et al. (2002) *The SAVI Report: Sexual Abuse and Violence in Ireland. A National Study of Irish Experiences, Beliefs and Attitudes Concerning Sexual Violence*, Dublin, Liffey Press.

Mantle, G., Moules, T., Johnson, K. et al. (2007) 'Whose wishes and feelings? Children's autonomy and parental influence in family court enquiries', *British Journal of Social Work*, 7(5), 785–805.

Morrow, V. (1999) '"We are people too": children's and young people's perspectives on children's rights and decision-making in England', *International Journal of Children's Rights*, 7, 149–70.

Murphy, C. and Holt, S. (2014) *Final Evaluation of the Barnardos/One Family Pilot Child Contact Centre*, Dublin, Barnardos/One Family.

Neale, B. (2002) 'Dialogues with children: children, divorce and citizenship', *Childhood*, 9(4), 455–75.

Neale, B. and Smart, C. (1999) 'In whose best interests? Theorising family life following parental separation or divorce', in Day Sclater, S. and Piper, C. (eds) *Undercurrents of Divorce*, Aldershot, Dartmouth.

Omer, H. (2004) *Nonviolent Resistance: A New Approach to Violent and Self Destructive Children*, Cambridge, Cambridge University Press.

Omer, H. (2011) *The New Authority: Family, School and Community*, Cambridge, Cambridge University Press.

Pagani, L., Tremblay, R., Nagin, D. et al. (2009) 'Risk factor models for adolescent verbal and physical aggression toward fathers', *Journal of Family Violence*, 24(3), 173–82.

Paterson, R., Luntz, H., Perlesz, A. and Cotton, S. (2002) 'Adolescent violence towards parents: maintaining family connections when the going gets tough', *Australian and New Zealand Journal of Family Therapy*, 23(2), 90–100.

Patuleia, N. and Alberto, I. (2014) Child to Parent Violence: Social Representations and Narratives of Parents, Children and Professionals, paper presented at RCPV Project International Conference on Child to Parent Violence – Innovations in Practice, Policy and Research, NUI Galway.

Piper, C. (1999) 'The wishes and feelings of the child', in Slater, S. and Piper, C. (eds) *Undercurrents of Divorce*, Aldershot, Dartmouth.

Piper, C. (2000) 'Assumptions about children's best interests', *Journal of Family Welfare and Family Law*, 22(3), 261–76.

Pryor, J. and Rodgers, B. (2001) *Children in Changing Families: Life after Parental Separation*, Oxford, Blackwell Press.

Rhoades, H. (2002) 'The "no contact mother": reconstructions of motherhood in the era of the "new father"', *International Journal of Law, Policy and the Family*, 16(1), 71–94.

Roche, J. (1999) 'Children and divorce: A private affair?', in Slater, S. and Piper, C. (eds) *Undercurrents of Divorce*, Aldershot, Dartmouth.

Rogers, M. (2009) *Helping Teenagers Cope with Domestic Abuse*, Dublin, Family Support Agency/Barnardos.

Sharry, J. and Fitzpatrick, C. (2004) *The Parent Plus Programme: The Children's Programme*. Dublin, Parents Plus/Child and Adolescent Mental Health Service, Mater Misericordiae Hospital.

Smart, C. (2002) 'From children's shoes to children's voices', *Family Court Review*, 40(3), 307–19.

Smart, C. and Neale, B. (1999) *Family Fragments?* Cambridge, Polity.

Smart, C., Neale, B. and Wade, A. (2001) *The Changing Experience of Childhood: Families and Divorce*, Cambridge, Polity.

Smith, A.B., Taylor, N.J. and Tapp, P. (2003) 'Rethinking children's involvement in decision-making after parental separation', *Childhood*, 10(2), 201–16.

Sturgess, W., Dunn, J. and Davies, L. (2001) 'Young children's perceptions of their relationships with family members: links with family setting, friendships, and adjustment', *International Journal of Behavioural Development*, 25(6), 521–9.

Tew, J. and Nixon, J. (2010) 'Parent abuse: opening up a discussion of a complex instance of family power relations', *Social Policy and Society*, 9(4), 579–89.

Thomas, N. and O'Kane, C. (2000) 'Discovering what children think: connections between research and practice', *British Journal of Social Work*, 30(6), 819–35.

Walsh, J.A. and Krienert, J.L. (2009) 'A decade of child-initiated family violence: comparative analysis of child-parent violence and parricide examining offender, victim and event characteristics in a national sample of reported incidents 1995-2005', *Journal of Interpersonal Violence*, 24(9), 1450–77.

Watson, D. and Parsons, S. (2005) *Domestic Abuse of Women and Men in Ireland: Report on the National Study of Domestic Abuse*, Dublin, National Crime Council.

Weinblatt, U. and Omer, H. (2008) 'Non-violent resistance: a treatment for parents of children with acute behaviour problems', *Journal of Marital and Family Therapy*, 34(1), 75–92.

Wilcox, P. (2012) 'Is parent abuse a form of domestic violence?', *Social Policy and Society*, 11(2), 277–88.

8

Intellectual Disability: Responding to the Life Course Goals and Challenges for Individuals and their Families

Bairbre Redmond and Anna Jennings

Introduction

This chapter looks at the development and professional approach of social work in the services of those with intellectual disability in Ireland, a system where social workers have been traditionally employed within specialist services. Taking a life course perspective, the chapter explores the key milestones in the lives of those with intellectual disability and their families, where person-centred social work can play an effective role. It looks at the impact of rapidly changing social and economic circumstances on this group and the social work response they can expect to receive. The changing relationship between voluntary bodies and the statutory services, moving social work out of specialized services into more generic primary care settings, is also discussed. There will be a focus on the divergent social work approaches to those with intellectual disability emerging from such a move, particularly within the contentious area of the capacity and rights of those with an intellectual disability to parent children. The chapter draws on international literature on past and current social work concerns and initiatives in the area of intellectual disability in Ireland, the UK, the US and Australia.

Developing social work in intellectual disability

Historically, the care of people with intellectual disability in Ireland was largely provided in large residential settings, typically former workhouses, with little emphasis on individual approaches or recognition of variation in needs. In the early 20th century, 'custodial' centres for children with intellectual disability, largely run by religious orders, were established, first in Dublin and later in Cork, Louth and Kildare. The mid-20th century saw the development of lay-run day facilities for people with intellectual disability, typically 'parents and friends' organizations, with a strong dependency on voluntary support (Redmond and Jennings, 2005). In its detailed recommendations, the Commission of Inquiry on Mental Handicap (1965) placed emphasis on skilled personnel playing an enhanced role in the lives of people with intellectual disability, with specialist teams of doctors, psychologists and social workers offering a diagnostic assessment and advisory service to families of people with intellectual disability. The social work role in such teams was to review 'social and environmental factors, to ascertain the behaviour of the patient and his attitude to people around him, to help parents and to advise them regarding the services available for their assistance' (Commission of Inquiry on Mental Handicap, 1965, p. 55). As a result of this report, a growing number of social workers were employed by specialist services across the country, playing an active role within these newly constituted multidisciplinary teams. The employment of social workers in the area of intellectual disability in such specialist services has remained largely unchanged until the early years of the 21st century.

A shift in the deployment of social work personnel occurred relatively recently with the arrival of the concept of primary care, as a result of the policy directive, *Primary Care: A New Direction* (Department of Health and Children, 2001). In line with international practice, this policy has sought to provide a comprehensive and accessible range of services that would be made available to a wide range of service users, on a self-referral basis. These developments in primary care have sought to map out a programme 'that includes a range of services deployed to keep people well, from promotion of health and screening for disease to assessment, diagnosis, treatment and rehabilitation as well as personal social services' (Department of Health and Children, 2001, p. 15). The essential interdisciplinary nature of the proposed structure involves social workers as part of the team. It is envisaged that families and people with intellectual disability can readily access such teams in their locality. However, primary care teams have not materialized as planned in all parts of Ireland, largely due to the decline in economic activity from 2008 onwards. Up to the time of writing, the traditional, voluntary service providers in the area of intellectual disability have continued to be the main employers of social workers in this domain, but the future development of social work for those with intellectual disability remains uncertain. Indeed, it is likely that national decisions as to the overall nature and location of services to those with intellectual disability and their families may remain undecided until Ireland returns to greater financial stability.

Unfortunately, there are no up-to-date figures available with regard to the specific number of social workers currently employed in the area of intellectual disability. The most recent figures date back to 2005, when there were 171 social workers employed in this field, representing 7.64 % of the total social work workforce (NSWQB, 2006). Social Workers in Disability (SWID), the special interest group of the Irish Association of Social Workers (IASW), comprises social workers who are employed in intellectual, physical, sensory and neurological disability in addition to social workers who are part of primary care teams and who deliver a service to people with disability. To an extent, this reflects the HSE's (2013) planned model of service delivery, *Progressing Disability Services for Children and Young People*, which will strive to offer a more unified approach across the country, irrespective of the nature of their disability.

Social work and the right to self-determination

The social work role is underpinned by the profession's stated ethics and values (Banks, 2008). Those working with individuals with intellectual disability and their families may find particular resonance in the values espoused by the IASW (2007), which highlight the unique and intrinsic worth of every individual, their entitlement to their own beliefs, to freedom of expression and action, and that truly valued, fully human life is generally realized by individuals living and acting interdependently in communities.

Earlier attitudes to those with intellectual disability tended to view them as persons with irrevocable impairment who would be more appropriately cared for at a remove from society in general (Robins, 1986). The normalization movement (Wolfensberger, 1972; Ramon, 1991) of the mid-20th century began to question the passive and non-inclusive nature of this approach and it championed the need for those with disability and their families to become a genuine part of the decision-making process about their own lives. This included their rights, where possible, to a job, personal friendships and relationships, and a say in how and where they might live in wider society. These new perspectives became enshrined in the introduction of approaches such as person-centred planning, an activity with a strong role for social workers acting as advocates for individuals and families, assisting them to articulate their needs and how best they might be met (Richie et al., 2003; Gaylard, 2012).

The fundamental rights of individuals with intellectual disability and their families to play a key role in making decisions about their own lives has been supported by those driving a rights agenda and a move away from medical dominance in the area of disability in general. Michael Oliver (1983), disability activist and author, initially expected that social work would be the most likely profession to embrace his rights-based vision for those with disability, working alongside those with disability to support their rights as equal citizens. More recently, Oliver et al. (2012) have been critical of the growing focus of social workers in the UK on the managerialization of welfare. Oliver et al. suggest that social work managers who primarily become brokers of scarce services will lack a full appreciation of the complexities of the needs of individuals with disability (particularly physical disability) who need those services.

The question of the appropriate social work role in the development of direct payments, allowing those with disability and their families a stronger and more self-directed role in 'purchasing' services, rather than participating in state-funded services, is well discussed in the literature. Often termed 'personalization', the value of this approach in the field of intellectual disability has been seen to be contested from the social work perspective, with some seeing it as an extension of service users' rights to self-determination (Stainton, 2002), while others argue that it leads to the closure of valuable services and increases the use of low-paid personal assistants (Scourfield, 2007). It should be borne in mind that, unlike service models in the UK and the US, traditionally Irish social workers have not had a role in the provision of direct payments to service users. With many Irish social workers still employed by voluntary intellectual disability agencies, their capacity to respond to the needs of individuals and their families remains constrained by the amount of state funding given to their agencies, rather than to service users themselves. There is no indication that the proposals to move Irish social work services into a primary care model in Ireland will change this position.

Social work approaches in intellectual disability

The generic model of training and education in social work has been the dominant one in Ireland since its inception, with some specific training provided in the area of disability along with exposing students to aspects of other 'specialist' areas. Research with Irish social work students, pre-qualification, reveals that the area of disability ranks third (14% of the cohort) in the areas of work into which they might consider working, after work in child protection and other child-related services (Redmond et al., 2012). The same research indicates that social work students and practitioners see it as an area of practice where social workers develop high levels of professional skills, and it is perceived as offering higher job satisfaction and significantly lower work stress than social work in child and family services (Redmond et al., 2012). Social workers who are employed in this area typically use a broad array of theories and approaches in their work, ranging from psychodynamic approaches to more contemporary solution-focused perspectives. As will be discussed further, a strengths perspective is well suited to person-centred practice (Saleeby, 1996). Traditionally, theories of grief and loss were viewed as offering specific insights and understanding of being disabled and having a child with a disability (Kübler-Ross, 1970; Worden, 1991), but this has largely been replaced by a social constructionist perspective (McClimens and Richardson, 2010), which is viewed as offering a more comprehensive and holistic view of this area.

Clearly, all legislation and practice guidelines that are enacted in Ireland have applicability to work with people with intellectual disability and their families, including those relating to child protection, such as *Children First* (Department of Children and Youth Affairs, 2011). However, many service providers felt that there was a need for clear guidelines in relation to the management of abuse in the intellectual disability services that would work in tandem with *Children First*. This recognizes the increased vulnerability of this particular population and the need for a specific response to this matter (Flynn and Brown, 2010). Social workers have played a pivotal role in the development of such procedures in many of the major service providers and have been instrumental in initiating comprehensive training programmes in relation to the management of abuse in their respective settings.

Social work in the intellectual disability service: appreciating a life course perspective

A key aspect of intellectual disability that differentiates it from many other personal situations to which social work responds is that it is an irrevocable, lifelong condition, allowing for a distinctive long-term service user–social worker partnership to develop. Heller et al. (2011) consider that using a life course approach is particularly important, as it takes into account the role of families, friends and the community/environment in supporting and expanding opportunities for people with disabilities to live fulfilled and useful lives (Olsen and Clarke, 2003; Sheldon and Macdonald, 2008).

National data, provided by the National Intellectual Disability Database (NIDD, n.d.), supports the fact that social work represents an important and well-used service for those with intellectual disability in Ireland. Figures from the NIDD show that, taking the adult and child cohorts together, social work is the most used therapeutic service by those with intellectual disability and their families in Ireland, with 40% of all those registered on the database (27,622 persons) availing themselves of a social work service (Kelly and O'Donohoe, 2014). This data continues a trend that has existed in previous years in earlier versions of the NIDD. The NIDD figures clearly illustrate the adaptability and capacity of social work to provide support to individuals with intellectual disability and their families across the life span, as envisaged by Heller et al. (2011). This begins with the role of the social worker in the multidisciplinary early intervention team.

Early intervention

The birth and diagnosis of a child with a disability represents a significant challenge to the coping capacities of any family. Research indicates that families do not feel that their concerns and opinions are well understood by some of the professionals they encounter (Redmond, 2006). In particular, they have articulated their need for better and more detailed information on the nature and prognosis of their child's condition and the services that are, and will be, available to them (Beckman and Bristol, 1991).

Tomasello et al. (2010) explored the importance for social workers of adopting a 'family-centred' approach in their practice, particularly at the point of early intervention – an approach that works with the existing strengths of the family as a whole, acknowledging their natural capabilities and coping powers, harnessing them to address the new challenges now facing the family (Dunst et al., 1988; Allen et al., 1997). This approach to social work with families who have a very young child with an intellectual disability allows the social worker to engage with the family on an equal footing, rather than one which emphasizes the imbalance between the 'expert' and the 'grateful recipient'. Saleeby (1996, p. 303) describes this strengths perspective dialogue with the family as one with 'a mutual sharing of knowledge, tools, concerns, aspiration and respect'. Families with babies and young children with an intellectual disability not only have their own distinct needs, but also distinct ways of coping with change and adversity. Irish research with families who had young children with severe and life-threatening disabilities revealed the importance of designing and delivering services in consultation with the families in a way that is sensitive to individual family functioning (Redmond and Richardson, 2004). Oliver and Sapey (2006) note that this requires social workers to become skilled communicators in assisting families to identify and express their views, rather than speaking for them. Social workers also need to be adept at brokering services, often becoming the 'human face' of the broader welfare system for families (Oliver et al., 2012).

Supporting transitions in times of austerity

Social work is the most commonly used service by those with intellectual disability in Ireland as they approach and enter adulthood. Periods of transition for young and older adults represent particularly stressful times for these individuals and their families as they move out of known services and supports into areas that may be far more vulnerable to funding cuts. Funding for disability services in post-boom Ireland has seen cumulative cuts of 15% since 2009. The large voluntary providers who provide specialist services for those with intellectual disability and their families have also been hit by a 17% reduction in fundraised income. Furthermore, service users and their families have suffered the generic cuts and transfer of costs from the state to all Irish people, economic approaches that have typified the six austerity budgets in Ireland since 2008 (Burke, 2013). In terms of the social work role, this represents a dual challenge in supporting people to plan for and cope with transitioning out of well-known services but also to do so in a period of considerable uncertainty in terms of national funding for those services. In general, social workers have advocated for scarce services for individual service users and their families. More general representations to government for improved funding for the sector have been made by parent-led groups, albeit with the support of individual social workers and their representative bodies. There is less evidence that social workers in intellectually disability see their role as making a significant contribution to national policy change, and SWID appears to be more focused on improving the standards and efficacy of direct social work practice than engaging in the policy process in the interests of their clients.

With the right to education enshrined under Article 42 of the Irish Constitution, more recent legislation has given greater rights for those with disability to be educated in inclusive educational settings (Education for Persons with Disabilities Act 2004; Education for Persons with Special Educational Needs Act 2004). However, the end of schooling often marks the start of very different life trajectories for those with intellectual disability in terms of training, employment and finding a place to live. For young people with more serious and profound levels of disability, parents and other family members face additional challenges in terms of the changing physical and medical care required as their child grows into adulthood, which is known to contribute to high levels of stress and worry for these families (Sloper, 1999). Longer term access to a reliable social work service can address some of these stress levels for families and also link them with developing essential resources, in awareness of their unique needs (Hepworth et al., 2012). The amount of time taken up by the care of a child with disability, particularly one with complex physical needs, can be considerable (Barnett and Boyce, 1995) and by supporting parents to continue to undertake paid work (leveraging reliable day services and respite breaks), social workers can also make a significant impact not just on the financial but also the psychological wellbeing of parents (Redmond and Richardson, 2004).

Having a job gives any individual a source of income, a purpose and a shape to the working day, a set of personal and professional goals, and the opportunity to meet and socialize with those outside their family (Jahoda, 1981). For those with intellectual disability, the gains of employment may be similar but the challenges of finding and keeping a job have added complexities, which may be addressed by a social work service (Weston, 2002). Until relatively recently, the employment of those with intellectual disability, where it existed, was primarily contained within specialist services and at a distance from wider society in the shape of 'sheltered workshops'. Writers have consistently highlighted the much higher benefits of supported employment, where those with intellectual disability enter open employment in the general workforce with varying degrees of support from external job coaches or through support within their place of work (see, for example, Walsh et al., 1998). Certainly, for those with higher levels of ability, entering employment with some support can be a transforming experience, not only improving the quality of life of the disabled person, but also creating gains for their co-workers and their employers. However, in recessionary times, fewer jobs exist overall and those with disability find themselves in stiffer competition for more limited employment opportunities. Ironically, the biggest barrier towards increasing open employment for those with disability has nothing to do with their ability or changing demands in the workplace. Rather, it relates to the potential loss of state benefits for those who begin to earn money (Simons, 1998). An internationally recognized problem, social welfare systems frequently threaten to thwart rather than encourage participation by those with intellectual disability in the labour force (Walsh and Linehan 2007), when individuals fear that, by taking a job, they may lose the entitlement to state payments related to their disability (Weston, 2002), a risk that may be too high to take.

Finding a home: temporarily and permanently

One of the major concerns for parents who have an intellectually disabled child is where they will live when their parents can no longer care for them (McGrath and Grant, 1993; Redmond, 1996; Walker and Walker, 1998; Gaylard, 2012). As those with intellectual disability live longer and healthier lives, their needs grow in terms of temporary respite breaks and longer term accommodation away from the family home. Many families will have interactions with a social worker in the planning and organization of respite care and more permanent accommodation needs. An Irish study on best practice in respite care in the area of intellectual disability brought together the views of social workers, carers and nurses as to the best way to organize and deliver effective respite services (Merriman and Canavan, 2007). Merriman and Canavan (2007) concluded that decisions about the timing, nature and setting of respite need to be person and family centred, designed in ways that facilitate individuals to build relationships in their community and be age appropriate as the individual grows older.

However good respite care is, it is not enough to replace a long-term alternative to a family home arrangement, where families are no longer in a position to continue the care of their disabled family member. There are also adults with intellectual disability who would like to move out of the family home, just as their siblings may have done at their age and where they can be supported by their families to move into a new adult home, rather than as a result of the death or illness of their parents. The NIDD Report (Kelly and O'Donohoe, 2014) shows that more than one in four of those who were over 35 who had a moderate, severe or profound intellectual disability lived at home with families in 2012.

The specific needs of those with intellectual disability who are growing older has been explored in the Intellectual Disability Supplement to The Irish Longitudinal Study on Ageing (IDS-TILDA; McCarron et al., 2011), which has collected data specific to the intellectual disability population (aged between 41 and 90) but is also measured against issues related to ageing in the general population. The study notes that about 20% of those in this older population use a social work service. While medical issues account for a lot of difficulties encountered by this ageing population, there are also significant psychosocial difficulties, with 50% of the cohort reporting that they feel lonely; and there is a higher prevalence of mental health and emotional problems in the cohort than in the general population of a similar age. Those in the longitudinal study were not living in their family home and the majority saw professional and support staff as their principal confidants (McCarron et al., 2011). Both NIDD and TILDA point to a changing age profile observed in the data over recent decades, which reflects an increase in the life span of people with intellectual disability, and, along with the general demographic trend, this has major implications for planning for services designed to meet the needs of older people with intellectual disabilities. In particular, there is an increasing demand for residential services, support services for ageing carers, and services designed specifically to meet the needs of older people with intellectual disability (Kelly and O'Donohoe, 2014). The impact of specific age-related difficulties that accompany some types of intellectual disability may also be considerable. For example, medical research shows that, beginning in their forties and continuing through their seventies, up to 75% of people with Down syndrome develop dementia (Zigman and Lott, 2007). This age-related complication has considerable impact on the capacity for many individuals to maintain a hard-won independent lifestyle that they may have achieved in early adulthood, creating demands for different types of services for the older population.

Different social work perspectives on those with intellectual disability

Aspects of the life course discussed so far have highlighted how social workers, primarily those based in specialist services, can make a positive impact in the lives of those with intellectual disability. However, social workers from other backgrounds and services who become involved with adults with intellectual disability and their families may approach their work from different perspectives. This can be seen particularly in regard to rights-based issues of sexuality and/or the parenting abilities of those with disability, which pose specific issues for those social workers who have specific duties in the area of child protection.

The idea that an individual with intellectual disability would develop adult sexual needs was largely denied up until the latter years of the 20th century, and traditionally many residential services were single sex. Many people with intellectual disability may be perceived as being perpetual children and, therefore, asexual. However, the reality is that most young adults with intellectual disability develop a full adult sexuality and they may need more help, not less, in making sense of these physical changes and the strong emotions that accompany them (Evans et al., 2009; Tattersall et al., 2009). Inclusive research with individuals with learning disabilities themselves (Bane et al., 2012) revealed, inter alia, that these adults wanted to be able to make their own decisions about personal relationships and that, at times, they wanted the support of families, parents, friends and staff to have and keep their friendships and relationships. For many social workers, the importance of supporting an individual with intellectual disability to achieve a full adult identity that incorporates their sexuality resonates with the basic social work appreciation of the right to self-determination, human dignity and worth. However, for others, including at times family members, social workers may not be seen as working in the best interests of protecting the individual adult with disability when they become involved in the provision of sex education or adopt what could be perceived as a permissive attitude towards their sexuality. If young adults are to become more independent and self-determined, care needs to be taken by social workers in acknowledging and negotiating a delicate balance between the diverse opinions and concerns of families and individuals with intellectual disability: 'carers have their own legitimate concerns and user empowerment should never be seen as a reason for ignoring families' (Simons, 2002, p. 173).

Parenting with an intellectual disability

IDS-TILDA found that 99% of those in the study (aged between 41 and 90) were not married, with less than 2% (n = 16) reporting having given birth to a child (McCarron et al., 2011). While the birth of a child to a mother or a couple with intellectual disability is rare, it can create situations in which the roles and indeed the attitudes of social workers can differ significantly, particularly between those social workers who work directly with those with disability and those charged with a specific child protection remit.

The capacity of those with intellectual disability to successfully raise their own children is generally considered poor (McConnell and Llewellyn, 2002), not least by their own family (Starke, 2011). There is also a wider belief among many professionals that all parents with an intellectual disability will be incapable of adequate parenting (McConnell and Llewellyn, 2002; Booth and Booth, 2003), with custody decisions frequently made prior to birth on the basis of the mother's disability (Mayes and Llewellyn, 2012).

The overriding concern in most cases is the impact on a child who is being parented by a mother with intellectual disability (May and Simpson, 2003), which is often the reason for the involvement of a social worker outside the disability services, operating under childcare legislation, in the best interest of that child. However, a UK study revealed that, contrary to popular belief, the level of risk to the child may not necessarily correspond to the level of cognitive impairment of the mother. Instead, high risk factors appear more related to previous childhood trauma and abuse of the mother and issues relating to the male partners of women with intellectual disability, many of whom were found to have antisocial and/or criminal behaviours (McGaw et al., 2010). Other research suggests that mothers with intellectually disability can be unsupported and at significant risk of isolation and poverty, factors that negatively impact on good parenting outcomes for any mother or couple (Kaiser and Delaney, 1996; Russell et al., 2008).

In the first qualitative study of the experiences of Irish women with intellectual disability who have children, Sheerin et al. (2013) found that, in the main, the women did not receive specialist support during pregnancy or after the birth of their child, but were dealt with within the broader social services, which were not geared towards their specific needs. This research suggests that women with intellectual disability had developed particularly negative attitudes towards the social workers based in child and family services who worked with them. While correctly acknowledging the requirement of these social workers to enact *Children First* guidelines in the best interests of the child, the research revealed that the women felt distanced from decisions made about their babies by their social workers, perceiving that they received little or no support to demonstrate adequate parenting skills. In contrast to the fundamental person-centred approach adopted by many social workers who work specifically in the area of intellectual disability, international research backs up the premise that child protection social work with intellectually disabled mothers tends to be deficit focused, lacking an appreciation of the potential strengths and competences these individuals may have (Llewellyn et al., 1998; Kroese et al., 2002; Mildon et al., 2003). Research also indicates that parents with an intellectual disability seek out and develop better parenting skills in services that have been designed with an awareness of these parents' specific needs, and which are offered to them on a long-term basis (Llewellyn et al., 1997; McConnell et al., 2006).

Future of social work in intellectual disability

The findings above highlight what may be a pertinent issue for social workers in the future development of Irish services for those with intellectual disability. Traditionally, social workers in the area have been based in specialized multidisciplinary services, their work underpinned by a rights-based, person-centred approach. The moving of some social work services from the specialist arena into more generic primary care, as is happening in Ireland, is viewed by some writers as a negative process, for the individual and their families and social workers themselves. Bigby and Atkinson (2010) note that the role of the specialist social worker in intellectual disability services started to disappear in Australia around the 1990s, with negative consequences for service users. Bigby and Atkinson also consider that, in the UK, the role of the social worker in intellectual disability services changed from being involved in person-centred work with individuals and their families to one that focused on more mundane care management and the commissioning of services. While the existing specialist services in Ireland may be associated with a lack of choice for service users, it is also important to note the continuing UK debate on what Ferguson (2007) calls the 'neo-liberal' economic roots of personalization, which he considers a threat to the viability of traditional services on which many vulnerable people rely.

Conclusion

If the positioning of social work services for those with intellectual disability in Ireland moves into a more generic social work setting, it will be essential that the necessary social work skills that appreciate the evolving life course goals and challenges for individuals and families are retained. When social work is developed and delivered in a specialist service, the focus remains on those with disability and their families. However, when services become shared between those with intellectual disability (who have lifelong and irrevocable limitations) and those whose temporary medical or social difficulties can be remedied, it is arguable that those with disability will be disadvantaged (Read, 2000). Furthermore, the longer term life course, prevention-focused approach to social work in intellectual disability may also run contrary to the shorter term crisis response nature of social work in community/primary care. However, there is an argument that social workers with expertise in the area of intellectual disability should also use their knowledge of those with whom they work in terms of seeking wider policy change and becoming a stronger public voice for those affected by intellectual disability.

Whatever way social work in intellectual disability develops, it is essential that it is informed by a robust understanding of the complex needs of those with disability and those who care for them, in social work training, ongoing professional social work practice and influencing policy. If the social work expertise developed over years in the specialist services in Ireland is lost, this will represent not only a diminution of professional social work capacity in the area but, more worryingly, the return of an older, less well-informed appreciation of the unique needs and rights of those with intellectual disability themselves.

References

Allen, R.I., Petr, C.G. and Brown, B.F. (1997) 'Family-centered professional behavior: frequency and importance to parents', *Journal of Emotional and Behavioral Disorders*, 5(4), 196–204.

Bane, G., Dooher M., Flaherty J. et al. (2012) 'Relationships of people with learning disabilities in Ireland', *British Journal of Learning Disabilities*, 40(2), 109–122.

Banks, S. (2008) 'Critical commentary: social work ethics', *British Journal of Social Work*, 38(6), 1238–49.

Barnett, W.S. and Boyce, G.C. (1995) 'Effects of children with Down syndrome on parent's activities', *American Journal on Mental Retardation*, 100(2), 115–27.

Beckman, P.J. and Bristol, M.M. (1991) 'Issues in developing the IFSP: a framework for establishing family outcomes', *Topics in Early Childhood Special Education*, 11(3), 19–31.

Bigby, C. and Atkinson, D. (2010) 'Written out of history: invisible women in intellectual disability social work', *Australian Social Work*, 63(1), 4–17.

Booth, T. and Booth, W. (2003) 'Self-advocacy and supported learning for mothers with learning difficulties', *Journal of Learning Disabilities*, 7(2), 165–93.

Burke, S. (2013) 'Further disability cuts are inexcusable', *The Medical Independent*, 12 September, www.medicalindependent.ie/34193/further_disability_cuts_are_inexcusable, accessed 31 December 2013.

Department of Children and Youth Affairs (2011) *Children First: National Guidance for the Protection and Welfare of Children*, Dublin, Stationery Office.

Department of Health and Children (2001) *Primary Care: A New Direction Quality and Fairness – A Health System for You Health Strategy*, Dublin, Stationery Office.

Dunst, C.J., Trivette, C.M., Davis, M. and Cornwell, J. (1988) 'Enabling and empowering families of children with health impairments', *Children's Health Care*, 17, 71–81.

Evans, D.S., McGuire, B.E., Healy, E. and Carley, S.N. (2009) 'Sexuality and personal relationships for people with an intellectual disability. Part II: staff and family carer perspectives', *Journal of Intellectual Disability Research*, 53(11), 913–21.

Ferguson, I. (2007) 'Increasing user choice or privatizing risk? The antinomies of personalization', *British Journal of Social Work*, 37(3), 387–403.

Flynn, M. and Brown, H. (2010) 'Safeguarding adults with learning disabilities against abuse', in Grant, G., Ramcharan, P., Flynn, M. and Richardson, M. (eds) *Learning Disability: A Life Cycle Approach*, Maidenhead, Open University Press.

Gaylard, D. (2012) 'Working with older people with mental health needs', in Hall, B. and Scragg, T. (eds) *Social Work with Older People: Approaches to Person Centred Practice*, Maidenhead, Open University Press/McGraw-Hill.

Health Research Board (n.d.) National Intellectual Disability Database, www.hrb.ie/ health-information-in-house-research/disability/nidd/, accessed 25 January 2014.

Heller, T., Schindler, A., Palmer, S.B. et al. (2011) 'Self-determination across the life span: issues and gaps', *Exceptionality: A Special Education Journal*, 19(1), 31–45.

Hepworth, D., Rooney, R., Dewberry Rooney, G. and Strom-Gottfried, K. (2012) *Direct Social Work Practice: Theory and Skills*, Belmont, CA, Brooks/Cole Empowerment Series.

HSE (Health Service Executive) (2013) *Progressing Disability Services for Children and Young People*, Dublin, HSE.

IASW (Irish Association of Social Workers) (2007) *Irish Association of Social Workers' Code of Ethics*, Dublin, IASW.

Jahoda, M. (1981) 'Work employment and unemployment: values theories and approaches in social research', *American Psychologies*, 36, 184–91.

Kaiser, A.P. and Delaney, E.M. (1996) 'The effects of poverty on parenting young children', *Peabody Journal of Education*, 71(4), 66–85.

Kelly, C. and O'Donohoe, A. (2014) *Annual Report of the National Intellectual Disability Database Committee 2013*, Dublin, Health Research Board.

Kroese, B.S., Hussein, H., Clifford, C. and Ahmed, N. (2002) 'Social support networks and psychological wellbeing of mothers with intellectual disabilities', *Journal of Applied Research in Intellectual Disabilities*, 15(4), 324–40.

Kübler-Ross, E. (1970) *On Death and Dying*, London, Tavistock.

Llewellyn, G., Bye, R. and McConnell, D. (1997) 'Parents with intellectual disability and mainstream family agencies', *International Journal of Practical Approaches to Disability*, 21(3), 9–13.

Llewellyn, G., McConnell, D. and Bye, R. (1998) 'Perception of service needs by parents with intellectual disability, their significant others and their service workers', *Research in Developmental Disabilities*, 19(3), 245–60.

McCarron, M., Swinburne, J., Burke, E. et al. (2011) *Growing Older with an Intellectual Disability in Ireland 2011: First Results from the Intellectual Disability Supplement of the Irish Longitudinal Study on Ageing*, Dublin, School of Nursing and Midwifery, Trinity College Dublin.

McClimens, A. and Richardson, M. (2010) 'Social constructions and social models: Disability explained?, in Grant, G., Ramcharan P., Flynn, M. and Richardson, M. (eds) *Learning Disability: A Life Cycle Approach*, Maidenhead, Open University.

McConnell, D. and Llewellyn, G. (2002) 'Stereotypes, parents with intellectual disability and child protection', *Journal of Social Welfare and Family Law*, 24(3), 297–317.

McConnell, D., Llewellyn, G., Matthews, J. et al. (2006) 'Healthy Start: A national strategy for children of parents with learning difficulties', *Developing Practice: The Child, Youth and Family Work Journal*, 16, 34–42.

McGaw, S., Scully, T. and Pritchard, C. (2010) 'Predicting the unpredictable? Identifying high-risk versus low-risk parents with intellectual disabilities', *Child Abuse & Neglect*, 34(9), 699–710.

McGrath, M. and Grant, G. (1993) 'The life-cycle and support networks of families with a person with a learning difficulty', *Disability, Handicap and Society*, 8(1), 25–41.

May, D. and Simpson, M.K. (2003) 'The parent trap: marriage, parenthood and adult-hood for people with intellectual disabilities', *Critical Social Policy*, 23(1), 25–43.

Mayes, R. and Llewellyn, G. (2012) 'Mothering difficulties: narratives of mothers with intellectual disability whose children have been compulsorily removed', *Journal of Intellectual Development Disability*, 37(2), 121–30.

Merriman, B. and Canavan, J. (2007) *Towards Best Practice in the Provision of Respite Services for People with Intellectual Disability and Autism,* Galway, Child and Family Research Centre, NUI Galway.

Mildon, R., Matthews, J. and Gavidia-Payne, S. (2003) *Understanding and Supporting Parents with Learning Difficulties*, Melbourne, Victorian Parenting Centre.

NSWQB (National Social Work Qualifications Board) (2006) *Report No. 3: Social Work Posts in Ireland*, Dublin, NSWQB.

Oliver, M. (1983) *Social Work with Disabled People*, Basingstoke, Macmillan.

Oliver, M. and Sapey, B. (2006) *Social Work with Disabled People*, 2nd edn, Basingstoke, Palgrave Macmillan.

Oliver, M., Sapey, B. and Thomas, P. (2012) *Social Work with Disabled People*, 4th edn, Basingstoke, Palgrave Macmillan.

Olsen, R. and Clarke, H. (2003) *Parenting and Disability: Disabled Parents' Experiences of Raising Children*, Bristol, Policy.

Ramon, S. (1991) 'Policy issues', in Ramon, S. (ed.) *Beyond Community Care: Normalisation and Integration Work*, Basingstoke, Macmillan.

Read, J. (2000) *Disability, the Family and Society: Listening to Mothers*, Maidenhead, Open University Press.

Redmond, B. (1996) *Listening to Parents: The Aspirations, Expectations and Anxieties of Parents about their Teenager with Learning Disability*, Dublin, UCD Family Studies Centre.

Redmond, B. (2006) *Reflection in Action: Developing Reflective Practice in Health and Social Services*, Aldershot, Ashgate.

Redmond, B. and Jennings, A. (2006) 'Social work and intellectual disability', in Kearney, N. and Skehill, C. (eds) *Social Work in Ireland,* Dublin, Institute of Public Administration.

Redmond, B. and Richardson, V. (2003) 'Just getting on with it: exploring the service needs of mothers who care for young children with severe/profound and life-threatening intellectual disability', *Journal of Applied Research in Intellectual Disabilities*, 16(3), 205–21.

Redmond, B., Guerin, S., Nolan, B. et al. (2012) *The Retention of Social Workers in the Health Services: An Evidence-based Assessment*, Dublin, University College Dublin.

Ritchie, P., Sanderson, H., Kilbane. J. and Routledge, M. (2003) *People, Plans and Practicalities: Achieving Change through Person Centred Planning*, Edinburgh, SHS.

Robins, J. (1986) *Fools and Mad: A History of the Insane in Ireland*, Dublin, Institute of Public Administration.

Russell, M., Harris, B. and Gockel, A. (2008) 'Parenting in poverty: perspectives of high-risk parents', *Journal of Children and Poverty*, 14(1), 83–98.

Saleeby, D. (1996) *The Strengths Perspective in Social Work Practice*, Boston, Allyn & Bacon.

Scourfield, P. (2007) 'Social care and the modern citizen: client, consumer, service user, manager and entrepreneur', *British Journal of Social Work*, 37(1), 107–22.

Sheerin, F., Keenan, P.M. and Lawler, D. (2013) 'Mothers with intellectual disabilities: interactions with children and family services in Ireland', *British Journal of Learning Disabilities*, 41(3), 189–96.

Sheldon, B. and Macdonald, G. (2008) *A Textbook of Social Work*, London, Taylor & Francis.

Simons, K. (1998) *Home, Work and Inclusion: The Social Policy Implications of Supported Living and Employment for People with Learning Disabilities*, York, Joseph Rowntree Foundation.

Simons, K. (2002) 'Empowerment and advocacy', in Malin, N. (ed.) *Services for People with Learning Disabilities*, London, Routledge.

Sloper, P. (1999) 'Models of service support for parents of disabled children: What do we know?', *Child Care Health Development*, 25(2), 85–99.

Stainton, S. (2002) 'Taking rights structurally: disability, rights and social worker responses to direct payments', *British Journal of Social Work*, 32(6), 751–63.

Starke, M. (2011) 'Supporting families with parents with intellectual disability: views and experiences of professionals in the field', *Journal of Policy and Practice in Intellectual Disabilities*, 8(3), 163–71.

Tattersall, J., Boycott-Garnett, R., Garbutt, R. et al. (2009) *Talking about Sex and Relationships: The Views of Young People with Learning Disabilities. The Final Report of the Sexuality Project by CHANGE 2007–2010*, Leeds, Centre for Disability Studies, Leeds University.

Tomasello, N.M., Manning, A.R. and Dulmus, C.N. (2010) 'Family-centred early intervention for infants and toddlers with disabilities', *Journal of Family Social Work*, 13(2), 167–72.

Walker, C. and Walker, A. (1998) *Uncertain Futures: People with Learning Difficulties and their Ageing Family Carers*, Brighton, Pavilion/Joseph Rowntree Foundation.

Walsh, P.N. and Linehan, C. (2007) *Living and Working in the Community*, in Carr, A., O'Reilly, G., Walsh, P.N. and McEvoy, J. (eds) *The Handbook of Intellectual Disability and Clinical Psychology Practice*, London, Brunner-Routledge.

Walsh, P.N., Lynch, C. and deLacey, E. (1998) 'Supported employment for Irish adults with intellectual disability: The OPEN ROAD experience', *International Journal of Rehabilitation Research*, 17(1), 15–24.

Weston, J. (2002) 'Supported employment and people with complex needs: a review of research literature and ongoing research', *Journal of Social Work*, 2(1), 83–104.

Wolfensberger, W. (1972) *Normalization: The Principle of Normalization in Human Services*, Toronto, National Institute on Mental Retardation.

Worden, W. (1991) *Grief Counselling and Grief Therapy: A Handbook for the Mental Health Practitioner*, New York, Springer.

Zigman, W.B. and Lott, I.T. (2007) 'Alzheimer's disease in Down syndrome: neurobiology and risk', *Mental Retardation and Developmental Disabilities Research Reviews*, 13(3), 237–46.

9

Responding to Psychosocial Aspects of Illness and Health: Challenges and Opportunities for Social Work

Erna O'Connor and Elaine Wilson

Introduction

Social workers in healthcare provide a broad range of services. However, a key focus of health-related social work is the interface of health and social issues such as interpersonal conflict, poverty, social isolation and social exclusion. Social workers work with individuals, families and communities to achieve positive change in their circumstances in order to address social determinants of health, as outlined by the World Health Organization (WHO, 2004), reduce health inequalities and improve their health status. Social work is also concerned with the emotional impact, meanings and implications of diagnoses and symptoms for individual service users and those affected by their illness.

This chapter traces the evolution of social work in healthcare in Ireland from the initial appointment of an almoner at the Adelaide Hospital in 1919 to the current day where social workers are employed across a wide range of public, non-profit and private healthcare providers. Contemporary healthcare provision is underpinned by the professional and often competing discourses of the health sciences, social sciences, management and corporate governance. It is also fundamentally shaped politically by the policies of successive governments, which, in Ireland, have delivered a very particular mix of private and public care. Although public hospital care is available to all, approximately 50% of the Irish population pay for private healthcare insurance, which affords faster access to hospital-based diagnostic and treatment services, resulting in an inequitable 'two-tier' system (Wren, 2003; Tussing and Wren, 2006; Burke, 2009; Considine and Dukelow, 2009; Burke and Pentony, 2011). The current government health strategy, *Future Health: A Strategic Framework for Reform of the Health Service 2012–2015* (Department of Health, 2012), proposes a single tier health service based on a system of universal insurance, signalling a major change in the delivery of health services in Ireland. To date, this reform has not been implemented.

In addition to complexity in healthcare delivery, there is a risk to the sustainability of adequate levels of health, social and continuing care in Ireland, as elsewhere, in light of the current budgetary climate. This is occurring at a time of increasing demands on healthcare due to an ageing population, an increase in the number of people with chronic illnesses such as diabetes and heart disease (Department of Health, 2012), and a growing dependence on the public healthcare system, as larger numbers of people experience unemployment, insecure and zero-hours employment contracts and reduced incomes. Increased demands have led to the introduction of measures to manage increasingly scarce resources.

For a number of decades, healthcare services and other public sector organizations have been subject to a managerialist ethos imported from the private sector. Epstein and Aldredge (2000) define managed healthcare as an integrated delivery system that manages healthcare services by approving and targeting services and following patients through the system, rather than simply financing or delivering services without supervision. As a consequence, health service users and social workers working on their behalf have to engage with increasingly complex administrative systems, negotiate multilevel assessment processes, and fulfil audit-led requirements in order to access and maintain basic resources and services. Social workers and other healthcare professionals have had to develop ways of working within an increasingly rationalized healthcare system to address the human consequences of cost containment policies.

Despite these difficulties, social work continues to develop and plays a significant role within the Irish healthcare system. This chapter examines the changes and continuities in the role of social work across the healthcare spectrum, with particular emphasis on hospital and primary care settings. Three key challenges for social work in the context of contemporary healthcare are identified, namely a context of competing professional paradigms, contracting resources, and the changing demographical profile of healthcare users. The possible implications of each of these challenges are considered in relation to social work practice. The particular contribution social work can continue to make within the Irish healthcare system is explored.

The evolution of health-related social work in Ireland

Social workers have worked in hospital settings since the turn of the 20th century (Horne and O'Connor, 2005; NASW, 2005; Judd and Sheffield, 2010). In Ireland, health-related social work developed from the creation of an almoner service at the children's dispensary of the Adelaide Hospital, Dublin in 1919. The Irish Hospitals Commission, established under the Public Hospitals Act 1933, promoted the almoner's role in relation to the provision of social services and the assessment of the financial contribution people could make towards the cost of their care. Almoner departments were established in 1936 at the Rotunda Hospital and Sir Patrick Dun's Hospital and subsequently almoners were appointed to a number of other Dublin hospitals. In the aftermath of the 1953 Health Act, which established categories of eligibility for free and reduced cost medical care, almoners moved to distance themselves from the role of financial assessor and focus instead on social casework (Horne and O'Connor, 2005). The 1970s were a time of significant social change coupled with increased economic prosperity in Ireland, thus changing the focus of social work from addressing material need and disadvantage to responding to personal and family issues (Horne and O'Connor, 2005).

Since the 1970s, the amalgamation of smaller Dublin hospitals resulted in the formation of large social work departments in the newly established acute teaching hospitals. Expansion allowed for specialization in areas such as rehabilitation, paediatrics, maternity services, oncology, infectious diseases, emergency medicine and palliative care. Although social work services were extended to hospitals in most regions in the latter decades of the 20th century, the distribution of posts has remained unevenly spread throughout the country, with a concentration of posts in the greater Dublin area (Horne and O'Connor, 2005). Nonetheless, social work had by then become an established hospital-based discipline in Ireland, commonly referred to as 'medical social work'. Research undertaken by the National Head Medical Social Workers' Forum (2008) found that in 2007 (just before the global financial crisis impacted on Ireland), there were 350 social workers employed across 52 acute hospital settings. These figures do not differentiate between public and private hospitals. However, more recent data from the Health Service Executive (HSE, 2013) identified a total of 49 public and 21 private hospitals (one of which closed in 2014) in Ireland. Currently, only 4 of these private hospitals employ social workers, and although the numbers of social workers in these hospitals are small, they are gradually increasing. While there are well-established links between socioeconomic status and health outcomes, there are many psychosocial issues associated with diagnosis and living with illness that arise regardless of economic status. Given that almost 50% of the population have private health insurance, the development of social work within private hospitals allows for the potential extension of social work services across the population. As a growing sector for social work, there is an opportunity to shape the development of the service to meet the evolving psychosocial needs of healthcare service users in the 21st century. However, more research is needed in order to maximize this potential.

A significant development since the turn of the century has been the introduction of a primary healthcare service to include social work as one of a number of allied health professions constituting primary care teams. Research carried out by Ní Raghallaigh et al. (2014) found that approximately 80 social workers were employed in primary care settings.

Hospital-based social work

A study undertaken by hospital-based social work managers suggests that significant social work time (60%) is spent in direct work with patients, focusing on assessment, risk interventions and counselling. Skills in liaison, complex network management and case management were also identified as key to the social work role (National Head Medical Social Workers' Forum, 2008). In another Irish study, 9,145 referrals to the social work department of a large acute Dublin hospital in a single year were audited; of which 43% were for review in relation to home supports and a further 16% were for counselling (Foreman et al., 2010). International studies have also highlighted the investment of social work time in discharge planning, suggesting it constitutes approximately 60% of social work time in hospitals (McAlynn and McLaughlin, 2008; Judd and Sheffield, 2010). McLead et al.'s (2008) study demonstrates the psychological and physical health benefits of service user-centred discharge planning in facilitating the re-engagement of older people in a variety of networks, including friendship, recreational and family groups, healthcare treatment programmes, and locality-based contacts and organizations.

In the Australian context, psychosocial assessment, education and information, discharge planning and referral were identified as the main activities of hospital social workers (Cleak, 2002). In a more recent paper, Cleak and Turczynski (2014, p. 209) identify an expanding role for social work in the context of increasing chronicity of health conditions and a contracting healthcare system:

> Social workers' role in the discharge of patients within limited time frames now appears to be balanced with their additional role of negotiating and managing more complex medical conditions and their psychosocial implications ... [which]

requires expansion of the social work role in the area of medico-legal issues, community supports, conflict management strategies and strengthening of the advocacy role in assisting those whose care needs exceed available resources.

In collaboration with service users, carers and others, social workers have established community-based support groups for people impacted by cancer and other illnesses, those who have sustained brain injuries, and family carers (Foreman et al., 2010).

Social workers have researched and developed therapeutic responses to a range of psychosocial issues that can arise in the healthcare context, including domestic violence (Allen, 2011, 2012) and the diagnosis of cancer (Wilson 2011, 2012; Wilson and Crown, 2011). Allen (2011) used a narrative approach to explore how women who experience domestic violence use strategies of resistance, and suggested that social workers have a role in strengthening women's identities, thereby contributing to their ability to employ such strategies. Wilson (2012) also employed this approach when examining how young women make the transition from treatment for early-stage breast cancer into survivorship, and devised a narrative framework for social workers to use to assist cancer patients as they make that transition.

Both Allen's and Wilson's work explored the importance of helping service users make meaning of their situations, so they may then be able to consider the dominant narratives or culturally dominant expectations, which can be oppressive in nature. The application of a narrative approach and the use of meaning-making are two of the many therapeutic approaches used by social workers in healthcare settings, where clients may face significant physical and/or emotional difficulties and challenges to their identity. In addition to therapeutic and discharge planning roles, social workers, particularly those working in maternity and children's hospitals, have responsibilities as part of the interdisciplinary team for assessment and initial interventions with children and families where children are deemed to be at risk. Social workers have an important liaison role between hospital and community-based child and family services to ensure continuity in the management of child protection issues.

From 1989 onwards, social workers were appointed to hospital-based HIV counsellor posts to support those diagnosed with HIV. Unlike other jurisdictions, their role included the provision of pre- and post-HIV test counselling (Foreman et al., 1992) as well as ongoing psychosocial support (Foreman and Mulcahy, 1997). The Irish Association of Social Workers' special interest group in HIV was established in 1989 (IASW, 1992). In an early initiative, members worked with HIV-positive parents to produce a book for children infected and affected by HIV (Fitzgerald, 1992). Social workers have researched the psychosocial aspects of HIV, including the experiences of ethnic minorities accessing HIV services (Foreman and Hawthorne, 2007). Working at a policy level, social workers have sat on the National AIDS Strategy Committee (NASC) since it was established in 1991. NASC reported twice, in 1992 and 2000, and recognized that the most effective way to deliver services was a coordinated civil society and statutory intersectoral approach.

Hospital-based social workers and those working in specialist palliative care settings have a long tradition of working with people who are facing life-limiting illness or are dying, and in supporting those close to them. Irish social workers have been central to the development and delivery of hospital-based services to respond to adult and child bereavement (Harney and Price, 1992; O'Driscoll, 2002, 2004; Farrelly, 2005; Walsh et al., 2008). Following intense media publicity on the issue of organ retention in Britain and subsequently in Ireland, the Madden Inquiry (Madden, 2006) provided an imperative to formalize hospital bereavement services with its recommendation for the appointment of hospital-based liaison officers to offer practical help and support to bereaved families. Social workers have been appointed to many of these hospital liaison positions (Walsh et al., 2008) to work with families and support and coordinate interdisciplinary bereavement care.

In the first Irish study of a hospital-based bereavement programme, Walsh et al. (2007) examined the Beaumont model of bereavement care (O'Driscoll, 2002, 2004). The Beaumont model is an innovative, tiered approach to service delivery, developed by social workers (and integrating pre-existing services), whereby a range of bereavement services are provided for individuals, families, groups and the wider community, with more intensive interventions available to those experiencing the greatest need. Participants in the study identified the three most helpful aspects of the bereavement care service as providing information and advice, speaking to someone about their feelings, and the sharing of experiences with other bereaved people (Walsh et al., 2007, 2008). The impact of broader principles that underpin the service, such as a strengths-based, non-pathologizing approach, is illustrative of the contribution social workers can make in the design and delivery of services in medical settings.

Social work in primary care

The framework for introducing a more comprehensive primary care service in Ireland was first introduced in the *Quality and Fairness Health Strategy* (Department of Health, 2001a), and developed in detail in the policy document, *Primary Care: A New Direction* (Department of Health, 2001b). The aim was to deliver significantly strengthened primary care services, with expanded access to GP care, free at the point of use, as a way to enhance service provision within the community and ensure effective and efficient delivery of services close to people's homes, at the lowest level of complexity and the lowest cost. According to *Primary Care: A New Direction* (Department of Health, 2001b), a more comprehensive primary care service would strengthen the capacity to improve population health approaches to service provision. As the *Mental Health in Primary Care in Ireland* document (Mental Health Reform, 2013, p. 3) comments: 'there is an international trend advocating the availability of mental health services through primary care'. The importance of primary care in the provision of palliative care has also been recognized with the establishment of the Primary Palliative Care programme in 2010. By the end of 2012, 426 primary care teams were operating, providing services for almost 4 million of the population (Department of Health, 2013); however, there are only approximately 80 social workers employed in primary care settings. This figure represents only 22% of the original target (Report of the Comptroller and Auditor General, 2010, cited in Jacob, 2013, p. 180). A lack of primary data from government sources makes it difficult to assess the causes for such low figures.

Van Hook (2004), Bikson et al. (2009) and Keefe et al. (2009) have examined the role of primary care social work in North American contexts. These studies illustrate high correlations between psychosocial issues such as financial, family, housing and work difficulties and the use of primary healthcare, and argue for social work as integral to primary care provision. Jacob (2013) makes a similar case in the Irish context. The most recent Irish research on social work in primary care (Ní Raghallaigh et al., 2014) examined the existing and potential role of social workers within these teams in Ireland. In common with other healthcare settings, the research found that the remit of social workers in primary care is broad and diverse in order to respond to the needs of the community. The focus of social work in primary care teams is to tackle health inequalities, promote self-determination, and work with people around issues that may be causing them distress. The primary care social work respondents in this study reported opportunities to engage in individual work, groupwork and community work, with flexibility to decide which level of intervention is appropriate. The study did not report on advocacy at a systemic level.

When reflecting on the role of social work in healthcare in general, and specifically in primary care, Lymbery's (2005, p. 52) conceptualization of social work as comprising the following three functions (often interwoven in practice) is helpful:

1. Working with individuals in problem-solving and therapeutic ways.

2. Working as a go-between ensuring that resources are mobilized to meet need, with particular stress on the tasks of liaison and coordination.

3. Working with groups and communities to develop new responses to problems.

Ní Raghallaigh et al.'s research (2014) showed that there was ample opportunity to fulfil the first two functions – working with individuals in a therapeutic and problem-solving way, and liaising with, and referral to, community-based resources. A majority of respondents were also engaged at Lymbery's third level, which involves groupwork and community work. This diversity within the role was found to be one of the most satisfying aspects of working in primary care. Other positive aspects of the work included:

- the opportunity to participate in an interdisciplinary team
- the ability to engage in early intervention or preventive practice
- operating an open-door policy
- working with communities.

The respondents also commented that they have the opportunity to work with non-mandated clients and felt that they were able to take the time to talk to clients, often in their own home, giving them space to fully tell their story. For the respondents, the capacity to give clients the time they need resonated strongly with the core values of social work (Ní Raghallaigh et al., 2014).

Current challenges for social work across the healthcare spectrum

Competing professional paradigms

The social worker–service user relationship is the vehicle for the delivery of social work services and is, in itself, therapeutic, particularly in the containment of anxiety (Howe, 1998; Sudbery, 2002; Trevithick, 2003; Ruch, 2005) and in responding to anger and other difficult emotions. Without the use of the therapeutic potential of the relationship, social work is reduced to a more functional task of coordination of services (Harlow, 2003). Wider practice relationships are also integral to effective social work. Engaging with carers and others close to the service user promotes inclusive healthcare practice. Collaborative practice with volunteers, service user organizations and campaigners facilitates access to wider resources and enables advocacy on health inequalities, discrimination and other social justice issues. Positive interprofessional and interagency relationships allow for a more comprehensive response and better solutions, especially in cases of complex needs.

Tensions can arise, however, between professionals who work from fundamentally different knowledge and value bases. Wilson et al. (2008) argue that the humanist tradition of social work can be at variance with the technical-rational scientific knowledge base of many of the other disciplines in healthcare. In addition, different professionals often occupy different power positions within the healthcare system. Beddoe (2011) discusses the attempt by social work in healthcare to define itself within the context of a health system with many other powerful players, describing it as a guest under the benign control of the nursing and medical professions. Bywaters (1986) identified a history that is seldom acknowledged, that of interprofessional conflict and what he refers to as the widespread emasculation of social work in hospitals. Wilson et al. (2008) suggest such tensions can be addressed at three levels:

- *structural-organizational:* by providing leadership that develops and empowers practitioners as well as management

- *professional-cultural:* by respecting different skills and having opportunities for collaboration, such as regular meetings

- *interpersonal:* by extending the principles and practices of relationship-based social work to relationships in the work environment, together with a high level of commitment to the wider aims and purposes of the team.

In practice, collaboration develops when disciplines come together to 'find solutions for clients that they have been struggling with alone' (Bronstein, 2003, p. 304).

Contracting economic resources

The pervasiveness of cutbacks to incomes and services is such that the amelioration of the worst effects of austerity has once again become a central focus of social work in healthcare. In a context of a shrinking public sector, cost containment policies, such as a review of medical card eligibility to achieve a €23 million cut (HSE, 2014), and the rationalization of the social welfare system require significant investment of social work time in advocacy in order to achieve safer or less risky discharges from hospital and access to basic resources in the community. Links can be made between austerity policies and extreme poverty such as homelessness; for example, the rent allowance has been reduced to a level that makes access to private rented accommodation difficult. Furthermore, new applicants must submit a housing application to the local authority, which can take a number of months to process, and only if they are deemed in need of housing can they then apply for a rent allowance. It is also difficult to access places in homeless accommodation, especially if, for health reasons, the person needs to be indoors during the day. These requirements make the discharge process precarious and inherently risky, with each case requiring intensive advocacy in order to access basic resources.

In addition, discharge planning with people needing support services in their homes has become more complex, with 'home care packages' now comprising services from multiple providers across public, non-profit and private sectors. There is also a significant reduction in the provision of public, long-term care beds for people who require extended care, with public care being replaced by a system of care in private nursing homes funded through the Nursing Homes Support Scheme, known as Fair Deal (HSE, 2009). Assisting service users and their carers in navigating application processes for these resources is an integral part of discharge planning. Again, advocacy is necessary on a case-by-case basis to maintain existing resources, negotiate new resources, and possibly slow down a discharge in order to put basic supports in place. Social work teams collate data on the incidence and prevalence of these issues and their impact on service users. This information is escalated to hospital and wider health services management with a view to addressing anomalies identified in practice, at systems and policy levels.

Spending considerable social work time on case-by-case advocacy for basic resources militates against the maintenance and development of therapeutic and preventive social work services, such as bereavement counselling, the facilitation of carer support groups and health promotion programmes. It also militates against more systemic advocacy to challenge the disproportionate burden that those most dependent on state services have been handed. Increased demands for social work services, at a time when teams are short staffed due to non-replacement of some personnel and salary reductions, longer working hours and job insecurity for people on contract-based employment are impacting on the remaining social work staff. The non-availability of adequate levels of support for people who are vulnerable in the community, or who are being discharged from hospital, creates anxiety for staff in relation to gaps in care and the associated risks for service users. These conditions can give rise to low morale. In an effort to manage increased demand with contracting resources and in response to external imperatives of professional registration and quality initiatives, the National Head Medical Social Worker's Forum (2014) has developed guidelines for hospital-based social work teams. The guidelines cover key areas for the implementation of caseload management systems for screening referrals and prioritization of cases, for example involving child or vulnerable adult protection, critical illness and bereavement.

However, writing in the Irish primary care context, Jacob (2013) suggests that an overfocus on case management and clinical practice may not meet the demands of a primary healthcare model that emphasizes prevention, health promotion, collaboration and community development. She argues that in addition to responding to individual psychosocial needs, social workers as 'systems specialists' should work towards the integration of service delivery and utilize community development approaches to population health.

Changing profile of healthcare service users

There are five societal trends, all applicable to the Irish context, which have the potential to pose significant challenges to social work in healthcare settings in the future (Berkman, 2011). The trends identified are:

- an increase in the number of people living with chronic illnesses
- the move from hospital-based to community-based services
- increased patient diversity
- family caring
- palliative and end of life care.

Social workers in Ireland are encountering increasing numbers of people with complex care needs associated with chronic illness, a trend that is evident internationally. This can result in longer hospital stays and the risk of failed discharge and readmission. In line with policy developments in health (Department of Health, 2001a) and in mental health (Department of Health, 2006), a move from hospital-based to community-based services is a longstanding aspiration in Irish healthcare. Improved coordination of community-based services is essential due to the model of mixed care provision, delivered through home care packages, which fund services according to assessed needs, drawing on public (HSE), voluntary and private home care providers, yet the low numbers of social workers employed in primary care jeopardize this ambition.

The concept of cultural diversity is well recognized within the health services (HSE, 2008). The profile of minority ethnic groups in Ireland comprises refugees, asylum seekers, family reunification, migrants and migrant workers, undocumented migrant workers, Travellers and foreign students (MacGabhann and Nobre, 2010). Demographic trends estimate further increases from 10.4% to 18% of non-Irish nationals living in Ireland by 2030, suggesting that ethnocultural diversity will be a long-term feature of Irish society. A report on cultural diversity in the Irish healthcare sector

(NCCRI and IHSMI, 2002) identified two specific challenges. The first is the need to ensure that healthcare services are accessible, user friendly and equitable to all, including people from minority ethnic backgrounds, seeking to avail themselves of services. The second challenge relates to fully integrating staff from minority ethnic backgrounds into the Irish healthcare workplace in a way that respects cultural diversity. Social workers, trained in non-discriminatory and anti-oppressive practice, are well placed to promote recognition of, and respect for, cultural diversity and could take a greater lead in driving this ambition in healthcare.

'Family carers' refer to relatives, primarily spouses and adult children, who provide assistance for their relative, but are unpaid for such care. In common with international trends, the proportion of older people in Ireland is expected to rise. From the current proportion of 11%, a 44% increase in the number of people over 65 is expected in the next 10 years, a doubling over the next 30 years, with the greatest increase occurring in the over-80 age group (Kenny and Barrett, 2011). The bulk of social care for older persons is provided by family carers, partly due to the relatively low (direct) cost of family care in comparison with state-financed long-term care. Another reason, according to Kamiya et al. (2012), is the belief that receipt of care in the community and family context helps to maintain central, often lifelong, social relationships and thereby contributes to the wellbeing of older persons. However, caring can be stressful, especially if the carer is an older person or is managing other demands. Social workers have taken a role in ensuring the wellbeing of carers as well as that of people receiving care. They were proactive in the establishment of the Carers Association in Ireland and work with individual carers in many contexts, including those caring for older people, parents of children who are ill, and family members caring for people living with disabilities or mental health issues.

When a person enters the terminal or palliative stages of a disease, there is significant emotional impact on the person who is dying, their family and those close to them. This may be further exacerbated where there is difficulty in accessing services that meet their needs in terms of where and how they want to die. Evidence suggests that older people may be disadvantaged in terms of their access to appropriate and acceptable services (Department of Health and Children, 2001; Irish Hospice Foundation, 2002, 2006; HIQA, 2007). The evidence indicates that there is an unevenness of provision, with geographical inequity in the distribution of services and lack of access to specialist palliative care for part of the population.

Social work has had a strong presence in the provision of palliative care services in Ireland, and a central role to play now and in the future in ensuring that the psychosocial needs of the person who is dying and their family are met. Applying Lymbery's (2005) framework in this context, there is a need to ensure that all three functions are carried out:

- meeting the individual and their family's psychosocial needs

- liaising with other service providers to ensure services are provided

- advocating for equality in the availability of, and access to, palliative care services.

Conclusion: implications for the future of social work across the health spectrum

Social work is a well-established discipline within interdisciplinary practice, in a range of hospital settings in Ireland. It is now also one of a number of allied health professions within the developing network of primary care teams. Hospital-based social work has traditionally had committed and organized leadership in Ireland, which managed and promoted social work services within hospital systems and ensured that practice adhered to the person-centred and social justice-oriented values of the profession. However, social work management and leadership structures have yet to be standardized in the private hospital sector and across the primary care network.

Much has been accomplished in gaining recognition of the psychosocial aspects of illness and health and developing good practice in the continuity of care between hospitals and the community, but social work in healthcare is also facing significant challenges. It operates within a complex healthcare system underpinned by competing professional paradigms and political ideologies. Economic recession and the ensuing austerity have led to contracting health and social care services. These challenges intersect with the changing profiles of health service users, presenting new areas of need and increased levels of complexity.

There is much potential for collaborative practice across the interface of hospitals and primary care in meeting the needs of individual service users and developing new initiatives and services to reduce stress and promote health and wellbeing. There is a need for social workers to research and evaluate issues in relation to the intersection of social issues and health, with particular emphasis on the impact of austerity. The findings of such research could contribute evidence to support advocacy and inform wider healthcare practices and policies. Social workers across the healthcare spectrum need to engage in systemic and public advocacy work, such as that undertaken on issues of HIV, direct provision and human rights (Foreman, 2008, 2014), to bring a focus to the social determinants of health and reduce health inequalities.

Throughout its history in Ireland, social work in healthcare has maintained a dual focus on the social and emotional aspects of illness and health. It continues to contribute psychosocial perspectives and services to an interdisciplinary healthcare system, endeavouring to meet the needs of increasingly diverse populations.

References

Allen, M. (2011) *Narrative Therapy for Women Experiencing Domestic Violence: Supporting Women's Transitions from Abuse to Safety*, London, Jessica Kingsley.

Allen, M. (2012) 'Domestic violence within the Irish travelling community: the challenge for social work', *British Journal of Social Work*, 42(5), 870–86.

Beddoe, L. (2011) 'Health social work: professional identity and knowledge', *Qualitative Social Work*, 12(1), 24–40.

Berkman, B. (2011) 'Gerontological social work research in health and mental health', *Generations Review*, www.britishgerontology.org/DB/gr-editions-2/generations-review, accessed 4 June 2014.

Bikson, K., McGuire, J., Blue-Howells, J. and Seldin-Sommer, L. (2009) 'Psychosocial problems in primary care: patient and provider perceptions', *Social Work in Health Care*, 48(8), 736–49.

Bronstein, L.R. (2003) 'A model for interdisciplinary collaboration', *Social Work*, 48(3), 297–306.

Burke, S. (2009) *Irish Apartheid: Healthcare Inequality in Ireland*, Dublin, New Island.

Burke, S. and Pentony, S. (2011) *Eliminating Health Inequalities: A Matter of Life and Death*, Dublin, TASC.

Bywaters, P. (1986) 'Social work and the medical profession: arguments against unconditional collaboration', *British Journal of Social Work*, 16(6), 661–7.

Cleak, H.M. (2002) 'A model of social work classification in health care', *Australian Social Work*, 55(1), 38–49.

Cleak, H.M. and Turczynski, M. (2014) 'Hospital social work in Australia: Emerging trends or more of the same?', *Social Work in Health Care*, 53(3), 199–213.

Considine, M. and Dukelow, F. (2009) *Irish Social Policy: A Critical Introduction*, Dublin, Gill & Macmillan.

Department of Health (2001a) *Quality and Fairness: A Health System for You, Health Strategy*, Dublin, Stationery Office.

Department of Health (2001b) *Primary Care: A New Direction*, Dublin, Stationery Office.

Department of Health (2006) *A Vision for Change: Report of the Expert Group on Mental Health Policy*, Dublin, Department of Health.

Department of Health (2012) *Future Health: A Strategic Framework for Reform of the Health Service 2012–2015*, Dublin, Department of Health.

Department of Health (2013) *Annual Report 2012*, Dublin, Department of Health.

Department of Health and Children (2001) *Report of the National Advisory Committee on Palliative Care*, Dublin, Department of Health and Children.

Epstein, M.W. and Aldredge, P. (2000) *Good but Not Perfect*, Needham Heights, MA, Allyn & Bacon.

Farrelly, M. (2005) 'The bereavement journey: the Irish experience', in Ling, J. and O'Siorain, L. (eds) *Facing Death: Palliative Care in Ireland*, Maidenhead, Open University Press.

Fitzgerald, G. (1992) *Ciara's Story*, Dublin, IASW/Health Promotion Unit.

Foreman, M. (2008) 'HIV and "direct provision": learning from the experiences of asylum seekers in Ireland', *Translocations: Migration and Social Change*, 4(1), 67–85.

Foreman, M. (2014) *Social Work, HIV and Direct Provision: Human Rights in Ireland*, http://humanrights.ie/immigration/directprovision14-social-work-hiv-direct-provision/.

Foreman, M. and Hawthorne, H. (2007) 'Learning from the experiences of ethnic minorities accessing HIV services in Ireland', *British Journal of Social Work*, 37(7), 1153–72.

Foreman M. and Mulcahy, F.M. (1997) 'Social work, HIV and Irish women', *Irish Journal of Social Work Research*, 1, 68–78.

Foreman, M., Flynn, S., Keane, A. and Lawler, C. (2010) Evaluating Medical Social Work in an Irish Hospital: The Service Users' Perspective, paper presented at 6th International Conference on Social Work in Health and Mental Health, UCD, Dublin.

Foreman M., McLoughlin, C., Flynn, D. et al. (1992) 'Study of patients presenting for pre-HIV test counselling in St. James's Hospital Dublin and implications for social work practice', *Irish Social Worker*, 11(1), 8–12.

Harlow, E. (2003) 'New managerialism, social service departments and social work practice today', *Practice: Social Work in Action*, 15(2), 29–44.

Harney, N. and Price, B. (1992) 'Groupwork with bereaved children', *Groupwork*, 5(3), 19–27.

HIQA (Health Information and Quality Authority) (2007) *Draft National Standards for Residential Care Settings for Older People: A Consultation Document*, Cork, HIQA.

Horne, M. and O'Connor, E. (2005) 'An overview of the development of health-related social work in Ireland', in Kearney, N. and Skehill, C. (eds) *Social Work in Ireland: Historical Perspectives*, Dublin, IPA.

Howe, D. (1998) 'Relationship-based thinking and practice in social work', *Journal of Social Work Practice*, 12(1), 45–56.

HSE (Health Service Executive) (2008) *National Intercultural Health Strategy 2007–2012*, www.hse.ie/eng/services/Publications/SocialInclusion/National_Intercultural_Health_Strategy_2007_-_2012.pdf, accessed 12 June 2014.

HSE (2009) *The Nursing Home Support Scheme: A Fair Deal*, Dublin, HSE, www.hse.ie/go/fairdeal, accessed 17 June 2014.

HSE (2013) *Accessing Healthcare in Ireland under CBD*, http://hse.ie/eng/services/list/1/schemes/cbd/acchealthcareireland/Accessing_Healthcare_in_Ireland_under_CBD.html, accessed 8 January 2015.

HSE (2014) *National Service Plan 2014*, www.hse.ie/eng/services/Publications/corporate/serviceplan2014, accessed 17 June 2014.

IASW (Irish Association of Social Workers) (1992) *A Resource Pack on HIV*, Dublin, IASW Committee on HIV.

Irish Hospice Foundation (2002) *End-of-life Care in General Hospitals: Developing a Quality Approach for the Irish Setting*, Dublin, Irish Hospice Foundation.

Irish Hospice Foundation (2006) *A Baseline Study on the Provision of Hospice/Specialist Palliative Care Services in Ireland*, Dublin, Irish Hospice Foundation.

Jacob, D. (2013) 'Primary care, social work and integrated care: A new way of delivering services?', in O'Connor, T. (ed.) *Integrated Care for Ireland in an International Context: Challenges for Policy, Institutions and Specific Service User Needs*, Cork, Oak Tree.

Judd, R.G. and Sheffield, S. (2010) 'Hospital social work: contemporary roles and professional activities', *Social Work in Health Care*, 49(9), 856–71.

Kamiya, Y., Murphy, C., Savva, G. and Timonen, V. (2012) *Profile of Community-Dwelling Older People with Disability and their Caregivers in Ireland*, Dublin, Irish Longitudinal Study on Ageing.

Keefe, B., Geron, S.M. and Enguidanos, S. (2009) 'Integrating social workers into primary care: physician and nurse perception of roles, benefits and challenges', *Social Work in Health Care*, 48(6), 579–96.

Kenny, R.A. and Barrett, A. (2011) 'Introduction', in Barrett, A., Savva, G., Timonen, V. and Kenny, R.A. (eds) *Fifty Plus in Ireland 2011: First Results from the Irish Longitudinal Study on Ageing (TILDA)*, Trinity College Dublin.

Lymbery, M. (2005) *Social Work with Older People: Context, Policy and Practice*, London, Sage.

McAlynn, M. and McLaughlin, J. (2008) 'Key factors impeding discharge planning in hospital social work', *Social Work in Health Care*, 46(3), 1–27.

MacGabhann, K. and Nobre, T. (2010) 'Managing ethno-cultural diversity in health care service delivery: the Irish experience: an exploratory study', International Conference of l'AIMS Luxembourg, 1–4 June.

McLeod, E., Bywaters, P., Tanner, D. and Hirsch, M. (2008) 'For the sake of their health: older service users' requirements for social care to facilitate access to social networks following hospital discharge', *British Journal of Social Work*, 38(1), 73–90.

Madden, D. (2006) *Report of Dr. Deirdre Madden on Post Mortem Practice and Procedures*, Dublin, Stationery Office.

Mental Health Reform (2013) *Mental Health in Primary Care in Ireland: A Briefing Paper*, Dublin, Mental Health Reform.

NASW (National Association of Social Workers) (2005) *Standards for Social Work Practice in Health Care Settings*, Washington DC, NASW.

National Head Medical Social Workers' Forum (2008) *Champions for Social Gain*, Dublin, National Head Medical Social Workers' Forum.

National Head Medical Social Workers' Forum (2014) *National Guidelines on Caseload Management in Medical Social Work*, Dublin, National Head Medical Social Workers' Forum.

NCCRI and IHSMI (2002) *Cultural Diversity in the Irish Health Care Sector: Towards the Development of Policy and Practice Guidelines for Organisations in the Health Sector*, Dublin, National Consultative Committee on Racism and Interculturalism and Irish Health Services Management Institute.

Ní Raghallaigh, M., Allen, M., Cunniffe, R. and Quin, S. (2014) 'Experiences of social workers in primary care in Ireland', *Social Work in Health Care*, 52(10), 930–46.

O'Driscoll, S. (2002) 'Responding to trauma and bereavement in an acute hospital', *Eisteach*, 15, 5–11.

O'Driscoll, S. (2004) 'Responding to bereavement in the acute care setting: a journey in service development', in Cruz, L. (ed.) *Making Sense of Dying and Death*, Oxford, Inter-Disciplinary Press.

Ruch, G. (2005) 'Relationship-based practice and reflective practice: holistic approaches to contemporary child care social work', *Child & Family Social Work*, 10(2), 111–23.

Sudbery, J. (2002) 'Key features of therapeutic social work: the use of relationship', *Journal of Social Work Practice*, 16(2), 149–62.

Trevithick, P. (2003) 'Effective relationship-based practice: a theoretical exploration', *Journal of Social Work Practice*, 17(2), 163–78.

Tussing, A. and Wren, M. (2006) *How Ireland Cares: The Case for Health Care Reform*, Dublin, New Island.

Van Hook, M. (2004) 'Psychosocial issues within primary health care settings; challenges and opportunities for social work practice', *Social Work in Health Care*, 38(1), 63–80.

Walsh, T., Foreman, M. and Curry, P. (2007) *Bereavement Care in Acute Hospitals: An Evaluation of the Beaumont Hospital Bereavement Care Service*, Dublin, Beaumont Hospital/Trinity College, Dublin.

Walsh, T., Foreman, M., Curry, P. et al. (2008) 'Bereavement support in an acute hospital: an Irish model', *Death Studies*, 32(8), 768–86.

WHO (World Health Organization) (2004) *Commission on the Social Determinants of Health* (CSDH): note by the Secretariat, Document number EB115/35.

Wilson, E. (2011) 'Every cloud has a silver lining', *Cancer Professional*, 5(4), 7–9.

Wilson, E. (2012) The Psychosocial Effects of Early Stage Breast Cancer on Young Women Exiting Treatment: Implications for Social Work Practice, unpublished PhD, UCD.

Wilson, E. and Crown, J. (2011) 'Premature menopause: information needs of young women undergoing adjuvant chemotherapy for early stage breast cancer', *Cancer Professional*, 5(3), 11–14.

Wilson, K., Ruch, G., Lymbery, M. and Cooper, A. (2008) *Social Work: An Introduction to Contemporary Practice*, London, Longman.

Wren, M. (2003) *An Unhealthy State: Anatomy of a Sick Society*, Dublin, New Island.

10

Opportunities for Social Workers' Critical Engagement in Mental Health Care

Liz Brosnan and Lydia Sapouna

Introduction

Mental health social workers in Ireland work in community and inpatient services as part of multidisciplinary teams (MDTs) aiming to provide a 'holistic seamless service' and a continuum of care for mental health service users (Mental Health Commission, 2007). The key structure of multidisciplinary service provision includes psychiatrists, community mental health nurses, addiction counsellors, social workers, clinical psychologists and occupational therapists, all led by a consultant psychiatrist. The unique skill social workers bring to the MDT is 'to take, as their primary perspective, a view of the individual in the context of their personal, family, cultural, and socioeconomic circumstances and to propose and carry out interventions in that context' (Mental Health Commission, 2006, p. 26). Mental health social work brings awareness of contextual/structural factors and interpersonal interactions through a diverse range of practices, including assessment of psychosocial needs, family work, counselling, advocacy, mobilizing community resources, community development, and social inclusion work.

Social work services in the Irish mental health context vary significantly. In many MDTs, social workers embrace, and often lead, a social recovery approach to practice, while in other MDTs social workers may find it difficult to promote a social perspective. The willingness of the consultant psychiatrist leading the MDT to support a social perspective is often quoted as the key factor in expanding or limiting possibilities for such practice. Given this inconsistent picture on the ground, this chapter does not aim to provide a detailed overview of mental health social work practice in Ireland. Instead, we explore social work in relation to some key pillars of a social perspective in the context of current conceptual and policy transformations in Irish mental health.

The past decade has seen significant changes in the field of mental health that have impacted on social work practices. These changes go beyond the shift from institutional to community care settings towards exploring experiences of human distress and recovery within a social context. The need to reform the Irish mental health services (MHS) is almost universally accepted as urgent (Sapouna, 2006; Higgins and McDaid, 2014). Key Irish policies, such as *A Vision for Change* (Department of Health and Children, 2006) and *A Recovery Approach within the Irish Mental Health Services* (Mental Health Commission, 2008), advocate a comprehensive, recovery-oriented, person-centred, biopsychosocial approach to MHS, as opposed to a purely biological orientation.

Despite the government's rhetoric of change, policy implementation has been slow and inconsistent across the country (Mental Health Commission, 2013). It has been argued that the economic crisis, with a range of cutbacks impacting disproportionally on MHS, is the main factor to have 'stalled' the process of change. However, in this chapter, we argue that by focusing on the lack of resources as *the problem*, professionals can fail to see that existing services are often experienced as unhelpful and/or damaging by people who use them. A preoccupation with the lack of resources tends to hide the problems that lie *within* the current MHS, including the attitudes and values of professionals, power imbalances between professionals and service users, and the hegemony of the biomedical model in defining and treating human experiences of distress. Despite a shift to the use of biopsychosocial discourses within MHS, the main responses to people in distress remain medical/pharmacological interventions (Bracken et al., 2012).

Within this predominantly medical framework, social workers in Irish MHS often consider themselves powerless to develop a 'social' approach to emotional distress. Yet, research indicates (Brosnan, 2013) that service users want a social approach to practice that can make their contact with services more meaningful and 'human'. This requires a paradigm shift towards 'person-directed' practice (Quinn, 2013) and creating genuine partnerships between service users and professionals to facilitate a recovery process that service users direct. We are conscious that the terms 'recovery' and 'user involvement' are in danger of being assimilated within the current biomedical discourse and losing their transformative potential as a consequence. Therefore, this chapter offers a critical insight into the use of these concepts. We propose that social workers become critically engaged in mental health practice by:

- addressing the context of people's lives
- challenging medical hegemony through recovery-informed practice
- promoting meaningful service user involvement.

Addressing the context of people's lives

Social work is located at the interface between the person and their social environment and is therefore ideally placed to critically engage with the context of people's lives, a long-neglected element within the biomedical approach. While there are several examples of social workers in Ireland engaging with a social practice perspective, overall, the profession has yet to articulate a confident social approach to mental health. Many MDTs still operate without a full-time social work post, and within a predominantly medical hegemony, this limits the space for a broader holistic practice. Such practice is essential in recognizing the connections between people's emotional distress and their life experiences.

Within interdisciplinary contexts, there is a tendency to view the primary role of social work as responding to practical concerns in people's lives, such as welfare benefits, housing and employment. Responding to these concerns is important; however, this role does not in itself imply a broader understanding of emotional distress. We argue for a social approach to practice, which views emotional distress as a meaningful response to problems of living, trauma and adverse life experiences, rather than a 'chemical imbalance'. We propose a social approach in which context, relationships and meanings are put at the centre of our interventions (Bracken and Thomas, 2005). As Tew (2011, p. 2) states:

> Fundamental to a social approach is the idea of being alongside people as they reclaim a life that is meaningful and satisfying to them – one that involves participating in the mainstream social world and taking roles that are valued within social, family, employment and other domains. As part of this, people may need help in making sense of what has happened to them – and how their social experiences may have contributed to their mental distress.

Social workers have distinctive practice capabilities in working alongside people and supporting them to overcome barriers to achieving their potential by adopting a community, as well as an individual, perspective. However, their potential to fully embrace this role can be seriously impeded by the way social work has developed over the past decade in Ireland, with practices being increasingly defined by managerial procedures and guidelines (Ferguson, 2010) that focus on individualized work and risk management. This definition of social work can limit the profession's potential to respond meaningfully to the unpredictable and complex situations of people's lives and address issues of injustice and discrimination.

In order to counteract these trends, social workers require a value base that is informed by the principles of empowerment, social justice, anti-oppressive practice, and genuine partnerships that recognize the expertise of people with experiences of distress. Social approaches are often considered to be lacking a coherent body of theory backed up by research compared to the medical perspective (Tew, 2011). Social workers need to be informed of the research evidence demonstrating the strong links between life adversity and emotional distress. Next, we highlight some key contributions in this area.

Injustice and adverse life experiences

A significant body of research challenges beliefs that 'madness' can be explained without reference to the context of people's lives and problematizes the excessive preoccupation with chemical imbalances and genetic predispositions as causes of human misery, including the conditions that are given the name 'schizophrenia' (Read and Dillon, 2013). Furthermore, the role of the pharmaceutical industry in promoting a narrow biomedical approach to treating human distress has increasingly been called into question (Rapley et al., 2011).

There is overwhelming evidence that life events and broader environments affect the likelihood of experiencing distress at some stage in our lives. Research confirms the relationship between inequality and poorer mental health, with particularly strong correlations between the incidence of distress and disadvantage, including unemployment, homelessness, lack of education, and being brought up in socially disadvantaged areas (Rogers and Pilgrim, 2010; Read et al., 2013). Furthermore, a considerable body of research has correlated membership of social groups that are subject to systematic experiences of oppression or disadvantage with higher rates of mental health difficulties (Fernando, 2011). A World Health Organization (WHO, 2009, p. III) report concluded that:

> levels of mental distress among communities need to be understood less in terms of individual pathology and more as a response to relative deprivation and social injustice, which erode the emotional, spiritual and intellectual resources essential to psychological wellbeing.

Irish policy identifies poverty as a key risk factor for poor mental health (Department of Health and Children, 2006). Irish health statistics consistently show that people from lower socioeconomic backgrounds are up to seven times more likely than their middle-/upper-class counterparts to enter the inpatient psychiatric system (Department of Health and Children, 2006; Daly and Walsh, 2013). Mental Health Reform (2012) highlighted the risk to the social and economic lives of people with poor mental health in Ireland and the social exclusion experienced by people with mental health difficulties. In the context of the economic crisis and austerity, mental health service users in Ireland are acutely affected by poor housing, loss of employment and service cutbacks. The subsequent increased stress has had an adverse effect on family relationships, in some cases contributing to relationship breakdown and the onset or deterioration of emotional distress. The link between poverty, disadvantage and use of mental health services is certainly not a new phenomenon. Asylums and madhouses have historically been filled by people living in poverty. Foucault's seminal work *Madness and Civilization* (1971) provides a critical insight into the social significance of the great confinement as a project of isolating the poor, the insane and other 'forms of uselessness' from society in order to protect social order.

International research indicates that the experience of injustice and inequality may be more damaging to mental health than the absolute levels of deprivation (WHO, 2009; Read et al., 2013). An influential contribution to this argument comes from the research of Wilkinson and Pickett (2009), which identifies the profound effects of living in unequal societies. Their research summarizes multiple studies demonstrating that poverty leads to exclusion from community life and from a sense of belonging and being valued, all of which result in people suffering 'social pain'. This argument fits in with other evidence suggesting that inequality and injustice feed into a sense of 'otherness', worthlessness and shame (Janssen et al., 2004).

A social justice framework can facilitate the consideration of explicit experiences of discrimination and injustice, such as sexism, racism, homophobia, ableism, ageism, and also more subtle experiences of being made to feel powerless or inferior. A consideration of identity and the intersectionality of oppression and discrimination, with consequent mental health challenges, is beyond the scope of this chapter. However, it is important to acknowledge the evidence from Irish and international research on distress within ethnic minorities, migrant populations (Lakeman and Mathews, 2010; Fernando, 2011) and lesbian, gay, bisexual and transgender groups (Higgins et al., 2011). Social workers need to consider the experiences of people from marginalized and/or disadvantaged groups on the basis of the personal story of the individual in the social context of their lives.

Childhood adversity and psychosis

Perhaps the most influential body of evidence that has emerged over the past two decades in relation to life events and psychiatric diagnoses is the research linking childhood adversity and psychosis, a condition that has traditionally been treated as a biochemical problem: 'Until very recently the hypothesis that abuse in childhood has a causal role in psychosis was regarded by many biologically oriented psychiatrists as heresy' (Read and

Bentall, 2012, p. 90). However, in the past decade, there have been a number of ground-breaking international studies showing that adverse life events, trauma, loss and neglect in childhood increase vulnerability to emotional distress. A recent meta-analysis by Varese et al. (2012) confirms this link between trauma and psychosis. In addition, many studies demonstrate the powerful relationship between all forms of child abuse and schizophrenia (reviewed by Read et al., 2004). People subjected to childhood abuse:

- are more likely to be admitted to a psychiatric hospital
- have earlier, longer and more frequent admissions
- receive more psychiatric medication
- are more likely to self-harm and try to kill themselves
- experience more severe symptoms (Read and Bentall, 2012).

One of the most robust of these studies was a prospective study of 4,000 people in the Netherlands, which found that those who had suffered 'moderate' abuse during childhood were 11 times more likely and those who had suffered 'severe' childhood abuse 48 times more likely to have 'pathology level psychosis' than people who had not been abused as children (Janssen et al., 2004).

Of particular interest is the work of Marius Romme and Sandra Escher, two Dutch social psychiatrists who pioneered a new approach to understanding voice-hearing experiences (Romme and Escher, 2005). Traditional psychiatric practice treats voice-hearing as a classic symptom of schizophrenia, a meaningless pathological phenomenon that is a product of genetic and cognitive brain faults. On this basis, medical practitioners have nothing to offer to voice-hearers who seek help other than medication to eliminate the voices (Corstens et al., 2008). In contrast to this approach, Romme and Escher's (2005) research with over 350 voice-hearers has firmly established that between 70 and 80% of people who hear voices have had some traumatic experience that they connect with hearing voices. As Dillon and Longden (2012, p. 130) propose: 'hearing voices in itself is a normal human experience that is often a reaction to a traumatic or intensely emotional event that has not been adequately resolved'. Voice-hearers who come to the attention of psychiatric services are often stuck in destructive communication patterns with their voices. An alternative approach is based on helping people make sense of their voices and learning to cope with them (www.hearingvoicesmaastricht.eu). This radical shift from the pathologizing language of *auditory hallucinations* to the ordinary language of *hearing voices* can be a tool to transform thinking and practice in mental health care.

Asking 'what happened' and listening to voices

These research developments are only significant for practice if professionals act on them by asking people 'what happened' in their lives and responding respectfully to the stories they hear. Social workers, as a profession carrying out psychosocial assessments, need to ask questions that haven't been asked before about people's lives, including questions about abuse, bullying, neglect and loss (Read, 2013). Through such questions, professionals can facilitate people to make connections 'between elements of experience that had previously seemed confusing or contradictory' (Tew, 2002, p. 146) and thereby take control of their own recovery.

Nevertheless, it is important not to always assume the existence or denial of experiences of trauma and abuse. Professionals can facilitate conversations about meanings, but are not the makers of the meaning. As Tew (2002) argues, such an approach would require a commitment to hear and take seriously what people may have to say about their emotional distress, their life experiences, and the meanings, histories and hopes that they attach to them. Listening to people in their own terms and language has been identified as a missing component from current practice (Hepworth and McGowan, 2012). This kind of listening can challenge traditions of biological psychiatry, in which the voice of the service user is primarily used to diagnose disorders and interpret experiences for people.

Meaningful listening is a key practice skill and requires a shift towards an active dialogue with the people concerned and their networks. An interesting example of dealing with psychosis through dialogue was developed in Northern Lapland by a group of innovative family therapists and has been piloted in some Irish MHS since 2012. The 'open dialogue approach', as it is called, works with people experiencing psychotic symptoms in their home with interventions involving the individual's social network. The general aim is to generate dialogue to construct words for the experiences, which exist in psychotic symptoms. Open dialogue involves working in groups because psychosis is viewed as a problem involving relationships, rather than something that happens to an individual. Additionally, open dialogue values the voice of everyone in the process, most especially the person directly in crisis. The open dialogue project changed a mental health system that once had some of Europe's poorest outcomes for schizophrenia into one that now gets the best statistical results in the world for those beginning to show psychotic symptoms (Seikkula et al., 2006).

In order to actively listen to service users' meanings and stories, it can be important to engage with forms of expression and language that may be unconventional and perhaps unfamiliar to social workers. Working with voices is a powerful example of this engagement. Professionals' willingness and ability to accept people's accounts of their experiences, including

Social Work in Ireland

voice-hearing experiences, can have a major influence on outcomes for people diagnosed with schizophrenia (Dillon and Longden, 2012). Practitioners who work with voice-hearers suggest that:

> in our experience, talking with voice-hearers doesn't provoke psychosis ... Most voice-hearers find it liberating to be respectfully questioned about their voice hearing experiences and feel acknowledged by it. For some, only this kind of assessment produces profound change. (Corstens et al., 2008, p. 321)

The Hearing Voices Network (www.hearing-voices.org) is an influential example of practice where voice-hearers have come together to develop shared understandings of voice-hearing experiences. In Ireland, since 2012, a number of voice-hearers and professionals, including social workers, have participated in three-day training on Hearing Voices Group Facilitation, facilitated by Jacqui Dillon (herself a voice-hearer). Subsequently, a number of groups have been set up within and outside MHS, with a number of mental health social workers being involved in them. Participating in this training enabled social workers to bring the principles of this approach into their individual and groupwork practice in Irish MHS. At an individual level, for example, social workers have started to work with service users around the meaning of voice-hearing. These practitioners report how people who were initially fearful to talk about their voices have gradually opened up about their experiences and have been helped to make sense of what has happened to them. At a group level, social workers using the Wellness Recovery Action Plan (see below) have started to incorporate voice management techniques as part of wellness, relapse-prevention tools. It is particularly important that exposure to a different understanding of voice-hearing experiences has facilitated social workers and service users to have more open conversations about trauma regardless of the existence of voices. International experience has demonstrated that hearing voices support groups are effective communal solutions that enable people to make profound positive changes in their lives (Dillon et al., 2013). Social workers can form alliances with service users and forward-thinking professionals within and outside MHS to facilitate the development of spaces that are conducive to the recovery process. Mental health recovery as a journey, but also as an ideology challenging the dominant medical hegemony, is discussed next.

Challenging medical hegemony through recovery-informed practice

Originally a user movement concept, recovery represents hopes and aspirations for the transformation of a paternalistic, coercive and institutionalized form of service provision. *A Vision for Change* (Department of Health and Children, 2006, p. 9) identified the need for MHS to adopt a recovery perspective and considered it a core principle to 'inform every aspect of service delivery'. While the concept of recovery in mental health is not a new one, there has been a redefinition during the past two decades involving a shift from the clinical understanding of recovery as the 'absence of symptoms', or equating it with a cure, to a process of 'recovering what was lost': citizenship, rights, meaningful roles, responsibilities, decisions, potential and support (see Bracken and Thomas, 2005; Mental Health Commission, 2008). In Ireland, *A Vision for Change* (Department of Health and Children, 2006) and the Mental Health Commission (2008) endorse a social recovery approach and emphasize the social inclusion aspect of recovery. Advancing Recovery in Ireland (ARI) is an initiative supporting Irish MHS in their efforts to implement a number of key concepts in *A Vision for Change*. ARI focuses on service-level structures, systems and practices that can maximize personal recovery opportunities and outcomes for service users. As Roberts and Wolfson (2004, p. 37) argue, the current 'redefinition of recovery as a process of personal discovery, of how to live (and to live well) with enduring symptoms and vulnerabilities opens the possibility of recovery to all'.

However, as Walsh et al. (2008, p. 251) observe, 'the shift from traditional psychiatry to recovery can be achieved on paper with a few deft strokes of a pen', but making a shift in organizational and cultural practice is altogether more challenging. Recovery as a concept and practice can contribute to a paradigm shift in mental health, in which the service user becomes the central driver of their own life, a life of their own choosing, in a community in which they are citizens with equal rights to all other citizens (Ryan et al., 2012). Mental health professionals can support or hinder this process.

There are common themes in recovery stories that are familiar to social work: enabling the voice of the service user, a commitment to anti-oppressive practice and social justice, and a focus on life contexts, systems, networks and relationships (Coppock and Dunn, 2010). At an individual level of practice, such themes can be acted on through hope-inspiring relationships, nurturing a vision of the life people want to live, being in charge of wellness, and focusing on strengths and resilience rather than pathology (Rapp and Goscha, 2012). In this process, social workers can use a social approach more as a basis of enquiry than as a way of giving expert insights. As Tew (2002, p. 151) suggests, social workers' 'most important role may be one of taking seriously and being the "enlightened witness" for the histories of trauma and powerlessness that may emerge, once connections start to be made'. At community and agency levels, such themes can be acted on through person-directed services, individualized self-management plans, service user-operated services, peer support and respect for 'experts by experience' (see Mental Health Commission, 2008).

Moving beyond the focus on the individual, social workers are also in a position to acknowledge and act on the impact of distress on families, friends and social networks. By locating the experience of distress in a social context, social workers can have an important role in supporting renegotiations within family, social and agency networks and challenging patterns of oppression and exclusion within these networks (Tew, 2002). Furthermore, recovery-oriented practitioners can challenge the organizational and institutional barriers to creating environments conducive to recovery, including professional attitudes and a resistance to 'let go' of the expert role.

An example of a recovery-focused intervention at an individual level is the Wellness Recovery Action Plan (WRAP). WRAP was developed by Mary Ellen Copeland (2002), an American survivor, as a self-management tool offering a practical framework for managing one's life, to understand, anticipate and ameliorate the stresses and triggers that may lead to mental health problems. It is currently the most widely used self-management strategy in Ireland, with many mental health social workers employing it as part of their practice. WRAP presents a format for people to detail how they are when well, as often professionals may not know them outside the context of acute services. It also encourages people to:

- develop a list of 'wellness tools', that is, daily routines and activities that help them stay well

- develop a circle of supporters

- identify triggers and warning signs

- make an action plan for when warning signs appear

- draw up an advance directive or, at minimum, a crisis plan, for example who might accompany the person to seek help from MHS, care for children, hold keys and so on

- do a post-crisis review, to assess what went well and what can be improved.

A recent evaluation of WRAP Education Programmes in Ireland (Higgins et al., 2012) identified the potential of WRAP to increase people's knowledge, promote positive attitudes towards recovery, and provide people with strategies to support mental health. While social workers in Irish MHS consider WRAP a central element of their recovery-oriented practice, much of this practice takes place within a highly medicalized culture. As Higgins et al.'s study identified, initiatives such as WRAP are only meaningful in the context of shifting the ethos of care from the current preoccupation with illness to one of wellness.

At a community/agency level, there are several examples of MHS that are seeking to reform their practices towards an ethos guided by a commitment to service user involvement, a recovery philosophy, a community develop- ment orientation and the importance of integrated partnership working. The Home Focus project in West Cork is one such example of a community-based approach providing outreach, home-based, individualized support for people with mental health difficulties in their own communities. Delivered by a team combining service user and professional expertise engaging in a diverse range of interventions, the project provided unique sources of support for its participants, resulting in reduction of hospitalization, individual gains, and, above all, a new experience of service provision where people felt respected, listened to and treated 'as a person rather than a symptom' (Sapouna, 2008).

A key dimension of the recovery philosophy is its organic link with the service user/survivor movement. For the survivor movement, recovery is about having a voice. As Bracken and Thomas (2005, p. 227) argue:

> through social action, the survivor movement has created safe spaces in which individuals can start the process of telling their own stories ... the meaning of recovery is very closely tied to the struggle of survivors to have the right to tell their own stories in their own way.

Higgins and McGowan (2014, p. 64) state that first-person accounts of recovery, as well as highlighting resilience and overcoming adversity, are 'discourses of resistance', which advocate civil and human rights for those who experience mental health problems:

> Such accounts also advocate actively for a radical shift in how mental health prac- titioners frame and respond to people's experience of mental health problems urging a greater distribution of power between the institution of psychiatry and people using the services.

What does recovery mean for social work practice? In Brosnan's (2013) study, professionals practising on a 'recovery track' were described by service users as people who can act as allies, who come into meetings as human beings and leave their 'hats outside the door'. Brosnan (2013, p. 135) also identified the prevalence of rhetoric about recovery in the absence of real change. As one participant put it: 'it's no good saying ... we're a recovery- focused service but all that we're offering you is a psychiatrist and drugs'.

A meaningful recovery approach does not involve the implementation of technical measures within a predominantly medical framework of service provision. The recovery approach we are proposing requires a fundamental shift in understanding, responding to, and being with, emotional distress. In this shift, the voice of service users in defining their own recovery is central (Sapouna, 2008).

Promoting meaningful service user involvement (SUI)

SUI is considered to be a necessary component of good practice internationally (Kemp, 2010) and a feature of MHS planning and management for decades in many countries (Gammon et al., 2014; Beresford, 2010). SUI in Irish mental health services first appears in the government policy *A Vision for Change* (Department of Health and Children, 2006). Chapter Three of this policy discusses SUI, asserting that service users and carers must be at the centre of decision making, from the level of decisions about their own care through to the strategic development of local services and national policy. It specifically recommends that service users be included in local management teams and that their perspectives inform national planning and regulatory bodies (Department of Health and Children, 2006, p. 27).

There are at least two directions for the impetus to include the voice of the service user (Beresford, 2002). The first is a push from top management committed to reform MHS. The second is the bottom-up demand of the user movement, inspired by civil and human rights movements. As social workers operate from within an increasingly managerial environment, there is a danger that collaborative working with service users becomes a 'tick box' procedure rather than a professional value. Meaningful involvement requires a change in the culture of professional superiority. It is important, therefore, not to lose sight of the profession's commitment to human rights and social justice as the underpinning principle of SUI.

SUI can occur at strategic, operational or individual levels (Brosnan, 2013). SUI at the individual level, such as making decisions about their own care, ideally being in control of their own care, is highly significant for service users. This is to be distinguished from operational and strategic levels of involvement, which have more potential to influence the change of current practice and ethos. Rose et al. (2010, p. 393) list eight different forms of SUI:

1. Being consulted about staff recruitment, having a role in candidate selection or staff performance evaluations

2. Advising on local MHS in committee work

3. Involvement in research, usually consultation but increasingly service user-led and controlled research

4. User-led service delivery

5. Training of professionals

6. Employment in services as peer workers

7.   Peer advocacy

8.   Campaigning.

Some of these forms of SUI are evident in an Irish context (Brosnan, 2014), but due to space limitations, this chapter focuses only on peer advocacy and peer support.

Peer advocacy and peer workers

A Vision for Change (Department of Health and Children, 2006) makes a clear recommendation that advocacy should be provided as a right in all parts of the country. The Irish Advocacy Network (IAN), a prominent peer-run organization established in 1999, evolved from a vision to develop a critical mass of empowered service users who would use peer advocacy skills and training to demand respect, dignity and control over how they are treated (McGowan, n.d.). The IAN provides independent peer advocacy services at approved centres (that is, licensed centres to detain people under the 2001 Mental Health Act) in all but one of the 26 counties of the Republic.

A similar yet distinct role to peer advocacy is that of peer support workers. In the past few years, peer support workers have been employed in the voluntary sector to work alongside a few pioneering statutory services. These peer worker projects are associated with the Advancing Recovery in Ireland (ARI) project. ARI is influenced by the Implementing Recovery through Organisational Change project in the UK (see www.imroc.org). Service user involvement is one of ARI's 10 organizational challenges. Also, as a result of ARI, Recovery Colleges have begun to emerge in Ireland where the emphasis is on co-production; peer educators and mental health professionals co-design a curriculum to support recovery. The ethos of Recovery Colleges is to move the emphasis from treatment to education and recovery.

Gosling (2010) describes in some detail how peer advocacy work and promoting self-advocacy can shift the balance of power and powerlessness in individuals' relationships with themselves, their peers and services. Other service user/survivor writers explain that peers best understand the support other service users need because they have been through the depersonalization and psychiatric mystification of the mainstream MHS (Dillon et al., 2013; Watts, 2014). Repper and Carter (2011) conclude that contact with peer support workers can result in many positive outcomes for those they work with, including increased self-esteem, self-management of difficulties, social inclusion and increased social networks.

The fact that no peer-led MHS, for example crisis houses, have emerged in Ireland to date, for reasons touched on elsewhere (see Brosnan, 2014), indicates the challenge to developing alternative models of care to the hegemonic statutory MHS. The Critical Voices Network Ireland emerged as a response to the lack of public space for debate as a coalition of service users, carers, professionals, academics, national campaigning and advocacy groups, all looking for a mental health system not based on the traditional biomedical model (Gijbels and Sapouna, 2011).

Challenges for service user involvement

There are many structural and cultural obstacles to the meaningful participation of service users: inadequate legal and policy-related support, complex, confusing jargon-loaded organizational procedures and rituals, discrimination and stigma generated by professionals, and feelings of powerlessness, low self-esteem, scepticism or apathy towards SUI among many service users and carers (Carey, 2009).

Power dynamics are ubiquitous throughout the MHS, in the construction of knowledge, hierarchical structures, interprofessional status, and relationships between service users and service providers (Brosnan, 2013). A common theme that emerged in Brosnan's (2013) research into SUI is the low level of control available to service users over the processes they become involved with. The overall findings in this research indicate that service providers have much to learn from service users about the conditions of participation (Brosnan, 2013, p. 289). Unless the various dimensions of power that maintain and reproduce unequal conditions are acknowledged, the risk of tokenistic SUI is ever present and likely to impede any of the potential of SUI to shift power relations within MHS. By contrast, projects developed in real partnerships with user-led groups from the ground up, for example building capacity in local groups through human rights-based approaches (see McMillan et al., 2009), can be the beginnings of meaningful participation for service users (Brosnan, 2013).

Working collaboratively is an essential value base in social work. However, meaningful SUI does not come naturally within the current power structures of the MHS. Such an approach requires a shift from a preoccupation with professional roles and status towards recognizing the insights and expertise of people with lived experience of distress.

Conclusion

This chapter considers the opportunities for social work to contribute to a paradigm shift in Irish mental health care towards a context-sensitive practice in which the user is the central driver of their own recovery. This shift requires social workers to engage with critical questions about the way emotional distress is understood and responded to and to challenge the dominant biomedical model of thinking and practice. Critical questions reframe emotional distress as a meaningful response to problems of living, trauma and adverse life experiences. Such questions consider life stories, the impact of injustice and inequality in people's life contexts, including the context of MHS where people often feel powerless. Considering these questions can enhance practice through conversations about 'what happened' in people's lives and through creating opportunities for people to articulate their experiences, hopes and expectations. It also involves engaging at a broader level of seeking structural change within and beyond MHS.

We also argue that a recovery approach, placing value on hope, choice and citizenship, is a key component in this paradigm shift. Social workers' knowledge and value base can facilitate the construction of environments conducive to recovery through hope-inspiring relationships, focusing on strengths and resilience, and negotiating relationships with family, social and agency networks. However, recovery is not a technical measure to be integrated in the existing culture of mental health care; it is a tool to transform it. In this transformation, the participation and involvement of service users is central. We then consider the importance of promoting meaningful user involvement, highlighting that the level of control service users have over the process, and to shape the agenda, remains a key concern if we are to move beyond tokenistic practices of involvement. A real risk remains that recovery and SUI, core components of the change that users and their allies demand of MHS, lose their transformative potential and are appropriated into cosmetic changes that sustain the 'bio-bio-bio' approach (Read et al., 2009).

Finally, while this chapter focuses on the contribution social work can make towards a social approach to emotional distress, we are not proposing that social workers become the 'new experts' in the field of mental health. We are not proposing a new 'social model' to replace the 'medical model' in order to establish some new domination in the way human distress is understood and responded to. As Tew (2002) argues, social work should approach this with humility and facilitate service users to understand their distress and recovery in the way that works most effectively for them. By engaging in a paradigm shift and forming meaningful partnerships with service users and people with self-experience, social work can reclaim its social identity and respond to human distress in a way that is user driven, respectful, context aware, and informed by human rights principles.

References

Beresford, P. (2002) 'User involvement in research and evaluation: Liberation or regulation?', *Social Policy and Society*, 1(2), 95–105.

Beresford, P. (2010) 'Public partnerships, governance and user involvement: a service user perspective', *International Journal of Consumer Studies*, 34(5), 495–502.

Bracken, P. and Thomas, P. (2005) *Postpsychiatry: Mental Health in a Postmodern World*, Oxford University Press.

Bracken, P., Thomas, P., Timimi, S. et al. (2012) 'Psychiatry beyond the current paradigm', *British Journal of Psychiatry*, 201(6), 430–34.

Brosnan, L. (2013) Service-User Involvement in Irish Mental Health Services: A Sociological Analysis of Inherent Tensions for Service-Users, Service-Providers and Social Movement Actors, unpublished thesis, University of Limerick.

Brosnan, L. (2014) 'Empowerment and development of an Irish advocacy movement', in Higgins, A. and McDaid, S. (eds) *Mental Health in Ireland: Policy, Practice and Law*, Dublin, Gill & Macmillan.

Carey, M. (2009) 'Critical commentary: Happy shopper? The problem with service user and carer participation', *British Journal of Social Work*, 39(1), 179–88.

Copeland, M.E. (2002) 'What is Wellness Recovery Action Plan (WRAP)?', www.mentalhealthrecovery.com/wrap, accessed 27 January 2015.

Coppock, V. and Dunn, B. (2010) *Understanding Social Work Practice in Mental Health*, London, Sage.

Corstens, D., Escher, S. and Romme, M. (2008) 'Accepting and working with voices: the Maastricht approach', in Moskowitz, A. Schafer, I. and Dorahy, M.J. (eds) *Psychosis, Trauma and Dissociation: Emerging Perspectives on Severe Psychopathology*, Oxford, Wiley-Blackwell.

Daly, A. and Walsh, D. (2013) *Activities of Irish Psychiatric Units and Hospitals 2012*, Dublin, Health Research Board.

Department of Health and Children (2006) *A Vision for Change: Report of the Expert Group on Mental Health Policy*, Dublin, Stationery Office.

Dillon, J. and Longden, E. (2012) 'Hearing voices groups: creating safe spaces to share taboo experiences', in Romme, M. and Escher, S. (eds) *Psychosis as a Personal Crisis: An Experience-based Approach*, London, Routledge.

Dillon, J., Bullimore, P., Lampshire, D. and Chamberlin, J. (2013) 'The work of experience-based experts', in Read, J. and Dillon, J. (eds) *Models of Madness: Psychological, Social and Biological Approaches to Psychosis*, London, Routledge.

Ferguson, I. (2010) '"I didn't come into social work for this!": Managerialism, modernisation and alternative futures', *Irish Social Worker*, summer, 12–16.

Fernando, S. (2011) 'Cultural diversity and racism', in Moncrieff, J., Ripley, M. and Dillon, J. (eds) *Demedicalising Misery: Psychiatry, Psychology and the Human Condition*, Basingstoke, Palgrave Macmillan.

Foucault, M. (1971) *Madness and Civilization: A History of Insanity in the Age of Reason*, London, Routledge.

Gammon, D., Strand, M. and Eng, L.S. (2014) 'Service users' perspectives in the design of an online tool for assisted self-help in mental health: a case study of implications', *International Journal of Mental Health Systems*, 8(1), 1–8.

Gijbels, H. and Sapouna, L. (2011) 'A broader platform to discuss mental health service concerns', *Irish Examiner*, 6 August.

Gosling, J. (2010) 'The ethos of involvement as the route to recovery', in Weinstein, J. (ed.) *Mental Health Service User Involvement and Recovery*, London, Jessica Kingsley.

Hepworth, I. and McGowan, L. (2012) 'Do mental health professionals enquire about childhood sexual abuse during routine mental health assessment in acute mental health settings?', *Journal of Psychiatric and Mental Health Nursing*, 20(6), 473–83.

Higgins, A. and McDaid, S. (eds) (2014) *Mental Health in Ireland: Policy, Practice and Law*, Dublin, Gill & Macmillan.

Higgins, A. and McGowan, P. (2014) 'Recovery and recovery ethos: challenges and possibilities', in Higgins, A. and McDaid, S. (eds) *Mental Health in Ireland: Policy, Practice and Law*, Dublin, Gill & Macmillan.

Higgins, A., Callaghan, P., DeVries, J. et al. 2012) 'Evaluation of mental health recovery and Wellness Recovery Action Planning education in Ireland: a mixed methods pre–postevaluation', *Journal of Advanced Nursing*, 68(11), 2418–28.

Higgins, A., Sharek, D., McCann, E. et al. (2011) *Visible Lives: Identifying the Experiences and Needs of Older Lesbian, Gay, Bisexual and Transgender (LGBT) People in Ireland*, Dublin, Gay and Lesbian Equality Network.

Janssen, I., Krabbendam, L., Bak, M. et al. (2004) 'Childhood abuse as a risk factor for psychotic experiences', *Acta Psychiatrica Scandinavica*, 109(1), 38–45.

Kemp, P. (2010) 'Introduction to mental health service user involvement', in Weinstein, J. (ed.) *Mental Health Service User Involvement and Recovery*, London, Jessica Kingsley.

Lakeman, R. and Matthews, A. (2010) 'The views and experiences of members of new communities in Ireland: perspectives on mental health and well-being', www.translocations.ie/docs/v06i01/Lakeman%20and%20Matthews.doc, accessed 12 December 2013.

McGowan, P. (n.d.) 'The Time is Right', www.irishadvocacynetwork.com/About%20 the%20Irish%20Advocacy%20Network%20Ltd.htm, accessed 21 January 2014.

McMillan, F., Browne, N., Green, S. and Donnelly, D. (2009) 'A card before you leave: participation and mental health in Northern Ireland human rights', *Health and Human Rights*, 11(1), 61–72.

Mental Health Commission (2006) *Multidisciplinary Team Working: From Theory to Practice* Dublin, Mental Health Commission.

Mental Health Commission (2007) *Quality Framework for Mental Health Services in Ireland*, Dublin, Mental Health Commission.

Mental Health Commission (2008) *A Recovery Approach within the Irish Mental Health Services: A Framework for Development*, Dublin, Mental Health Commission.

Mental Health Commission (2013) 'Implementation of a Vision for Change is slow and inconsistent across the country, according to the Mental Health Commission', press release, www.mhcirl.ie/File/Press_Release_7th_Anniversary_ AVFC.pdf, accessed 10 January 2014.

Mental Health Reform (2012) *Guiding A Vision for Change: Manifesto*, Dublin, Mental Health Reform.

Quinn, G. (2013) 'Age: from human deficits to human rights – reflections on a changing field', in *Human Rights and Older People in Ireland – Policy Paper*, Dublin, www. nuigalway.ie/lifecourse/downloads/hr_and_old_age__gqfinal.pdf.

Rapley, M., Moncrieff, J. and Dillon, J. (2011) *Demedicalising Misery: Psychiatry, Psychology and the Human Condition*, Basingstoke, Palgrave Macmillan.

Rapp, C. and Goscha, R. (2012) *The Strengths Model: A Recovery-oriented Approach to Mental Health Services*, Oxford, Oxford University Press.

Read, J. (2013) 'Childhood adversity and psychosis', in Read, J. and Dillon, J. (eds) *Models of Madness: Psychological, Social and Biological Approaches to Psychosis*, London, Routledge.

Read, J. and Bentall, R. (2012) 'Negative childhood experiences and mental health: theoretical, clinical and primary prevention implications', *British Journal of Psychiatry*, 200, 89–91.

Read, J. and Dillon, J. (eds) (2013) *Models of Madness: Psychological, Social and Biological Approaches to Psychosis*, London, Routledge.

Read, J., Bentall, R. and Fosse, R. (2009) 'Time to abandon the bio-bio-bio model of psychosis: exploring the epigenetic and psychological mechanisms by which adverse life events lead to psychotic symptoms', *Epidemiologia e Psichiatria Sociale*, 18(4), 299–310.

Read, J., Johnstone, L. and Taitimu, M. (2013) 'Psychosis, poverty and ethnicity', in Read, J. and Dillon, J. (eds) *Models of Madness: Psychological, Social and Biological Approaches to Psychosis*, London, Routledge.

Read, J., Goodman, L., Morrison, A. et al. (2004) 'Childhood trauma, loss and stress', in Read, J., Mosher, L.R. and Bentall, R.P. (eds) *Models of Madness: Psychological, Social and Biological Approaches to Schizophrenia*, London, Routledge.

Repper, J. and Carter, T. (2011) 'A review of the literature on peer support in mental health services', *Journal of Mental Health*, 20(4), 392–411.

Roberts, G. and Wolfson, P. (2004) 'The rediscovery of recovery: open to all', *Advances in Psychiatric Treatment*, 10, 37–49.

Rogers, A. and Pilgrim, D. (2010) *A Sociology of Mental Health and Illness*, Maidenhead, Open University Press.

Romme, M. and Escher, S. (2005) 'Trauma and hearing voices', in Larkin, W. and Morrison, A. (eds) *Trauma and Psychosis: New Directions for Theory and Therapy*, London, Routledge.

Rose, D., Fleischmann, P. and Schofield, P. (2010) 'Perceptions of user involvement: a user-led study', *International Journal of Social Psychiatry*, 56(4), 389–401.

Ryan, P., Ramon, S. and Greacen, T. (eds) (2012) *Empowerment, Lifelong Learning and Recovery in Mental Health: Towards a New Paradigm*, Basingstoke, Palgrave Macmillan.

Sapouna, L. (2006) 'Tracing evidence of institutionalisation in the process of de-institutionalisation: the Irish case', in Sapouna, L. and Herrmann, P. (eds) *Knowledge in Mental Health; Reclaiming the Social*, New York, Nova Science.

Sapouna, L. (2008) *Having Choices: An Evaluation of the Home Focus Project in West Cork*, University College Cork, Department of Applied Social Studies/HSE.

Seikkula, J., Aaltonen, J., Alakare, B. et al. (2006) 'Five-year experience of first-episode nonaffective psychosis in open-dialogue approach: treatment principles, follow-up outcomes, and two case studies', *Psychotherapy Research*, 16(2), 214–24.

Tew, J. (2002) 'Going social: championing a holistic model of mental distress within professional education', *Social Work Education: The International Journal*, 21(2), 143–55.

Tew, J. (2011) *Social Approaches to Mental Distress*, Basingstoke, Palgrave Macmillan.

Varese, F., Smeets, F., Drukker, M. et al. (2012) 'Childhood adversities increase the risk of psychosis: a meta-analysis of patient-control, prospective- and cross-sectional cohort studies', *Schizophrenia Bulletin*, 38(4), 661–71.

Walsh, J., Stevenson, C., Cutcliffe, J. and Zinck, K. (2008) 'Creating a space for recovery-focused psychiatric nursing care', *Nursing Inquiry*, 15(3), 251–9.

Watts, M. (2014) 'Peer support and mutual help as a means to recovery', in Higgins, A. and McDaid, S. (eds) *Mental Health in Ireland: Policy, Practice and Law*, Dublin, Gill & Macmillan.

Wilkinson, R. and Pickett, K. (2009) *The Spirit Level: Why More Equal Societies Almost Always Do Better*, London, Allen Lane.

WHO (World Health Organization) (2009) *Mental Health, Resilience and Inequalities*, Copenhagen, WHO.

11

Reforming, Reframing or Renaming Irish Probation Practice in the 21st Century?

Anthony Cotter and Carmel Halton

Introduction

Positivism, radical and realistic criminologies and feminist perspectives have examined the causes of crime and have come up with various and multifaceted theories. These different perspectives evoke strong opinions, emotions and beliefs, not only in terms of the origins of crime, but more immediately in terms of solutions. These range from retribution, restitution, rehabilitation, decriminalization and their various combinations. Importantly, deviance and crime are defined by legislation and are conceptualized in a societal context. What is criminal in one society may be lawful in another. What is considered 'criminal' changes over time, for example homosexual acts between men were decriminalized in 1993 under the Criminal Law (Sexual Offences) Act 1993.

In the public mind, criminal behaviour is construed through high-profile cases of murder, rape, robbery and assaults. Such offences are readily understandable. By way of contrast, offences committed by business organizations, banks and corporations are more complicated, difficult to investigate, and may have been perpetrated over a long period of time. Such offences tend to be committed 'in private' and the victims are not readily identifiable. However, according to Sutherland (1949, pp. 9–10), 'the financial loss from white-collar crime, great as it is, is less important than the damage to social relations. White-collar crime violates trust and therefore creates distrust; this lowers social morale and produces social disorganisation.' The global financial crisis, which began in 2008, has shown in stark terms the veracity of Sutherland's critique of white-collar crime, including the social disorganization it caused in Ireland, economically, socially and psychologically. It impacted the Probation Service (2013a) in terms of a reduction in budget allocations and the referral of high-profile, white-collar offenders to the service.

Against this backdrop, the authors examine how the Probation Service has been impacted and how recent developments represent pragmatic shifts in probation policies and priorities. The chapter will critique the Probation Service, in the context of privatization and managerialism where state services have to adopt more commercial management skills and work practices. It will discuss whether the service has been able to retain its relevance in the criminal justice system.

Probation in Ireland

Probation in Ireland has its origins in a relatively small service with a handful of probation officers in the 1960s, operating exclusively in the Dublin Metropolitan District Court (O'Dea, 2002; McNally, 2009). Since the mid-1980s, it has undergone numerous reviews (Whitaker, 1985; Department of Justice, 1994; McCarthy, 1999). Today, the Probation Service (2007a) represents a large organization that employs over 500 staff. It has a professional hierarchy of personnel – deputy, deputy directors, assistant principals, senior probation officers and probation officers. Probation services are offered in a variety of contexts, that is, courts, prisons and communities. According to the most recent Annual Report (Probation Service, 2013), probation officers worked nationwide, with 15,984 offenders in the community and 1,580 offenders in the prisons.

Probation is directly influenced by changing public attitudes to crime and political and economic considerations. The Irish Probation Service has undergone significant change in the past 30 years. Since 2007, the focus has been on developing a more managed bureaucratic service that has brought both losses and gains for the service, its personnel and service users. Recent public service agreements dictate developments within the service and provide the main rationale for realizing improved efficiencies, greater cost-effectiveness and value for money. Balancing the provision of good quality, professional services with economic principles presents many challenges. While the Probation Service continues to occupy a marginal position within the criminal justice system (O'Dea, 2002; McNally, 2009), a succession of government reports and policy initiatives represent expansion and developments that have taken place over time. *The Report of the Committee of Inquiry into the Penal System* (Whitaker, 1985) strongly recommended the use of more community-based sanctions and the use of prison only where danger and risk to the offender and the community was clearly identified. *The Management of Offenders: A Five Year Plan* (Department of Justice, 1994) reiterated these recommendations, advocated for an expanded Probation Service and the use of more community-based sanctions. Recently, a number of significant pieces of legislation were enacted by the Oireachtas. These served to extend and consolidate the role of the Probation Service as the designated authority for the administration and provision of community-based sanctions (Sex Offenders' Act 2001, Children Act 2001, Criminal Justice Act 2006, Criminal Justice (Community Service) Act 1983, 2011). Today, the Probation Service is a key player in the delivery of community-based services to offenders (Probation Service, 2007a, 2008a, 2012a, 2012b, 2013a, 2013b; Maguire and Carr, 2013).

As the largest provider of community-based services, researchers have argued that the work of the Probation Service is poorly understood outside the courts and indeed within the criminal justice system itself (McCarthy, 2011; Maguire and Carr, 2013). Furthermore, they argue that the development and growth of probation may be attributed to its survivalist strategies and its reflexivity, and because it has 'seen the adaption and adoption of various rationales – managerial, punitive, rehabilitative and (potentially) reparative' (Maguire and Carr, 2013, p. 4). Maguire and Carr (2013, p. 4) suggest that its survival may also be linked to a recognition of and willingness to respond to 'wider cultural and socio-political imperatives'.

Despite the political and economic challenges posed for probation in the 21st century (Healy and O'Donnell, 2005; Maguire and Carr, 2013; Robinson et al., 2013), the Irish Probation Service has developed far beyond its formative and historical links with the UK (O'Dea, 2002; McNally, 2009). Its close links with the Confederation of European Probation have been formative. The Confederation of European Probation was established in 1981 and campaigns for the development of community-based services for offenders, including probation, community service, mediation and conciliation. The authors will consider how the Probation Service has developed its profile as a previously poorly understood and little known service to become the largest provider of community-based sanctions in the state.

In 1907, when the Probation of Offenders Act was enacted, it provided the statutory basis for probation supervision in Ireland and the UK. Although it has undergone a number of revisions in the UK, today the Act remains the primary legislation for probation supervision. It outlines the supervisory functions of the probation officer as 'advising, assisting and befriending' the offender. These supervisory duties provide a significant, if somewhat debated, point of reference for contemporary probation practice. As Vanstone (2004) acknowledges, the 'welfare' emphasis of the Act, as reflected in its use of the language 'help' and 'assistance', has over time exerted a formative, if at times contentious, influence on the work of the Probation Service.

Undoubtedly, probation has changed considerably since 1907. However, research undertaken with Irish probation officers in 2007 demonstrates a strong support for the more traditional values of help and welfare that is captured in the content and spirit of the 1907 Probation of Offenders Act (Halton, 2007). Recently, the mission of the Irish Probation Service was clearly articulated by Vivian Geiran, its director (Probation Service, 2012a):

> continuing to deliver on our strategic goals of reducing reoffending and victimisation, promoting supervised community sanctions, providing alternatives to custody, further strengthening our interagency and partnership working, and enhancing our organisational capability to do this.

Ideas of community building, public protection and crime prevention through challenging offenders' behaviour and promoting the identification and use of community-based sanctions have gained international acceptance in probation circles (van Kalmthout and Derks, 2000).

Moreover, recent changes to Irish probation policy and legislation reflect the increased emphasis on public protection and victimization, with consequent changes to definitions and understandings of probation officers' roles and responsibilities (Healy and O'Donnell, 2005).

In 2006, the Probation and Welfare Service was rebranded as the Probation Service, resulting in a change in focus and direction for the service. At this time, the needs of individual offenders came to be considered alongside community interests and economic efficiencies (McNally, 2009). Welfare principles competed with justice principles: the former linked probation intervention to rehabilitation and reform, the latter to principles that carry a more retributive and punitive emphasis. These changes in ideology and mission were not specific to Ireland. They represented a change in focus and direction for probation services worldwide (van Kalmthout and Derks, 2000; Smith, 2005).

The Probation Service in Ireland is located within the Department of Justice and Equality and this positioning has had a formative influence on its progress and development to date. Probation practice is constructed and practised within a criminal justice system where dominant discourses of law and penal policy exert a direct influence. Unlike other professionals working in the criminal justice system, probation officers are dependent on criminal justice personnel for their clientele. They work in the court system where the judiciary has primary responsibility for protecting the interests of the wider citizenry. While in certain situations, judges are obliged to seek the assistance of the Probation Service in the preparation of pre-sentence reports, ultimately, they retain sole decision-making responsibility for placing offenders on probation (Sex Offenders' Act 2001, Children Act 2001, Criminal Justice Act 2006, Criminal Justice (Community Service) Act 1983, 2011). Probation officers who work in the court system act in an advisory capacity to the judiciary at the point of sentencing. When reporting back to the court, they do not act solely on behalf of the offender, they are charged with responsibility for balancing the needs of the offender with wider public interests. Their work often involves mediating complex and sometimes contradictory concepts, that is, of 'care' and 'control', 'welfare' and 'justice', 'punishment' and 'rehabilitation'.

Probation work involves the application of a diversity of knowledge and skills. Probation officers are required to work within clearly articulated ethical boundaries that are guided by recognized professional values. In contrast with the UK, the majority of Irish probation officers are professionally qualified social workers (Probation Service, 2007a; Halton, 2007). In Ireland, social work provides an important theoretical and practice lens from which to review developments in probation discourse, policy and practice. For the most part, probation officers are guided by the ethics and values of their profession, as articulated by the Irish Association of Social Workers (IASW, n.d.) and the Social Work Registration Board (n.d.). Research demonstrates that tensions do exist in the focus and representation of the Probation Service, between the more traditional humanistic reference of its social work personnel, the more community justice reference of probation policies (Halton, 2007), and the dominance of what Kilcommins (2000) refers to as a culture of control within penal discourse. Social workers in the service are challenged personally and professionally to find ways of practising that are in accordance with the ethics and values of the profession (social work), while still attending to designated roles and responsibilities and continuing to practise within the highly politicized criminal justice domain.

The influence of managerialism

Working in the criminal justice system, probation officers are continually reminded of the constraints placed on their professional autonomy. Jones (2001) states that social workers and probation officers increasingly are working within domains where professional autonomy is monitored and restricted by bureaucratic requirements. In addition, organizational structures place policy, legislative and financial constraints around the construction of professional roles and responsibilities. It is hardly surprising that in everyday probation practice, conflicts of priorities and objectives between service users, managers and professionals can arise, resulting in ambiguity and uncertainty around definitions of roles and responsibilities (Halton, 2007).

Traditionally, probation officers focused their interventions on working with offenders and their families, using practices that stressed 'relationship building', and 'individual casework' (Vanstone, 2004; Smith, 2005; Healy and O'Donnell, 2005). More recently, the growing popularity of implementing value for money practices presents a formidable challenge to the more traditional help and welfare emphases of the Probation Service (2012a, 2013a). New practice developments in probation reflect a change in service emphasis: priority is now given to the development of evidence-based practice, the production of empirical research and the application of risk assessment instruments with all offenders (van Kalmthout and Derks, 2000; Probation Service, 2007a, 2012a, 2013a; McNally, 2009; Maguire and Carr, 2013). On an organizational level, demands for increased public accountability have resulted in practices and protocols that are designed to closely monitor professional activity. Consequently, bureaucratic structures have emerged to help standardize and regulate professional practice (Robinson et al., 2013). These practice changes can be linked to a wider public demand for the exercise of greater managerial control over the activities of professionals. The increased emphasis on managerial power in public services, represented by developments in the structure and organization of the Probation Service, can also be attributed to a wider process of deprofessionalization. The latter has been criticized by professional practitioners and researchers alike. According to Thompson (2003, p. 172), this movement was 'associated with attempts to reduce the autonomy and professional standing of social workers', and resulted in what Winter et al. (1999, p. 193) term the devaluation and deskilling of professionals. Today, many professionals, including probation officers, have experienced a significant reduction in their discretionary powers that has impacted the form and content of their intervention practices with offenders (Coulshed and Mullender, 2001; Halton, 2007).

The probation literature explores the ambivalence and unease associated with probation officers' attempts at balancing the conflicting care and control functions of their work (Raynor and Vanstone, 2002; Innes, 2003; Vanstone, 2004). Evidence-based practice and research and, in particular, cognitive behavioural programmes are gaining in popularity in probation (Probation Service, 2007a, 2012a, 2012b, 2013a, 2013b). Writing on evidence-based practice, Trotter (2006), while acknowledging its important contribution, has warned against an overreliance on this form of research because many issues familiar to social workers and probation officers are not easily measured, that is, self-esteem, social justice and empowerment. It is generally acknowledged that researching practice outcomes is desirable in terms of supporting practice improvement and practitioner development. However, finding appropriate ways of measuring outcomes that do justice to the work of probation and social work poses a real challenge to practitioners and researchers. Efforts on the part of the Probation Service to respond to these challenges are represented in recent reports and documents (Probation Service, 2007a, 2012a, 2012b, 2013a, 2013b).

A significant challenge for the Probation Service as it moves into the 21st century lies in its ability to reconcile some of the traditional values of welfare and care, on which probation practice was founded, with a more contemporary penal discourse, where issues of justice and control dominate (Kilcommins et al., 2004). The current focus in probation, on forging a strong professional identity within the criminal justice system, by developing and supporting collaborative partnerships within community-based initiatives, is certainly reflected in contemporary probation documents (Probation Service, 2007a, 2012a, 2012b, 2013a, 2013b). These documents highlight the service's efforts to work alongside other criminal justice services and personnel in promoting change. Recent developments in the Probation Service have undoubtedly helped to shape the form that probation has taken and continues to take. In the past 30 years, Irish probation services have grown and developed in line with international best practice. Recent service developments reflect its efforts to develop a strong professional identity within the criminal justice system, promote ongoing partnerships with community-based programmes, and work alongside other organizations and professionals to support the ideals of offender integration and reintegration (Probation Service, 2007a, 2012a, 2012b, 2013a, 2013b).

Developments in probation

Community service

The Criminal Justice (Community Service) Act 1983 was the first piece of legislation since the Probation Act of 1907 that gave probation officers responsibility for the supervision of offenders in the community. The Act empowers a court to substitute a community service order for a prison sentence for convicted offenders over 16 years. A community service order obliges the offender to perform unpaid work for a specified number of hours, commensurate with the seriousness of the offence, from a minimum of 40 to a maximum of 240 hours. The Probation Service manages, develops and evaluates community service projects throughout the state. Community service permits convicted offenders to make reparation for the damage they have done to the community. The benefits of community service to offenders and the community are well documented in research. The challenges presented in terms of its development and expansion as a sentencing option in the courts are also clearly identified (Walsh and Sexton, 1999; Kilcommins, 2000; Kilcommins et al., 2004; Trainor, 2010).

In 2011, the Criminal Justice (Community Service) Amendment Act was passed. This Act enhances the original provisions of the 1983 Act and encourages the increased use of community service by the courts, as an alternative to imprisonment. Launching the legislation, Alan Shatter, minister for justice and equality, said: 'This Act will address those concerns that the sanction of community services orders is not being sufficiently used by our courts in the sentencing of offenders' (Department of Justice and Equality, 2011). In 2008, at the beginning of the economic downturn, 1,385 community service orders were made (Probation Service, 2008b). In 2012, 2,569 orders were made and in 2013, 2,354 orders were made (Probation Service, 2012a, 2013a).

Community Return Programme

Like all areas of Irish society, the criminal justice system was negatively affected by the economic downturn in 2008. The building of the super prison, Thornton Hall in North County Dublin, to accommodate 2,200 prisoners was deferred indefinitely. The increasing number of prisoners leading to overcrowding in the existing prisons and the 'increase in the number of prisoners granted temporary release' (Thornton Hall Review Group, 2011, p. i) had prompted Alan Shatter, minister for justice and equality, to commission a review of the prison system. The Thornton Hall Review Group Report was published in July 2011, and stated that: 'we are of the view that there is scope within the prison system to introduce a form of structured *"earned release"* for suitable offenders so as to encourage active engagement by prisoners in rehabilitation and progression, prior to release into the community' (p. iii). Thus began a process that led to a more formal structured cooperation between the Irish Prison Service and the Probation Service, resulting in the establishment in 2011 of the Community Return Programme. Inevitably, this development, brought about by the economic downturn, placed increased pressure on the personnel and resources of the Probation Service. The Community Return Programme extends and develops the concept and use of community service by providing a structured framework whereby some prisoners may be released early into the community. This scheme is a collaborative strategy between the Probation Service, the Irish Prison Service and is supported by the Department of Justice and Equality. During 2013, a total of 396 offenders had completed their supervised community return time and the scheme had a 90% compliance rate (Probation Service, 2013a). It is too early to comment on the success of this initiative in terms of helping to combat recidivism; however, early signs in terms of compliance rates are positive.

Sex offenders

Sex offending commands a high media profile everywhere. Society generally, interest groups and communities increasingly demand that offenders, especially high-risk offenders, do not pose any danger to public safety. Sex offenders are the most high-profile offender population and the Probation Service

has had to develop and implement specialized training for probation officers, new supervision practices and intervention strategies to address the issues
presented by this particular group of offenders. Beginning in 1885 with the
Offences against the Persons Act, there has been a raft of legislation in Ireland
governing a variety of sexual assaults. However, the Sex Offenders Act 2001
introduced many new provisions not included in previous legislation, notably:

- A notification system, which requires sex offenders to notify the Gardaí
  where they are living within seven days of their conviction or on their
  release from prison.

- A post-release supervision order whereby the offender is subject to a
  period of statutory supervision by the Probation Service for a specific
  period of time on release from prison (Cotter et al., 2005, pp. 78–9).

It is within the context of the 2001 Sex Offenders Act that the Probation
Service (2007b) developed an assessment process, personal history compilation skills, effective community supervision, a set of goals leading to a new
non-offending personal identity, and an interagency cooperation strategy.
During 2013, there were 211 sex offenders subject to statutory supervision
orders. Wilson et al. (2013, p. 178) reflect:

> Twelve years after the enactment of the legislation, there are almost 1300 con-
> victed sex offenders subject to the requirement to notify with approximately 12%
> of these subject to probation supervision.

In reviewing the challenges posed by this particular group of offenders,
the Department of Justice, Equality and Law Reform established a High Risk
Offender Working Group in 2007, to examine how best to enhance the
management and supervision of sex offenders, in prison and in the community, especially those on post-release supervision by the Probation Service.
In 2009, the Probation Service and An Garda Síochána developed the Sex
Offender Risk Assessment and Management Model (SORAM), which began
as a pilot project in a number of selected areas and was launched nationally in May 2013. The SORAM model is similar to the Multi-Agency Public
Protection Arrangements introduced in England in 2003. It represents an
important development in the supervision and management of convicted
sex offenders in the community. SORAM has a dual objective, offender
rehabilitation and community safety. It is a structured, multiagency model
that ensures that appropriate and relevant information can be shared by
the relevant agencies – Probation Service, Prison Service, Gardaí and Health
Service Executive – thus providing a focused and individually tailored intervention strategy for each offender, supporting them in their effort to avoid
further offending.

Young Persons' Probation

The Report of the Committee of Inquiry into the Penal System (Whitaker, 1985) outlined its analysis of juvenile delinquency and pointed to a new way forward for juvenile justice practice in Ireland. In considering the principal factors that contributed to juvenile crime – parental neglect, unemployment, abuse of drugs and alcohol, and homelessness – it recommended (Whitaker, 1985, pp. 79–80):

- As far as possible juvenile offenders should be kept out of the criminal justice system.

- Juveniles should only be placed in detention where they are a danger to themselves or society and all non-custodial interventions have been tried.

It was not until the enactment of the Children Act 2001, amended by the Criminal Justice Act 2006, that community sanctions rather than punishment and detention were given the force of law. Under the Act, statutory agencies, including the Probation Service, were given responsibility for the delivery of a number of community-based sanctions for young offenders: 'The Act introduces the principle of minimum intervention and prevention (Blake, 2007) which necessarily implies decisions being made regarding prediction of future risk' (O'Leary and Halton, 2009, p. 97). Young Persons' Probation, a specialized division of the Probation Service, was established in 2006 and works closely with the Irish Youth Justice Service, developing and enacting community-based rehabilitation programmes. Under section 99 of the Children Act 2001 (pp. 67–8), the court is now obliged to seek a probation officer's report when considering a community sanction, detention or detention and supervision.

Two factors are applied in managing young offenders under the Children Act 2001:

1. *Assessment:* Young Persons' Probation provides pre-sanction assessment reports to the court on young offenders found guilty of an offence. The assessment involves the use of a risk assessment instrument. A research study (O'Leary and Halton, 2009, p. 109) evaluating the use of the Youth Level of Service/Case Management Inventory (YLS/CMI) in probation practice in Ireland found that 'the YLS/CMI is a useful addition to clinical practice by providing a consistent and approximate measure of likelihood of reoffending'.

2. *Family conferences:* The court can order the Probation Service to convene a family conference, which has as its objective the diversion of young

people away from custody, stresses the importance of the victim being heard, and highlights the role of parents in supporting their child to desist from future offending.

The Children Act 2001 is clearly having an impact on juvenile justice practice; in 2012, the courts made 888 supervision orders involving young people (Probation Service, 2012a).

Restorative justice

The concept of restorative justice in the criminal justice system is relatively new to Ireland, although it has been an integral part of how particular crimes are dealt with in other jurisdictions like the UK. Within the context of restorative justice, the offender accepts responsibility for the offence, the victim's victimization, and personal needs are explicitly recognized. Furthermore, the community benefits because the damage done has been repaired within the community itself. There are many definitions of restorative justice, but all reflect its belief in encouraging dialogue between the offender and the victim that ensures that the offender is made accountable for their behaviour. The victim can achieve a level of satisfaction not possible in more orthodox criminal justice procedures. However, it must be kept in mind that the dialogue is primarily between the offender and the victim. As Russell (2010, p. 125) states:

> the journey from the margins of community life into the centre as a contributing active member will not be achieved solely by building bridges between offenders and probation professionals (trained people), regardless of how skilled those professionals may be.

The increase in the prison population has resulted in a renewed impetus for reform of the criminal justice system, including the introduction of a restorative justice strategy. In 2006, two restorative justice projects were developed in Tallaght, County Dublin and Nenagh, County Tipperary. In March 2007, a National Commission on Restorative Justice was established by Michael McDowell, minister for justice, equality and law reform. He commented (Department of Justice, Equality and Law Reform, 2007):

> Restorative justice puts the victims at the centre of the process. I want to see how it can be extended in Ireland with appropriate structures and a sound funding base.

The National Commission on Restorative Justice (2009) published its final report in 2009, a year after the economic collapse in Ireland, thus ensuring that the availability of funding for the establishment of a national restorative justice system would not be forthcoming and that any extension of restorative justice would proceed piecemeal. In 2010, a restorative justice project for young offenders on probation was established in Limerick under the management of Le Chéile, an agency funded by the Probation Service to provide a mentoring service for young people and their parents, and in cooperation with the Probation Service. The primary aim of the programme was to reduce the level of youth crime and antisocial behaviour in the city. A report, *Building Bridges* (Quigley et al., 2014), outlines the benefits of the programme for young offenders, victims and the wider community. While the Probation Service (2013c) published its strategy document, *Repairing the Harm: A Victim Sensitive Response to Offending* in 2013, the incorporation of restorative justice for all offenders into a more nuanced, targeted, multilayered criminal justice system has not yet taken place because of the effects of the recession on the public finances.[1]

Risk assessment

Risk assessment became an integral part of probation practice (Bracken, 2010) because of the perceived deficiencies in clinical knowledge to competently and accurately determine the level of risk posed by offenders' behaviour to themselves and others in a multiplicity of settings. The development and application of risk assessment instruments is now an integral part of much probation practice. The level of risk posed by an offender determines the level and intensity of supervision that any one person will receive, ensuring that scarce resources are deployed differentially towards those who would most benefit.

Probation officers work with involuntary clients who are mandated by the courts to become involved with the Probation Service or other criminal justice agencies. Undoubtedly, the process of assessment and supervision demands a professional ability to positively engage with the offender, especially by accepting the offender as an individual. Writing on assessment, Healy (2012) identifies two purposes for assessment – the assessment of individual needs and strengths, and the assessment of individual risk.

Risk assessment instruments are now an integral part of the offender assessment process completed by probation officers. The LSI-R (Level of Service Inventory-Revised) is the instrument applied to general cases and is therefore the most widely used. It is a combined risk and needs assessment tool. The assessment, frequently carried out within the context of a pre-sentence report to the court, provides the basis on which an intervention/supervision plan is developed and outlined to the court.

In probation, risk assessment tools are primarily used to assess the risk of future offending. In this context, it is important to be mindful that: 'Research consistently points to the need to work with client definitions of problems and goals with both voluntary and involuntary clients' (Trotter, 2006, p. 27). Over the past 10 years, the Probation Service has gradually introduced assessment tools to support and enhance its assessment work, not only to determine the risk of an offender reoffending but to design a supervision strategy to achieve that goal. However, Healy (2012, p. 99) warns that it is important to 'ensure that such assessment tools are used to assist in the decision making process rather than replacing the views of service providers and service users in the assessment process'. The collaborative aspect of risk assessment, which involves the use of an assessment instrument, ensures that, rather than using it as a checklist exercise, it is expanded with a collaborative undertaking (between client and probation officer) by the application of the skills of listening and judicious questioning. Researchers support the use of risk assessment tools as part of a process of intervention that involves offender participation and attention to motivational concerns (Robinson, 2003; Doel and Shardlow, 2005).

Conclusion

Since the word 'probation' was first introduced in Ireland at the beginning of the last century, it was regarded for many decades as the Cinderella of the criminal justice system, used sparingly in the courts. Today, the Probation Service is actively involved with other organizations in helping to refocus and reshape penal discourse. It is committed to researching and evaluating probation practice and has recently gathered empirical evidence that demonstrates that, while retribution will always be part of sentencing in the courts, there is a benefit to society in a criminal justice system that supports the application of community-based services across a wide spectrum of offending behaviours (Probation Service, 2012b, 2013b).

Robinson (2003) is critical of developments that have resulted in the essential principles of probation and social work practice being undermined by the adoption of managerialist ideology and practices. Undoubtedly, the current hierarchical structure of the Irish Probation Service, which increasingly focuses on management by objectives, has resulted in a changed and challenged Probation Service. The emphasis on solving administrative and organizational challenges through resource management and its allied corporate language has given probation managers a more central role in determining the objectives of probation. Consequently, the influence of practitioners and service users has been reduced and managerialism, with its emphasis on quality control, objective setting and time management, has come to dominate.

Theoretical developments and increases in the knowledge base of those working in the helping professions, coupled with economic downturns in the 1980s and 90s, has brought reduced funding to public services and attendant changes to the way public services are delivered. In 2012, the Probation Service budget provision was €40,171 million, but in 2013, this was reduced to €38,119 million, representing a decrease of more than €2 million (Probation Service, 2013a). Service documents represent these reductions in terms of cost savings. However, it would indeed be interesting to discover how these savings are reflected in terms of the quality and content of service provision, something that is difficult to ascertain from service documents and reports.

The authors have drawn on the literature and Probation Service publications to outline developments over time in probation in Ireland. This chapter highlights the changes that have taken place in the service in recent times. It draws attention to the some of the ideological and practice challenges facing professional social workers/probation officers in their efforts to forge a strong professional identity within the criminal justice system. Attention has been drawn to many of the complexities associated with attempts to reconcile professional and organizational tensions associated with the Probation Service's public service identity and its location within the criminal justice system. On a professional level, maintaining the professionalism of social work, which represents the core identity of the majority of probation officers, is important. However, continued efforts to define probation must be balanced against the possibility that such debates could lead to an undermining of its role in the criminal justice system and a weakening of its position among other criminal justice personnel. Many of the organizational challenges referred to in this chapter relate to resourcing issues, which result from continuing austerity measures that threaten the humanistic traditions on which probation and social work were founded. In a political climate where economic expediency takes precedence, principles of welfare are undermined, making it increasingly difficult for probation officers to retain their professional affiliation with social work and its central mission to work towards achieving social justice and inclusion for all. It is significant that in the recently published Criminal Justice (Community Sanctions) Bill 2014, it is recommended that all probation officers be registered with the Social Work Registration Board. This development appears to represent a firm commitment on the part of government to preserving the traditional link with social work and its values. This link is reflected by Vivian Geiran (2011), director of the Probation Service, when he states that probation has always maintained its link to its fundamental core and values – in the first instance, to help people to do something better, and in the case of probation work, to make good for the wrong they have done and become better and more positively contributing citizens.

Note

1. Vivian Geiran announced in May 2015 that the restorative justice scheme will be developed on a nationwide basis, coinciding with the emergence of the country from the worst effects of the recession.

References

Bracken, D. (2010) 'Differing conceptions of risk and need in Irish probation officers', *Irish Probation Journal*, 7, 108–18.

Cotter, A., Doyle, U. and Linnane, P. (2005) 'Sex Offender's Act 2001: implications for the Probation and Welfare Service, policy and practice', *Irish Probation Journal*, 2(1), 78–83.

Coulshed, V. and Mullander, A. (2001) *Management in Social Work*, 2nd edn, Basingstoke, Palgrave.

Department of Justice (1994) *The Management of Offenders: A Five Year Plan*, Dublin, Stationery Office.

Department of Justice and Equality (2011) Commencement of Criminal Justice (Community Service) (Amendment) Act 2011, press release.

Department of Justice, Equality and Law Reform (2007) 'National Commission on Restorative Justice Established', press release.

Doel, M. and Shardlow, S. (2005) *Modern Social Work Practice: Teaching and Learning in Practice Settings*, Farnham, Ashgate.

Geiran, V. (2011) 'Defining what we do: the meaning of "supervision" in Probation', *Irish Probation Journal*, 8, 6–27.

Halton, C. (2007) Making Sense of Probation: Changing Contexts and Constructions of Probation Practice in Ireland, unpublished PhD, University College Cork.

Healy, D. and O'Donnell, I. (2005) 'Probation in the Republic of Ireland: contexts and challenges', *Probation Journal*, 52(1), 56–8.

Healy, K. (2012) *Social Work Methods and Skills: The Essential Foundations of Practice*, Basingstoke, Palgrave Macmillan.

IASW (Irish Association of Social Workers) (n.d.) *Code of Ethics*, www.iasw.ie/attachments/8b37e75a-26f6-4d94-9313-f61a86785414.PDF.

Innes, M. (2003) *Understanding Social Control*, Buckingham, Open University Press.

Jones, C. (2001) 'Voices from the front line: state social workers and New Labour', *British Journal of Social Work*, 31(4), 547–62.

Kilcommins, S. (2000) 'Cultural determinates and penal practices: an analysis of the introduction of community service orders', *Mountbatten Journal of Legal Studies*, 4, 20–54.

Kilcommins, S., O'Donnell, I., O'Sullivan, E. and Vaughan, B. (2004) *Crime, Punishment and the Search for Order in Ireland*, Dublin, Irish Institute of Public Administration.

McCarthy, B. (1999) *Final Report of the Expert Group on the Probation and Welfare Service*, Dublin, Department of Justice Equality and Law Reform.

McCarthy, S. (2011) 'Perceptions of restorative justice in Ireland: the challenges of the way forward', *Irish Probation Journal*, 8, 185–99.

McNally, G. (2009) 'Probation in Ireland, Part 2: the modern age, 1960s to 2000', *Irish Probation Journal*, 6, 187–228.

Maguire, N. and Carr, N. (2013) 'Changing shape and shifting boundaries: the media portrayal of probation in Ireland', *European Journal of Probation*, 5(3), 3–23.

National Commission on Restorative Justice (2009) *Final Report*, Dublin, Department of Justice, Equality and Law Reform.

O'Dea, P. (2002) 'The probation and welfare service: its role in criminal justice', in O'Mahony, P. (ed.) *Criminal Justice in Ireland*, Dublin, Institute of Public Administration.

O'Leary, P., and Halton, C. (2009) 'Young Persons' Probation in the Republic of Ireland: an evaluation of risk assessment', *Irish Probation Journal*, 6, 97–112.

Probation Service (2007a) *A Century of Change, Challenge and Service, Annual Report 2007*, Dublin, Probation Service.

Probation Service (2007b) The Management and Supervision of Sexual Offenders: A Practical Guide for Probation Officers, unpublished, Probation Service, Dublin.

Probation Service (2008a) *Strategy Statement 2008-2010*, Dublin, Probation Service.

Probation Service (2008b) *Annual Report 2008*, Dublin, Probation Service.

Probation Service (2012a) *Annual Report 2012*, Dublin, Probation Service.

Probation Service (2012b) *Probation Service Recidivism Study 2007–2011*, Dublin, Probation Service.

Probation Service (2013a) *Reduce Re-offending to Create Safer Communities, Annual Report 2013*, Dublin, Probation Service.

Probation Service (2013b) *Probation Service Recidivism Study 2008–2013*, Dublin, Probation Service.

Probation Service (2013c) *Restorative Justice Strategy. Repairing the Harm: A Victim Sensitive Response to Offending*, Dublin, Probation Service.

Quigley, M., Martynowicz, A. and Gardner, C. (2014) *Building Bridges: An Evaluation and Social Return on Investment Study of the Le Chéile Restorative Justice Project in Limerick*, Limerick, Le Chéile.

Raynor, P. and Vanstone, M. (2002) *Understanding Community Penalties: Probation, Policy and Social Change*, Maidenhead, Open University Press.

Robinson, G. (2003) 'Technicality and indeterminacy in probation practice: a case study', *British Journal of Social Work*, 33(5), 593–610.

Robinson, G., McNeill, F. and Maruna, S. (2013) 'Punishment in society: the improbable persistence of probation and other community sanctions and measures', in Simon, J. and Sparks, R. (eds) *The Sage Handbook of Punishment and Society*, London, Sage.

Russell, C. (2010) 'Making the case for an ASSET Based Community Development (ABCD) approach to probation: from reformation to transformation', *Irish Probation Journal*, 7, 119– 32.

Smith, D. (2005) 'Probation and social work', *British Journal of Social Work*, 35(5), 621–37.

Social Work Registration Board (n.d.) *Code of Conduct*, www.swrb.govt.nz/complaints/code-of-conduct.

Sutherland, E.H. (1949) *White Collar Crime*, New York, Holt, Reinhart & Winston.

Thompson, N. (2003) *Promoting Equality*, Basingstoke, Palgrave Macmillan.

Thornton Hall Review Group (2011) *Report of the Thornton Hall Project Review Group*, Department of Justice and Equality.

Trainor, M. (2010) 'Tackling graffiti in South County Dublin: the community service response to a community problem', *Irish Probation Journal*, 7, 152–60.

Trotter, C. (2006) *Working with Involuntary Clients: A Guide to Practice*, Sydney, Allen & Unwin.

Van Kalmthout, A.M. and Derks, J.T. (eds) (2000) *Probation and Probation Services: A European Perspective*, Nijmegen, Wolf Legal.

Vanstone, M. (2004) *Supervising Offenders in the Community: A History of Probation Theory and Practice*, Aldershot, Ashgate.

Walsh, D. and Sexton, P. (1999) *An Empirical Study of Community Service Orders in Ireland*, Dublin, Stationery Office.

Whitaker, T.K. (1985) *Report of the Committee of Inquiry into the Penal System*, Whitaker Report, Dublin, Stationery Office.

Wilson, M., McCann. J. and Templeton, R. (2013) 'SORAM: towards a multi-agency model of Sex Offender Risk Assessment and Management', *Irish Probation Journal*, 10, 177–92.

Winter, R., Buck, A. and Sobiechowska, P. (1999) *Professional Experience and the Investigative Imagination: The Art of Reflective Writing*, London, Routledge.

12

Substance Misuse and Social Work in Ireland: Must Do Better?

Shane Butler and Hilda Loughran

Introduction

In light of this book's overall focus on changes and continuities in the issues dealt with by social workers, we begin this chapter on substance misuse by briefly reviewing levels and patterns of psychoactive drug use in Ireland over recent decades. Starting with alcohol, the obvious continuity is that, as the cliché has it, alcohol is still our favourite drug: a legal commodity that is consumed by a majority of Irish adults, regardless of age, gender and social class. There have, however, been significant changes in our drinking habits, the most remarkable being that, in recent decades, we have started to drink much more heavily than in the past. Irish drinking habits have been recently reviewed in the Department of Health's (2012) *Steering Group Report on a National Substance Misuse Strategy*, which noted that while consumption levels have dropped and stabilized from the unprecedented heights of the Celtic Tiger years, our consumption remains high in comparative international terms. The fact that the 'average Irish adult drank 11.9 litres of pure alcohol in 2010' meant that 'adults in 2010 were still drinking more than twice the average amount of alcohol consumed per adult in 1960' (Department of Health, 2012, p. 7). Furthermore, while this average per capita consumption statistic is accepted by international public health researchers (Babor et al., 2010) as being a useful marker of the prevalence of alcohol-related problems in any given society, its application to Ireland – a country with an unusually high proportion of abstainers, with as many as 20% of the adult population abstinent or virtually abstinent (Ramstedt and Hope, 2005) – masks the true extent of heavy, problematic drinking by those adults who are regular drinkers. What also emerges with great clarity is that Irish drinkers are especially prone to heavy episodic or 'binge' drinking, a pattern of consumption where drinkers may abstain for four or five days of the week while consuming large amounts of alcohol at weekends, with all the health and behavioural problems attendant on this style of consumption. A further recent change in Irish drinking habits noted in the Steering Group Report (Department of Health, 2012) is the increase in the purchasing of alcohol from supermarkets and off-licences and the concomitant decline in pub drinking. Following the abolition of the Groceries Order in 2006, it became legally permissible for supermarkets and smaller grocery businesses to sell alcohol below cost as a 'loss leader', thereby providing the drinking public with a cheaper product than had previously been available. From a somewhat longer historic perspective, it is noteworthy that Irish women, while continuing to consume less than their male counterparts, have now become regular and, in many cases, heavy drinkers in a way that would have been unconscionable in the mid-20th century. This increased alcohol consumption among Irish women has been reflected in increased alcohol-related morbidity in general health terms and in relation to drinking during pregnancy (Mongan et al., 2007).

Although the use of illicit drugs in Ireland dates only from the late 1960s, it is by now – as in all developed countries – a well-established phenomenon. Drug prevalence surveys of the general population (e.g. National Advisory Committee on Drugs, 2012) show that illicit drug use is more common among younger people but also that the drugs most commonly used, particularly cannabis, are relatively low risk in health and behavioural terms. If we wish to know more about problematic drug use, we can best turn to the National Drug Treatment Reporting System, which, although formally initiated in 1990, built on earlier work by the Health Research Board throughout the 1980s (e.g. Bellerose et al., 2011). Perhaps the most significant and consistent finding from this stream of epidemiological research is that risky drug use, initially injecting heroin use and more recently polydrug use (the simultaneous use of a combination of psychoactive drugs, in which illicit drugs are mixed with alcohol and prescription drugs such as benzodiazepines), is not distributed randomly across the population but is closely related to socioeconomic deprivation.

Finally, we have some research on drug and alcohol problems among marginalized groups in Irish society. It is well documented, for instance, that such problems are a prominent feature of the lived experience of homeless people, but whether substance misuse is a cause or a consequence of homelessness remains a moot question (e.g. Mayock et al., 2008). Similarly, it has been noted over several decades that the prevalence of drug and alcohol problems is much higher among prisoners than the general population, but recent research has indicated some improvement in this regard and, in particular, a decline in the practice of injecting drug use among prisoners (Drummond et al., 2014). While there is no research to indicate how ethnic minorities in Ireland fare with regard to substance misuse, research has consistently suggested that the Traveller community has a high prevalence of alcohol problems and an established, if as yet unquantified, problem associated with illicit drug use (All Ireland Traveller Health Study Team, 2010).

Social work and substance misuse

In its third and final research publication on *Social Work Posts in Ireland*, the National Social Work Qualifications Board (NSWQB, 2006, p. 13) reported that, between 1999 and 2005, there had been an increase of 131% in social work posts specifically dedicated to 'addiction'. Any impression that this increase was indicative of a major expansion of specialist addiction posts for Irish social workers would be immediately dispelled by a closer look at the absolute numbers to which this percentage refers. In fact, the statistics show that, in 1999, there were eight specialist addiction social work posts, which constituted just 0.6% of the total number of social work posts in the country at this time; by 2005, this had risen to 18.5 posts or 0.82% of all Irish social work posts. As of June 2014, it appears that there are just six specialist addiction social work posts in Ireland, five at the Health Service Executive's (HSE) National Drug Treatment Centre in Dublin and one in the voluntary drug treatment system. The HSE's specialist addiction service has evolved since the early 1980s and is currently linked managerially to the general provision of 'social inclusion' services. Outside the National Drug Treatment Centre, this service opted to employ addiction counsellors rather than social workers, and Butler (2011) reported that, in 2009, there were 158 addiction counsellors employed directly in the HSE addiction service.

This is not to say, however, that the vast majority of professional social workers in Ireland do not regularly encounter alcohol and drug problems in their caseloads; and commonsense and anecdotal evidence – perhaps not always backed up as much as it might be by valid and reliable statistical data – suggests that, across all settings in which they are employed, Irish social workers constantly deal with such problems.

If, for instance, we look at statutory social work with children and families – undoubtedly the single biggest source of employment for Irish social workers and, since the beginning of 2014, operating from a new Child and Family Agency outside its previous base in the HSE – it seems clear that substance misuse impinges significantly on the child welfare and protection concerns of these social workers. This occurs because children and adolescents are themselves prone to use psychoactive drugs problematically, but more commonly because parental substance misuse causes or contributes to children's problems. As part of a methodologically rigorous attempt to estimate the nature and scale of the risks posed to Irish children by parental drinking problems, Hope (2011, p. 7) pointed out the virtual impossibility of deriving any useful, national information on this topic from the child protection datasets published annually by the HSE, noting in a charitably understated criticism that: 'Validity and reliability issues are major limitations of the child protection data set'. However, focusing on the northwest where she conducted detailed research into this topic, she was in no doubt about the role played by substance misuse in child welfare concerns that were reported to the statutory authorities. Hope (2011, p. 38) concluded:

> The involvement of family drug/alcohol abuse as a primary reason for child welfare concerns was particularly high (almost one in every four cases) and increased between 2008 and 2009 [and] Donegal had the second highest level (one in twenty children) where the child abusing drugs/alcohol was the primary reason for the welfare concern.

The relaxation of the in camera rules governing family law cases promises to shed light on many previously obscure aspects of Irish childcare practice and, in her initial report on the *Child Care Law Reporting Project*, Coulter (2013) reported that in 18.6% of the first 333 cases studied the principal reasons given by the HSE for seeking a care order was parental alcohol or drug abuse. While it would be foolish to presume that the precise mechanisms whereby parental substance misuse puts children at risk are simple and readily understood, or that substance misuse generally operates independently of other risk factors, there has long been acceptance at international level (e.g. Forrester, 2000; Seay and Kohl, 2013) that, in epidemiological terms, parental substance misuse is a major contributory factor to the immediate and longer term welfare of children who grow up with such experiences.

In 2005, the Probation Service was, as it presumably still is, the second largest employer of Irish social workers. Whatever doubt may exist about the prevalence of substance misuse problems in the caseloads of child protection social workers, there has long been detailed and reliable evidence on this matter in relation to the work of the Probation Service within the wider criminal justice system. Most recently, the Probation Service (2012) conducted its own research on problem drinking and drug use in adult and young offenders on probation supervision in the community, reporting that 89% of a large sample of adult offenders had misused alcohol or drugs either in the past or currently, and 87% of offenders aged 20 years or less had misused drugs or alcohol or both (Probation Service, 2013).

Proceeding then on the basis that Irish social workers who are not defined as addiction specialists and who work across a wide range of human services continue to encounter clients experiencing drug and alcohol problems, our task for the remainder of this chapter is to attempt a critical review of the manner in which they engage with these problems. We will begin by focusing on changing conceptualizations of substance misuse over the past 30 years, with a view to understanding how national and international research and policy on this topic has challenged and altered our understanding of this phenomenon. And, in light of this review of what might be considered best practice or an evidence-based approach to health and social service management of substance misuse, we will conclude by looking at the reality of Irish social work practice and the obstacles to the implementation of best practice in this area.

Changing conceptualizations of substance misuse

It would be impossible to summarize all the research and policy developments that have occurred in relation to substance misuse over the past 30 years, so our ambition here is to identify some of the major shifts in thinking that have characterized the field over this period. These are changing conceptualizations that, in our view at least, have been of universal importance as well as specific relevance to the Irish social work scene. We should, of course, make it clear that in so doing, we are not adopting a positivistic biomedical approach, which would see developments in this area as reflecting scientific consensus and linear progress – characterized by greater understanding of causal factors, the use of more precise diagnostic systems, and the implementation of evidence-based treatment modalities. Neither, it should be said, do we subscribe to the view that public policy on psychoactive drug use is primarily a rational, evidence-based process. On the contrary, we approach this task from a critical, sociological perspective, taking it for granted that the field is highly contested and marked by conflicting value systems, which are unlikely to be resolved by developments in pharmacology or the neurosciences. On this basis, we regard attempts at problem definition and diagnosis (including the use of all conventional terminology such as 'substance misuse', 'addiction' and 'dependence') as social construction rather than the product of objective, value-free science (Reinarman, 2005; Room, 2011). Similarly, we see policy making in this area as an essentially political process, albeit one influenced in a somewhat limited and complex way by empirical research findings (Stevens and Ritter, 2013).

Bearing these caveats in mind, the three changing conceptualizations we have selected as being of most importance are:

1. A new appreciation of how environmental/contextual/setting factors shape individual drug-using choices, and how these factors can also contribute to the amelioration of problems arising from such drug use.

2. An understanding that personal motivation to change is a key element in successful 'recovery' from substance misuse, whether recovery be defined in terms of abstinence or harm reduction; but that personal motivation of this kind cannot be elicited or reinforced through the use of aggressively confrontational or punitive interventions with problem drug users.

3. An awareness that since drug-related problems vary in type and severity, not all these problems either need or will benefit from specialist addiction service intervention, and that there is much more scope for all health and social service professionals to play a constructive role with problem drug users than was hitherto believed.

The importance of setting

By coincidence, the 30-year period with which we are concerned began with the publication in 1984 of what is now considered a classic text in the addictions, Zinberg's (1984) *Drug, Set, and Setting.* Zinberg's thesis was that psychoactive drug use can only be fully understood through the use of a biopsychosocial model: that is, one which, while recognizing the importance of pharmacology (the *drug* component) or individual psychological (*set*) factors, is willing to accept the key role played by sociocultural, political and economic (or *setting*) factors in influencing people's choices to use particular drugs in a particular way. This ecological approach clearly challenged the tendency at this time to attribute drug problems solely to the evils inherent in drugs per se, and to suggest that the most beneficial policy approach was to create a drug-free world by waging a 'war on drugs'. Similarly, it challenged the view that problems were caused by individuals, randomly distributed in geographic and socioeconomic terms, who made foolish behavioural choices but who could be prevented from doing so by educational programmes that exhort them – in the words of Nancy Reagan, wife of the US President Ronald Reagan – to 'just say no'. A decade prior to this, the sociologist Lee Robins and colleagues (1974) had published research that challenged the notion of 'once an addict, always an addict' by demonstrating that the vast majority of American soldiers who had become addicted to heroin during the Vietnam War recovered from this addiction once they returned to their more salubrious home environments in the US. But Zinberg's work appeared to have a wider impact in terms of alerting researchers, policy makers and clinicians to the way in which drug problems were affected by the wider social context.

Even before Zinberg had published his book, Irish epidemiologists (Dean et al., 1983) who were studying the then new phenomenon of injecting heroin use in Dublin had concluded that such problem drug use had less to do with individual psychopathology than with the harshness of the inner-city environments in which this new phenomenon was mainly to be found. It was not until 1996, however, that the First Report of the Ministerial Task Force on Measures to Reduce the Demand for Drugs (1996) acknowledged this connection between social exclusion and problem drug use, and official policy finally conceded – in the form of Local Drugs Task Forces – that scarce preventive and treatment resources should be selectively targeted at socioeconomically deprived areas that had an identified high prevalence of injecting drug use. It may be argued that, in relation to alcohol, public health advocates have been arguing fruitlessly over a 30-year period that the prevalence of alcohol-related problems in Ireland can only be reduced through the implementation of environmental policies that challenge the normalization of heavy drinking. This, for instance, was the burden of the alcohol policy recommendations contained in *The Psychiatric Services: Planning for the Future* (Study Group on the Development of the Psychiatric Services, 1984), which unceremoniously abandoned the previous policy commitment to the individualistic 'disease concept of alcoholism', and over the succeeding three decades numerous health policy documents in this country have made similar recommendations but to little avail (Butler, 2009).

Motivation for change

In 1983, American psychologist William Miller (1983) published a seminal paper, 'Motivational interviewing with problem drinkers'. Over the subsequent three decades, the ideas presented in this paper have been developed and applied to a range of substance misuse problems under the rubric of motivational interviewing (MI); and outcome studies have generally found MI to be an effective counselling style for work with clients of this kind (Miller and Rollnick, 2013). The role of professionals who use this approach is to act as a catalyst or midwife to client-determined change, not – as might be the norm in medical or surgical situations – to be the active drivers of change in the lives of passive clients.

Essentially, MI is based on a belief that substance misusers make positive changes to their lives when they persuade themselves that they wish to change and that they are capable of change. In many ways, MI does not seem radically different from traditional ideas about casework or counselling to which social work students have always been exposed, but in Ireland in the early 1980s, it challenged much of the conventional wisdom of Irish addiction treatment. Specifically, it challenged the belief, endemic in other US imports to the Irish addiction treatment scene of this period, that addicts were clinically defined by the rigidity of their defence mechanisms, so that the only effective counselling styles with such clients were those that 'broke them down' through interpersonal confrontation. This, for instance, was the essence of the Minnesota Model (e.g. Johnson, 1973), which had gained considerable popularity among voluntary treatment agencies working with 'alcoholics' at this time; and beliefs of this kind also underpinned the work of the Coolmine Therapeutic Community, Ireland's first voluntary drug treatment centre, which had its origins in Synanon, a Californian residential treatment agency that openly advocated 'attack therapy' (Yablonsky, 1965) and eventually degenerated into a full-blown cult (Janzen, 2001).

Motivational interviewing took as its starting point the fact that there was no empirical evidence to support the view that substance misusers or addicts had any personality traits that distinguished them from other people, although research confirmed that – like other people – they reacted badly to being confronted. Generally, MI counsellors:

- reviewed the positive and negative consequences of psychoactive drug use with their clients

- elicited motivation to change by emphasizing that negatives outweighed the positives, while acknowledging that responsibility for change rested with the clients

- avoided pushing clients dogmatically towards any single option for change

- reinforced them in the view that they were capable of change.

All this was done empathically, eschewing anything that smacked of confrontation or punishment; and MI's emphasis on client self-efficacy also served to support and legitimate the movement towards harm reduction strategies within the wider addiction treatment sphere. The development and dissemination of MI was also important, in that it directly facilitated the third conceptual shift we have identified: namely, the view that there has been an excessive emphasis on the necessity for and value of specialist addiction treatment, and that generic professionals are capable of playing a much more useful role in working with substance misusers than was usually appreciated.

Involving generic professionals with substance misusers

The final conceptual shift arose from critical scrutiny of the mystique that had grown around specialist addiction treatment and its implicit suggestion that non-specialists were out of their professional depth when it came to working with substance misusers. In the UK, this conceptual shift gained impetus through the work of Shaw et al. (1978) on the Maudsley Alcohol Pilot Project. This research project, which was conducted in South

London, was aimed at exploring the potential for family doctors and other generic health and social service professionals to play a greater role in the management of problem drinkers than was the norm at this time. The publication of this research coincided with the discovery that official confidence in the value of specialist, intensive rehabilitation programmes was seriously misplaced, and that brief and relatively inexpensive community-based interventions – whether delivered by addiction specialists or generic workers – led to outcomes that were at least as good as those of intensive and expensive residential treatment systems (e.g. Orford and Edwards, 1977). Shaw et al. (1978) used role theory (specifically, the concepts of role legitimacy, role adequacy and role support) in devising a training framework they hoped would build 'therapeutic commitment' towards substance misusers by generic workers, and their work contributed to the expansion of community alcohol and drug services across the UK during the 1980s and 90s. It was not until a decade later that comparable policy work was initiated in the US with the publication of the Institute of Medicine's (1990) *Broadening the Base of Treatment for Alcohol Problems*, a report that clearly challenged the dominant role played by what one critic, Peele (1995), has described as that country's addiction 'treatment industry'.

In Ireland, official support for the notion that professionals (such as social workers) who were not addiction specialists could legitimately engage with these issues and were broadly adequate to do so if supported by management was slow to emerge. The mental health policy document, *The Psychiatric Services: Planning for the Future* (Study Group on the Development of the Psychiatric Services, 1984), was emphatic in its denunciation of the disease concept of alcoholism and in its recommendation that the routine practice of admitting problem drinkers into psychiatric hospitals and units should be radically scaled back; but it did not offer much support for expanding the work of generic professionals with substance misusers. It was not until well into the new millennium that official health policy in Ireland, drawing on the work of the British National Treatment Agency, explicitly proposed that health and social service responses to substance misuse should be based on a coherent model that recognized that, depending on the type and severity of the specific problem involved, all varieties and levels of human service professionals could play a useful role, and specialist and intensive interventions should not be considered unless or until generic or less intensive interventions had been tried and found wanting. This approach is commonly presented as a 'four-tier' model of response and was first endorsed by Irish policy makers in the *Report of the Working Group on Treatment of Under 18 Year Olds Presenting to Treatment Services with Serious Drug Problems* (Department of Health and Children/HSE, 2005) and then in the *Report of the HSE Working Group on Residential Treatment and Rehabilitation (Substance Abuse)* (HSE, 2007). The logic of this four-tier model would suggest, for instance, that a child protection social worker managing a case where a parental alcohol problem is the root cause of the childcare concerns should at least assess this problem and have an open mind to engaging directly with it, rather than automatically referring the parent to a specialist addiction service. Indeed, when combined with the previous emphasis on motivation, the four-tier model suggests that contrary to the view that the statutory child protection role is incompatible with playing a therapeutic role, this statutory role can add therapeutic leverage to the social worker's capacity to engage effectively with the parental alcohol problem. Similarly, it may be argued that a proba-tion officer's statutory authority adds therapeutic leverage to direct work with substance misusing offenders.

However coherent the four-tier model may be, it is clear that there are huge logistical difficulties in implementing a framework of this kind that depends for its success on the integration of such a wide range of public ser-vice and voluntary sector domains – all of which have traditionally operated as separate 'silos' (Rush, 2010).

Irish social work and substance misuse

On the face of it, it would seem that the three research and policy develop-ments we have reviewed are all broadly consonant with the general ethos of social work, in Ireland and elsewhere. We could, indeed, go further and argue that social work offers the ideal professional ethos for societal responses to substance misuse. As Specht and Courtney (1994) point out, the emphasis on setting was an integral element of early social work theory when, at the beginning of the 20th century, Mary Richmond explicitly promoted the idea of social work as a distinctive form of practice that would focus on 'person in environment'. Later developments that conceptualize such forms of practice in terms of ecology or systems (e.g. Germain, 1979) may be seen as con-tinuing this insistence that individual problems can only be understood and remedied when viewed in an environmental context. Similarly, the refine-ment of the concept of motivation as a critical factor in understanding positive change in problem drinkers and drug users is one that could expect to find general favour among social workers. Specifically, a counselling approach like motivational interviewing – with its de-emphasis on labelling clients as 'alcoholics' or 'addicts', and its insistence on clients' capacity to change if they wish to do so – overlaps considerably with social work's 'strengths perspective' and its disinclination to focus on diagnostic labels and deficits (Saleebey, 1997; Rapp and Goscha, 2012). And, finally, the idea that manag-ing substance misuse should be a shared responsibility across a range of types and levels of human services rather than the sole responsibility of specialist addiction services would seem to fit with the overall commitment to generic social work in Ireland and the UK in the post-Seebohm era.

It should also be noted that, in recent years, academic social work, in Ireland and elsewhere, has explicitly taken up and promoted various aspects of these conceptual developments: demonstrating, for instance, how motivational interviewing can be integrated into child protection and welfare practice (Hohman et al., 2005; Hohman, 2012) and generally legitimating work with alcohol and drug problems as part of the 'business' of social work outside the specialist addiction sphere (Walsh, 2013).

There is, however, no indication that Irish social work has in any coherent or systematic way taken up these ideas or, outside the handful of social workers employed in specialist addiction agencies, manifested any sustained therapeutic commitment to engaging directly with problem drinkers and drug users. On the contrary, it would seem impressionistically as though Irish social workers who are not addiction specialists routinely and immediately opt to refer identified substance misusers to specialist addiction services, without first attempting to engage directly with these issues themselves. In seeking to explain this, it is still helpful to invoke Shaw et al.'s (1978) framework, which identified three main impediments to the development of such therapeutic commitment by non-addiction specialists to working with clients of this kind:

1. *Role legitimacy:* This suggests to us that Irish social workers may still operate on the basis of internalized assumptions that substance misuse or addiction are the proper domain of the specialist, and that engagement with such issues is not a legitimate professional activity for social workers who are not addiction specialists.

2. *Role adequacy:* This suggests that Irish social workers who are not employed as addiction specialists may still be intimidated by the mystique of addiction specialism, believing that, as generalists, they simply lack the necessary degree of knowledge and skill that would make them adequate to engage with clients with these difficulties.

3. *Role support:* This sensitizes us to the importance of organizational and professional support for generic workers in relation to their engagement with problem drinkers and drug users. Put simply, even when generic workers are persuaded that it is legitimate to engage directly with their clients' substance misuse issues and that their existing knowledge and skill bases are broadly adequate for this task, they are unlikely to incorporate this into day-to-day practice unless supported or encouraged to do so by wider management systems.

It is this final concept of role support that seems most helpful in allowing us to understand how and why Irish social work has not become more energetically and consistently involved in direct work with substance misuse issues. Regardless of the conceptual developments we have reviewed and with which, it seems reasonable to assume, social work students have been familiarized as part of their professional education, Irish social work practitioners are unlikely to operationalize any of these concepts without the support of their employing organizations and, specifically, without the support of their line managers. And the reality is that the major public bureaucracies that employ Irish social workers (in particular the new Child and Family Agency) have not philosophically embraced the 'four-tier' model or developed practical strategies that might enable their employees to play a fuller role as 'tier one' or 'tier two' professionals responding to substance misuse.

From a sociological perspective (e.g. Freidson, 1986), professional activity has traditionally been viewed as a form of work in which, by virtue of their specialist knowledge and expertise, practitioners retain considerable power or discretion over what they do on a daily basis. And, if we look at 'clinical social work' with substance misusers within private practice settings as is commonplace in the US, it would seem that such social workers do exercise a high degree of autonomy. Such private practitioners would, however, be subject to criticism that by moving into private psychotherapeutic practice in this way and focusing solely on individual pathology to the exclusion of 'setting' factors, they have abandoned American social work's historic mission towards the poor and the socially excluded: they have become, in the phrase of Specht and Courtney (1994), 'unfaithful angels'. Social work practice in Ireland and the UK, on the other hand, is most commonly located within statutory agencies, where the power of individual social workers to make practice decisions is greatly circumscribed by the legally mandated functions of these welfare bureaucracies. Social work decisions within these large welfare bureaucracies are routinely made in compliance with the relevant legislation, regulations and guidelines, with minimal room for individual professional autonomy or 'reflective practice'. What David Howe (1991) has referred to as the 'shape of social work practice' is now dominated by managers rather than by individual practitioners or by academic researchers and educators; and if these managers do not support frontline social workers in engaging more fully with substance misuse issues – which by and large they appear not to – then the likelihood is that social workers will continue to see their role with substance misusing clients primarily in terms of referral to specialist addiction agencies and services.

Conclusion

One of the main points, therefore, to emerge from this discussion of how Irish social work has adapted and responded to problems associated with psycho-active drug use over the past 30 years is that it is illusory to speak of social work as though it enjoys the status and privileges of the more established professions and is, effectively, in charge of its own destiny. However distasteful it may be to practitioners and academics, the truth of the matter would appear to be that with the exception of those 'unfaithful angels' who have maximized their professional autonomy by becoming private psychotherapists, Irish social workers are mainly employed in statutory agencies where they work with involuntary clients within managerial systems that afford relatively little room for individual professional autonomy – whether in relation to substance misuse or the management of other issues. In the interests of balance, it should be pointed out that Irish social work is not unique in this regard and that there is no evidence to indicate that social work in other jurisdictions (such as the UK, for instance) has shifted to any great extent to incorporate or reflect the research and policy developments discussed here. Neither, it should be added, are other areas of generic health and social care significantly better when it comes to operationalizing the idea that management of substance misuse should be a shared responsibility across a range of professions and service sectors, rather than the preserve of addiction specialists. In particular, it should be noted that despite several decades of development and promotion by the World Health Organization of the concept of early identification and brief intervention by primary care doctors (GPs) into their patients' alcohol problems, it has not proved possible to mainstream such practice in any of the countries where it was proved – under research conditions – to be highly effective (Heather, 2007). It would appear that the main 'role support' obstacle to this integration of early identification/brief intervention of problem drinkers into primary healthcare is financial; GPs mainly operate as independent professionals, running their practices as businesses, and in the absence of specific financial incentives from service purchasers, they are unwilling to add this new element to their existing practices.

On a positive note, it should be pointed out that the Probation Service (2009, p. 4) has explicitly taken stock of the developments discussed here and produced a thoughtful policy document on its own role with regard to substance misuse, concluding:

> The Probation Service is a tier two agency whose primary role is to 'encourage problem substance misusers to engage with and avail of treatment services'. The Probation Service also engages in brief interventions to assist those with substance misuse problems to address their problems as part of their case management plans.

It remains to be seen how effective or consistent the Probation Service proves to be in developing practice that reflects these ideas, but this policy document displays a degree of management openness to expanding work with substance misusers that must obviously be welcomed. In the wider context of professional social work in Ireland, it would seem important that the new Child and Family Agency would take a similar initiative, given what we know of the prevalence of parental substance misuse in its employees' caseloads. How academic social work within the universities can contribute to further development of practice with substance misusers is less clear; already this aspect of social work practice jostles for place in an overcrowded curriculum, and academic teaching of 'best practice' may not be especially influential if the ideals promoted in an academic setting are ignored or contradicted in students' practice placement experiences.

In recent years, the Irish Association of Social Workers (IASW), a professional body representing professional social workers across all areas of practice, has regularly incorporated education and training on substance misuse into its continuing professional development activities, and there may be further opportunities for the IASW to develop this area of practice in Ireland. Given their lack of involvement at practice level, it comes as no surprise that Irish social workers – individually and collectively – have made no significant contribution to the policy process either in relation to alcohol or illicit drugs. Were this to change, one could expect that a social work input to the policy process would most likely reflect the emphasis on the environmental or setting factors discussed above, with social workers arguing for a greater commitment to drug prevention strategies that recognize the importance of social exclusion in the genesis of high-risk drug use, or for health promotion strategies that recognize that the prevalence of alcohol-related problems is unlikely to decline where public policy effectively makes alcohol cheaper and more readily available.

In conclusion, it would appear that Irish social work has not adapted as coherently or effectively as it might have to our continuing alcohol problems and our relatively newly established illicit drug problems. We have argued that, to a large extent, this failure is attributable to management systems rather than a lack of interest by individual practitioners; but we have also argued that the overall ethos of professional social work is ideally suited to work with substance misusers and that this is an area of professional social work in Ireland that deserves to be developed.

References

All Ireland Traveller Health Study Team (2010) *All Ireland Traveller Health: Our Geels*, University College Dublin, School of Public Health, Physiotherapy and Population Science.

Babor, F., Caetano, R., Casswell, S. et al. (2010) *Alcohol: No Ordinary Commodity: Research and Public Policy*, Oxford, Oxford University Press.

Bellerose, D., Carew, A.M. and Lyons, S. (2011) *Trends in Treated Problem Drug Use in Ireland 2005 to 2010*, Dublin, Health Research Board.

Butler, S. (2002) *Alcohol, Drugs and Health Promotion in Modern Ireland*, Dublin, Institute of Public Administration.

Butler, S. (2009) 'Obstacles to the implementation of an integrated national alcohol policy in Ireland: nannies, neoliberals and joined-up government', *Journal of Social Policy*, 38(2), 343–59.

Butler, S. (2011) 'Addiction counsellors in the Republic of Ireland: exploring the emergence of a new profession', *Drugs: Education, Prevention and Policy*, 18(4), 295–302.

Coulter, C. (2013) *Child Care Law Reporting Project: Interim Report*, Dublin, Child Care Law Reporting Project.

Dean, G., Bradshaw, J. and Lavelle, P. (1983) *Drug Misuse in Ireland 1982–1983: Investigation in a North Central Dublin Area and in Galway, Sligo and Cork*, Dublin, Medico-Social Research Board.

Department of Health (2012) *Steering Group Report on a National Substance Misuse Strategy*, Dublin, Department of Health.

Department of Health and Children/HSE (2005) *Report of the Working Group on Treatment of Under 18 Year Olds Presenting to Treatment Services with Serious Drug Problems*, Dublin, Department of Health and Children/HSE.

Drummond, A., Codd, M., Donnelly, N. et al. (2014) *Study on the Prevalence of Drug Use, Including Intravenous Drug Use, and Blood-Borne Viruses Amongst the Irish Prison Population*, Dublin, National Advisory Committee on Drugs.

Forrester, D. (2000) 'Parental substance misuse and child protection in a British sample', *Child Abuse Review*, 9(4), 235–46.

Freidson, E. (1986) *Professional Powers*, Chicago, University of Chicago Press.

Germain, C. (ed.) (1979) *Social Work Practice: People and Environments: An Ecological Perspective*, New York, Columbia University Press.

Heather, N. (2007) 'A long-standing World Health Organization collaborative project on early identification and brief alcohol intervention in primary health care comes to an end', *Addiction*, 102(5), 679–81.

Hohman, M. (2012) *Motivational Interviewing for Social Workers*, New York, Guilford Press.

Hohman, M., Kleinpeter, C. and Loughran, H. (2005) 'Enhancing motivation, strengths and skills of parents in the child welfare system', in Corcoran, J. (ed.) *Building Strengths and Skills: A Collaborative Approach to Working with Clients*, Oxford, Oxford University Press.

Hope, A. (2011) *Hidden Realities: Children's Exposure to Risks from Parental Drinking in Ireland*, Letterkenny, North West Alcohol Forum.

Howe, D. (1991) 'Knowledge, power and the shape of social work practice', in Davies, M. (ed.) *The Sociology of Social Work*, London, Routledge.

HSE (Health Service Executive) (2007) *Report of the HSE Working Group on Residential Treatment and Rehabilitation (Substance Abuse)*, Dublin, HSE.

Institute of Medicine (1990) *Broadening the Base of Treatment for Alcohol Problems*, Washington DC, National Academy Press.

Janzen, R. (2001) *The Rise and Fall of Synanon: A California Utopia*, Baltimore, MD, Johns Hopkins University Press.

Johnson, V. (1973) *I'll Quit Tomorrow*, New York, Harper & Row.

Mayock, P., Corr, M.L. and O'Sullivan, E. (2008) *Young People's Homeless Pathways*, Dublin, Homeless Agency.

Miller, W. (1983) 'Motivational interviewing with problem drinkers', *Behavioural Psychotherapy*, 11(2), 147–72.

Miller, W. and Rollnick, S. (2013) *Motivational Interviewing: Helping People Change*, London, Guilford Press.

Ministerial Task Force on Measures to Reduce the Demand for Drugs (1996) *First Report of the Ministerial Task Force on Measures to Reduce the Demand for Drugs*, Dublin, Department of the Taoiseach.

Mongan, D., Reynolds, S., Fanagan, S. and Long, J. (2007) *Health-related Consequences of Problem Alcohol Use: Overview 6*, Dublin, Health Research Board.

National Advisory Committee on Drugs (2012) *Drug Use in Ireland and Northern Ireland (Drug Prevalence Survey 2010/2011)*, Dublin, National Advisory Committee on Drugs.

NSWQB (National Social Work Qualifications Board) (2006) *Social Work Posts in Ireland: NSWQB Report No. 3*, Dublin, NSWQB.

Orford, J. and Edwards, G. (1977) *Alcoholism: A Comparison of Treatment and Advice, with a Study of the Influence of Marriage*, Oxford, Oxford University Press.

Peele, S. (1995) *The Diseasing of America: How We Allowed Recovery Zealots and the Treatment Industry to Convince Us We Are Out of Control*, New York, Lexington Books.

Probation Service (2009) *Principles of Probation Practice in Working with Substance Misusers*, Dublin, Probation Service.

Probation Service (2012) *Drug and Alcohol Misuse Among Adult Offenders on Probation Supervision in Ireland (Findings from the Drugs and Alcohol Survey 2011)*, Dublin, Probation Service.

Probation Service (2013) *Drug and Alcohol Misuse Among Young Offenders on Probation Supervision in Ireland (Findings from the Drugs and Alcohol Survey 2012)*, Dublin, Probation Service.

Ramstedt, M. and Hope, A. (2005) 'The Irish drinking habits of 2002: drinking and drinking-related harm in a European comparative perspective', *Journal of Substance Use*, 10(5), 273–83.

Rapp, C. and Goscha, R. (2012) *The Strengths Model: A Recovery-oriented Approach to Mental Health Services*, Oxford, Oxford University Press.

Reinarman, C. (2005) 'Addiction as accomplishment: the discursive construction of disease', *Addiction Research and Theory*, 13(4), 307–20.

Robins, L., Davis, D. and Nurco, D. (1974) 'How permanent was Vietnam drug addiction?', *American Journal of Public Health*, 64(suppl. 12), 38–43.

Room, R. (2011) 'Substance use disorders: a conceptual and terminological muddle', *Addiction*, 106(5), 878–81.

Rush, B. (2010) 'Tiered frameworks for planning substance use service delivery systems: origins and key principles', *Nordic Studies on Alcohol and Drugs*, 27, 617–36.

Saleebey, D. (ed.) (1997) *The Strengths Perspective in Social Work Practice*, New York, Longman.

Seay, K. and Kohl, P. (2013) 'Caregiver substance abuse and children's exposure to violence in a nationally representative child welfare sample', *Journal of Social Work Practice in the Addictions*, 13(1), 70–90.

Shaw, S., Cartwright, A., Spratley, T. and Harwin, J. (1978) *Responding to Drinking Problems*, London, Croom Helm.

Specht, H. and Courtney, M. (1994) *Unfaithful Angels: How Social Work Has Abandoned its Mission*, New York, Free Press.

Stevens, A. and Ritter, A. (2013) 'How can and do empirical studies influence drug policies? Narratives and complexity in the use of evidence in policy making', *Drugs: Education, Prevention and Policy*, 20(3), 169–74.

Study Group on the Development of the Psychiatric Services (1984) *The Psychiatric Services: Planning for the Future*, Dublin, Stationery Office.

Walsh, J. (2013) *Theories for Direct Social Work Practice*, Stamford, CT, Cengage Learning.

Yablonsky, L. (1965) *The Tunnel Back: Synanon*, London, Macmillan.

Zinberg, N. (1984) *Drug, Set and Setting*, New Haven, CT, Yale University Press.

13

Growing Old with Dignity: Challenges for Practice in an Ageing Society

Sarah Donnelly and Anne O'Loughlin

Introduction

Ireland's ageing population, which is characterized by increased heterogeneity, provides an opportunity for social work with older people to fully establish itself as a significant and valued area of social work practice. Our ageing population and their unique needs are receiving greater attention, not only from health and social care professionals and policy makers, but also from each of us personally, in the context of parents, relatives and older people in our local communities. Care of older people is a rapidly expanding area of social work practice and employment, meaning that most social workers will inevitably become more exposed and involved with older people, carers and their families (Duffy and Healy, 2011). Therefore, it is critical that social workers are equipped with the necessary skills and knowledge as they come into contact with older people from a variety of social, cultural, economic, generational and ethnic circumstances. Increasingly, social workers are likely to work with those older people who experience poverty, ill health, depression, dementia, substance abuse or those with unresolved traumas from previous years (Ray and Phillips, 2012).

In this chapter, we set the scene for social work with older people by discussing some of the critical issues and key themes. It begins with an outline of the current demographic landscape, the social policy backdrop and an argument for the need for social workers to address issues of ageism. Key ethical issues for social work with older people including elder mistreatment, self-neglect and care planning are discussed. The chapter then considers developments and challenges in this field, outlines a framework for practice with older people, and addresses critical factors in primary care including home supports, and working with older people with a dementia. The chapter concludes by highlighting some of the future challenges for social work with older people.

Demographics, diversity and addressing ageism

A global transformation is taking place as the world's population is rapidly ageing, with the proportion of people over 60 years expected to double from about 11% to 22% (WHO, 2014). This is a cause for celebration as well as a challenge for society and the social work profession to maximize the health, functional capacity, social security and participation of older people. The need for long-term care, which includes home-based nursing, community, residential and hospital-based care, is also increasing (WHO, 2014). These global changes are reflected in the Irish context; one of the age groups that experienced greatest growth over the period 2006–11 were those aged over 65 (535,393), a group that has increased by 14.4% since 2006, while the population aged 85 and over increased by 22% (CSO, 2011). This increase, combined with a predicted dramatic increase in the number of people with dementia, referred to in a recent report as 'the global dementia epidemic' (Prince et al., 2013, p. 4), has significant implications for the resourcing of services for older people and targeted forward planning in order to meet future demands.

A specific policy document dedicated to addressing the needs and preferences of older people in a comprehensive manner did not exist until the publication of the *National Positive Ageing Strategy* (Department of Health, 2013). This strategy is put forward as 'a new departure in policy-making for ageing in Ireland' by addressing the broader determinants of health and requiring 'stronger engagement, interaction and joint working' across government departments and society (Department of Health, 2013, p. 11). The strategy highlights particular issues of vulnerability for some older people, which are relevant to the role of social workers. These include the risk of poor health or loss of independence, financial vulnerability, and social isolation. It also highlights the particular vulnerability of marginalized, hard-to-reach and minority groups, such as those aged 80 years and over, people living in rural areas, persons with impaired capacity, older migrants, older people with intellectual disabilities, members of the Traveller community, lesbian, gay, bisexual and transgender older people, and those subjected to elder mistreatment (Department of Health, 2013). While the Irish government has recently made a commitment to develop a National Dementia Strategy and implement it over a five-year period (Department of Health, 2012a), its implementation and that of the *National Positive Ageing Strategy* and the *National Carers Strategy* (Department of Health, 2013, 2012b) are all constrained by the reduction in financial resources available to the state. Implementation concentrating 'on actions for the short to medium term, which can, to the greatest extent possible, be achieved on a cost neutral basis' (Department of Health, 2012c, p. 4), offers little hope for the further development and resourcing of comprehensive service provision to older people or a national social work service for this section of the population.

Ageing is not only a biological process, but is also socially constructed, as it is created by social interactions and power relationships in society; thus ageism may occur at many levels (Pierce and Timonen, 2010). The argument has been advanced that the macro-level (state and economy) influences the experience and condition of ageing. However, older people also actively construct their world at a micro-level through social interactions and at a meso-level by engaging with the organizational and institutional structures that are part of their everyday lives in society (Phillipson and Baars, 2007). Legislation and service provision for older people in Ireland has been given low priority until recent years, which, it could be reasoned, is reflective of systemic and legislative discrimination. Recently, however, there are indications that ageing is beginning to be constructed in a more positive framework and older people are now almost universally perceived as a deserving group who are entitled to better quality and increased resourcing of services from the state (Scharf et al., 2013). Individually and collectively, members of the Special Interest Group on Ageing of the Irish Association of Social Workers have played a key role over the past 20 years in macro-level advocacy and campaigning in order to influence social policy on the needs of older people.

Kerr et al. (2005) argue that a key function of the social work role with older people involves addressing ageism. This view complies with the International Federation of Social Workers' code of ethics and the strong social work commitment to issues of social justice and anti-discriminatory practice. Within the social work profession, there has been a tendency to focus on dysfunction in older people at the expense of recognizing the strengths and resources of our older generations (Ray and Phillips, 2012). Writers such as Ray and Phillips (2012) have argued that even the increased usage of the term 'elderly' by professionals and policy makers contributes to the stereotyping of older people as they are lumped together as a homogeneous group with uniform needs. Social work practice must encompass the goals of the *National Positive Ageing Strategy* by removing barriers to participation for older people, advocating strongly for their human rights, promoting intergenerational solidarity, and striving to eradicate ageism, thus helping to create a society for all ages that is underpinned by equality.

Ireland has finally moved from a situation of having virtually no access to community-based social work services for older people (O'Neill et al.,

2003) to one where a number of dedicated posts have been created through the establishment of senior caseworker posts for the protection of older people in 2007. In the sphere of mental health and ageing, there have also been developments, with the expansion of social work posts in psychiatry of later life teams nationally. Gerontology has also rapidly grown as a clinical specialty, and the resourcing of social work posts in the acute sector, it could be argued, reflects the value that has been placed on social work by consultant geriatricians. However, it also reflects the Health Service Executive's (HSE) prioritization of social work posts in the hospital sector to free up acute beds, rather than focusing on a more integrated approach to the care of older people. While the roll-out of primary care teams (PCTs), with their emphasis on early intervention and assuming a more preventive approach to the care of older people, must be welcomed, it also signifies a missed opportunity, with the omission of social work posts from a number of PCTs.

However, we know little about social workers' ability and capacity to respond to a growing number of older people with diverse and complex care needs (Richards et al., 2013). Social work with older people is still relatively invisible in terms of learning and research (Emilsson, 2013). Currently, there is some increase in research focused on social work and older people (Powell and Orme, 2011). High-quality research on social work and older people is clearly required to effectively address the needs of a diverse ageing population (Berkman, 2011), with a parallel need to strongly embed ageing in the social work curriculum (Ray et al., 2014). Indeed, students may be choosing not to work with older people as they are unclear about what this role entails (McCormack, 2008). Interestingly, research has shown that if students have the opportunity to undertake work with older clients in a practice placement, their interest in social work with older people is stimulated, leading to changes in perception about working with this client group (Jack and Mosley, 1997; Cummings et al., 2005).

Complexity and critical issues in relation to ageing

Research indicates that most older people would prefer to live in their own homes and have support services provided to enable them to do so for as long as possible (Barry, 2010). However, there is an evident tension between this objective and the lack of expansion of supported housing options or the promotion of 'ageing in place', with the consequent heavy reliance on the Nursing Home Support Scheme (NHSS) in the Irish context. There is also no official policy framework for integrated home care service provision to older people and without any legislation governing home care in Ireland, it remains unregulated (Timonen et al., 2012). The introduction of the Home Care Package (HCP) Scheme in 2006 signified a conscious move away from institutional care and gave rise to the concept of 'a package of care', which purports to offer older people individually tailored support packages. The majority of HCPs include a mix of public, private and voluntary care providers, resulting in a situation where several organizations or teams of people may be involved in caring for an older person, which can lead to difficulties in communication and coordination between services. Tensions also exist as HCPs can only be delivered within the framework of what is available in that particular geographical area, which limits the effectiveness of this scheme (Brennan, 2010), while the near complete absence of home support to assist with night-time care needs requires urgent attention and resourcing. Meanwhile, the growing emphasis on responding only to those with the most severe level of need, coupled with increased budgetary constraints, has meant that little or no support can now be accessed through home help services to assist older people with domestic, household tasks. Thus, while there has been an increased focus on the overarching goal of promoting independence and choice for older persons (Lymbery, 2010), this has ultimately been stymied by reducing budgets to core services.

The introduction of new integrated service areas in 2012 has added an additional complexity for social workers trying to negotiate and arrange community supports for older people. Waiting lists for community services operate in some areas and the concept of 'joined-up' services resembles more of a 'patchwork quilt' in reality, often with no designated healthcare professional formally being held responsible for case management. As a result, social workers must strongly advocate for services that the older people have been independently assessed as requiring. Moreover, communication between agencies is often poor, service provision fragmented, and there is pressing need for more integrated care pathways to be developed between the acute and community sector. While the introduction of national guidelines for the standardized implementation of HCPs (HSE, 2010) may allow for flexibility in delivery, it has also led to inconsistencies, inequities and duplication of work, including double or triple assessment of need (EPS Consulting, 2013).

Another challenge facing social workers is that it is estimated that there are 42,000 people in Ireland with dementia and the pressing need for a National Dementia Strategy is best understood in the context of projected increases in the number of people with dementia to between 65,000 and 140,000 over the next 30 years (Cahill et al., 2012). A research review found that community support services for those with dementia, including social work, 'were under-developed and fragmented' (Cahill et al., 2012, p. 13). The role of social workers in supporting persons with dementia and their carers, assessing need, protecting rights and safeguarding health and welfare is acknowledged as important, but access to this service and other community supports is described as extremely limited (Cahill et al., 2012). Each person's experience of dementia is unique and the illness can be experienced as stigmatizing, particularly for those who have retained insight, and it is often viewed as a 'hidden disability'. Social workers can help people explore what having a dementia means in the context of their lives and identities. However, uncertainty about how the illness will progress can be frustrating and makes forward planning challenging. When an older person develops memory problems or a dementia, their capability to make independent decisions may be compromised as a result of an inability to fully understand their care needs, or the risks associated with some of their presenting behaviours, for example leaving the cooker on or wandering. In such situations, social workers have a key role in creating a supported decision-making process for the person with dementia.

Dementia is different from other illnesses, in that for every one person diagnosed, three other family members will be significantly affected (Cahill et al., 2012). The bulk of care in Ireland is still provided by what Fanning (1999) labels the 'informal sector', which has historically and culturally been largely composed of family carers or friends and neighbours who carry out unpaid work (Timonen and McMenamin, 2002). To date, the majority of care provision to people with dementia continues to be provided by family and informal carers in the home, frequently by adult children and spousal carers, many of whom are frail and elderly themselves (http://dementia.ie). One of the main tenets of age-related care is the importance of holistic care and acknowledgement that family involvement is appropriate and is to be encouraged (Archbold and Stewart, 1996). However, these relationships can also serve to disempower older people with dementia through families being overly concerned and protective, thus promoting undue dependence (Nussbaum, 1985). In addition, many family carers may feel guilty about asking for help and often allow their own health to be adversely affected by the demands of the caring role. This is compounded by the fact that the responsibility for home respite or 'supervisory' carer support hours predominantly falls to voluntary non-profit organizations, such as the Alzheimer's Society and the Carers Association of Ireland, both of which have experienced increased demands on services and funding cuts in recent years.

Elder mistreatment, self-neglect and supported decision making

The investigation of, and intervention into, the alleged abuse of older people has become a dominant feature of social work in Ireland. The international definition of elder mistreatment adopted in most Western countries, including Ireland, is: 'Elder abuse is a single or repeated act or lack of appropriate action occurring within any relationship where there is an expectation of trust which causes harm or distress to an older person' (WHO/INPEA, 2002; WHO, 2008). Operationalizing this abstract definition is to describe types or categories of abuse that older people can be subjected to – physical, sexual, psychological, financial and neglect. Although valuable, the limitations of these narrow and mutually exclusive categories are increasingly recognized (O'Brien et al., 2011; Naughton et al., 2012; Anand et al., 2013). There is a major lack of understanding of the voice and experiences of older people in relation to abuse (INPEA/WHO, 2002; Anand et al., 2013; Charpentier and Souliéres, 2013). Recent Irish research has demonstrated that older people conceptualize elder abuse as the loss of voice and agency, diminishing status in society, violation of rights, and wider societal influences that undermine a sense of individualism and 'personhood' (O'Brien et al., 2011; Naughton et al., 2013).

Elder abuse policy in Ireland has been driven by key publications, including the first reports of elder abuse in the Irish literature (O'Loughlin, 1990, 1993; O'Neill et al., 1990; O'Loughlin and Duggan, 1998). The recommendations of the report *Protecting Our Future* (Department of Health and Children, 2002) include the formulation of a clear policy on elder abuse and the recruitment of senior elder abuse caseworkers (later known as 'senior caseworkers for the protection of older people') to whom all referrals of elder abuse were to be directed. The national policy, *Responding to Allegations of Elder Abuse* (HSE, 2012a, p. 4), was 'specifically concerned with people aged 65 and over'. In December 2014, however, this was replaced by a new national policy, *Safeguarding Vulnerable Persons at Risk of Abuse* (HSE, 2014), which was developed by the HSE's Social Care Division who hold responsibility for the provision of services for older people and people with a disability. The annual report, *Open your Eyes* (HSE, 2013), notes that the number of referrals to the elder abuse service continued its upward trend, with a total of 2,460 referrals in 2012 – an increase of 7% on 2011. Moreover, it acknowledges that significant underreporting of abuse is still likely. *Protecting Our Future* (Department of Health and Children, 2002) and *Safeguarding Vulnerable Persons at Risk of Abuse* (HSE, 2014) recognize that social work training provides the core competences required for assessing, investigating and intervening in cases of elder abuse and safeguarding vulnerable adults. However, when confronting situations of maltreatment, social workers are often faced with ethical dilemmas. This is particularly so in dealing with:

- controversies regarding balancing self-determination with protection from harm

- barriers to disclosure and help-seeking

- assessing cognitive capacity

the challenges of working collaboratively with others to resolve the complexity of elder abuse cases (Donovan and Regehr, 2010).

Recent research on the experience of senior caseworkers highlights the complexities and challenges they faced in managing cases of elder abuse (O'Donnell et al., 2012).

In the same research, senior caseworkers for the protection of older people also work with cases of serious self-neglect (O'Donnell et al., 2012). Models of self-neglect encompass a complex interplay between mental, physical, social and environmental factors. Differentiation between inability and unwillingness to care for oneself and capacity to understand the consequences of one's actions are important (Braye et al., 2011). With referrals increasing and a majority of cases relating to those in the 75–84 age category, this is a serious issue to be addressed (HSE, 2013). Self-neglect referrals should be viewed as alerts to potentially serious underlying problems, requiring evaluation and treatment (Naik et al., 2007). The *HSE Policy and Procedures for Responding to Allegations of Extreme Self-Neglect* (HSE, 2012b) emphasizes the need for a multidimensional approach, holistic assessment, and building relationships of trust. Research in Ireland demonstrates the complexity of the concerns and the personal challenges and powerlessness faced by social workers in such cases (Day et al., 2012).

The *National Quality Standards for Residential Care Settings for Older People in Ireland* came into force in July 2009 (HIQA, 2009). Of particular relevance is Standard 8, which requires that 'each resident is protected from all forms of abuse' (HIQA, 2009, p. 10). Many older people in long-term care are frail individuals with multiple medical and cognitive impairments. Their dependency on others for care may make them particularly vulnerable to abuse and neglect (Beaulieu and Belanger, 1995; Joshi and Flaherty, 2005; Post et al., 2010). In addition, there are many difficulties for them in reporting abuse or behaving in an assertive way due to fear of reprisal (Clough, 1999; Hawes, 2003; Joshi and Flaherty, 2005). Internationally, social workers have been part of staff teams in nursing homes for many years, although they are not normally employed in nursing homes in Ireland. Responding to elder mistreatment in nursing homes is a significant challenge in Ireland, given the context of an underresourced specialist elder abuse social work service, faced with increasing referrals predominantly concerning community-based older people.

The inadequacy of Irish law in relation to older people with a cognitive impairment or dementia has been frequently criticized and is of particular significance when dealing with cases of elder mistreatment and neglect. There is an urgent need to enact capacity legislation to replace the current legal system for substitute decision making in Ireland, that is, the ward of court system set out in the Lunacy (Regulation) Ireland Act 1871. The long-awaited Assisted Decision-making (Capacity) Bill 2013 will replace the existing ward of court system and provide a new legal framework supporting decision making by adults, which will enable them to retain the maximum amount of autonomy possible in situations where they lack, or may shortly lack, capacity. The current system employs an 'all-or-nothing' approach to capacity, whereas the new Bill encompasses a functional approach to decision making assessed on an issue- and time-specific basis. The Bill also makes provision for a range of assisted decision-making structures, advance care directives, and the establishment of an Office of the Public Guardian with supervisory powers to protect vulnerable people and overhaul the existing power of attorney structure. In this way, the Bill provides an important legal framework that recognizes and supports an older person's right to self-determination. The guiding principles broaden the assessment of 'best interests' to make central the lived realities of the person for whom the decision is made (Assisted Decision-Making (Capacity) Bill, 2013, S8). Its application poses many dilemmas for practitioners grappling with the meaning of 'capacity' and 'decision making', which will require training and guidance.

A framework of practice for social work with older people

Social work with older people can occur in a variety of settings, including hospitals, day care and respite facilities, community/primary care, psychiatry of later life teams, and adult protection services. Research has highlighted the value older people place on 'social workers' knowledge about specialist services, persistence, commitment, reliability and being supportive, sympathetic and prepared to listen' (Manthorpe et al., 2007, p. 1142). A social worker's main priority should be the maintenance and enhancement of their older adult clients' quality of life. This may include developing an understanding not only of the physical complications of ageing, but mental health, cultural barriers, and the organizational challenges faced by the older adult. The knowledge and skill set of social workers uniquely equips us to manage the diversity of issues that impact on our ageing population: frailty, multiple health needs, balancing autonomy and risk, life transitions, carer stress, and end of life care (Ray et al., 2014). Effective social work with older people requires practical skills (such as securing home supports) and 'people skills' (such as engaging with the older person's biography in order to promote strengths and resilience), active listening and striving to achieve the right balance between self-determination and protection (Kerr et al., 2005).

Older people are the largest group of users of community support services and are likely to have a complex and diverse range of problems requiring skilled multidisciplinary team assessments, ongoing interventions and review (Richards et al., 2013), coupled with the need to work with the older person's family/support network (Statham et al., 2006). Studies indicate that social workers need to proactively facilitate the involvement of older people and their family/carers in decisions related to their care and carefully consider the older person's wishes (Abramson, 1990). Older age can be characterized by multiple losses, therefore social workers have a key role in helping older people to adapt and cope with loss and bereavement, and rebuild self-esteem and social networks (Milne et al., 2007).

Social work expertise in issues relating to palliative care and end of life care are also pertinent. Providing support in relation to life transitions such as discharge from hospital or moving from independent to supported or residential care may be required. Social workers can offer psychological and emotional support to help manage anxieties and offer a bridge between settings. Social workers also play a crucial role in assisting older people and their families to apply for the Nursing Home Support Scheme (Department of Health and Children, 2009), as well as helping to identify a suitable long-stay facility and deal with any problems that arise during this transfer period. They provide support, information and advocacy for older people and their families through this process, recognizing that it is more than simply a form-filling exercise but a time of crisis and change. Often, tensions can arise in relation to the decision making around an older person entering nursing home care. It is pertinent to note that some 4.5% of older people are living in long-term residential care in Ireland – 40% above the EU average (Houses of the Oireachtas, 2012) – most probably due to the underdevelopment of community-based services and supported housing options.

Older people may have multiple healthcare needs requiring an integrated, coordinated approach to their discharge home from acute hospital and their care in the community (Donnelly et al., 2013). Multidisciplinary involvement is recommended for older people and the facilitation of 'involvement in decision-making' is therefore an interprofessional issue (NHS QIS, 2004). Older people may feel disempowered within this process and social workers have a key role to play at the interface between older people, their families, hospital staff and community services (Gibbons and Plath, 2009). Because age-related losses in vision, hearing and cognitive capacity have a direct impact on the older person and their environment, a 'person in environment' perspective is helpful as it is based on the premise that the older person cannot be understood adequately without consideration of the various aspects of their environment: social, political, familial, temporal, spiritual, economic and physical (Wahl and Lang, 2006). Negotiation is an integral part of social work with older people and may include situations such as exploring and agreeing on possible home supports to maximize the older person's independence in their home. Social workers must strive to work in a person-centred way through keeping the older person at the centre of this process as it is possible that family members or care providers may have differing views on the best course of action, which can make the negotiation process complex and challenging (Ray and Phillips, 2012).

It has been suggested that in the current climate, there has been a loss of identity and confidence in social work with older people (Lymbery, 2010) and that a more procedural approach to case management has been adopted (Taylor, 2012). Social workers are now faced with the dual challenge of advocating for older people within a system of increasingly scarce resources, while also striving to carry out holistic person-centred assessments. Opportunities for social workers to engage with older people in direct work that takes a life course approach have been 'replaced with resource finding' (McDonald et al., 2008, p. 7), which, in turn, frustrates any attempts to address issues of socioeconomic or structural inequalities (Richards, 2000). According to Hall (2012, p. 24): 'Particular emphasis has been placed on the role and skills of the social worker not just in coordinating packages of care but in building and sustaining high quality interpersonal relationships with service users.' However, Hall (2012, p. 24) points out that social workers' attention to interpersonal relationships within the case management role has been 'actively discouraged'. The increased bureaucracy of working with older people has largely stemmed from the fact that 'social care entrepreneurship' (Payne, 2000, pp. 82–91) is now a feature of Irish community services, where a range of care services from different providers may be negotiated and coordinated by a social worker. In addition, legislative changes have had a major impact on the roles and responsibilities of social work with this client group, creating challenging dilemmas for social workers at the interface of acute, community and social work systems (Jones, 2000; Postle, 2002; Phillips and Waterson, 2002).

Care planning meetings: a model for working in partnership with older people

A key part of the social work role in working with older people is care planning, which brings together the principles of involvement, shared decision making, support and person-centred care. Care planning requires multidisciplinary collaboration between the professional care providers, older people and their family/carers (Jones et al., 1997) and often culminates in what is known as a 'care planning meeting' (CPM). CPMs were originally convened in response to a crisis situation, but increasingly they are viewed as exemplifying 'good practice' and are used in a more preventive manner. It is an area of practice that social workers have found extremely challenging as they have usually take a lead role in organizing and facilitating these meetings (Donnelly et al., 2013). The desired outcome of the CPM is that:

- all participants are satisfied with the amount of information exchanged
- decisions are made with clarity
- the older person feels a sense of control (Ever, 1981).

The focus of CPMs should be to assist older people and their family members and carers to reach mutually agreed goals in an inclusive, supportive and positive environment (Dersteine and Hargrove, 2001). However, the physical involvement of older people in CPMs does not necessarily guarantee genuine involvement and it is not uncommon for older people to be talked 'about', rather than talked 'to' (Donnelly, 2012). Social workers must help support each older person to define their own needs, invite them to engage in dialogue, and develop the skills and a method to communicate their needs (Mullaly, 2007). For older people to feel comfortable expressing their views and preferences openly, the fostering of a therapeutic relationship is paramount to help create an emotionally secure environment (Sahlsten et al., 2006). Pre-meeting preparation should occur and issues of potential conflict identified. Active listening skills should be employed and social workers should demonstrate an awareness of both expressed communication (verbal) and tacit (body language and eye contact) in older people (Donnelly, 2012). The guiding principle is that the inclusion of cognitively impaired older people in their care planning is imperative. The importance of CPMs has been formally articulated in the Irish context since the introduction of the Nursing Home Support Scheme (Department of Health and Children, 2009), which states that older people must be involved in decisions relating to nursing home placement, thus bringing the issue of participation, capacity, and consent to the fore. A social citizenship approach should, therefore, be promoted, which assumes that an individual has the ability to participate at some level regardless of their cognitive ability, and that the principle of maximizing and valuing their participation should be respected (Bartlett and O'Connor, 2010).

Conclusion

Social workers are in a unique position to work with other professionals in clarifying the reality of the limits to choice and the involvement of older people and families. They can provide expertise in the facilitation of care planning meetings and support the older person and the family in their participation of problem solving, advocacy, negotiations and mediations.

A particular strength of social work is its attention to the holistic picture of the needs of older people, as well as their family needs, strengths and circumstances (Taylor, 2012), along with a focused attention to issues of social justice. Postle (2002, p. 335) argues that social work with older people is often carried out in a state of uncertainty, involving care and control, and mediating between the state and the individual, 'working between the ideal and the reality'. Paradoxically, despite an apparently flourishing policy agenda, which increasingly articulates a notion of 'good practice', major challenges exist in the current provision and delivery of social and healthcare services to older people (Lymbery, 2010). A task now facing the social work profession is to move away from the current prevailing discourse where older people with complex needs are viewed in a negative manner and old age as a period of decline (Ray and Phillips, 2012), and to help create conditions whereby a more positive narrative and lived experience of the ageing process exist. Ultimately, skilled and effective social work practice with older people depends on highly trained and critical practitioners, which, in turn, relies on an evidence-informed research base (Richards et al., 2013). These are the challenges for social work with older people – a client group set to increase significantly in the coming decades – the need to offer support and help to those who are sick, frail or vulnerable, while balancing the need to promote and emphasize a strengths-based approach that fosters positive ageing.

References

Abramson, J.S. (1990) 'Enhancing patient participation: clinical strategies in the discharge planning process', *Social Work in Health Care*, 14(4), 53–71.

Anand, J., Begley, E., O'Brien, M. et al. (2013) 'Conceptualising elder abuse across local and global contexts: implications for policy and professional practice on the island of Ireland', *Journal of Adult Protection*, 15(6), 280–9.

Archbold, P. and Stewart, B.J. (eds) (1996) 'The nature of the family caregiving role and nursing interventions for caregiving families', in Swanson, E.A. and Tripp-Reimer, T. (eds) *Advances in Gerontological Nursing*, vol. 1: *Issues for the 21st Century*, New York, Springer.

Barry, U. (2010) *Elderly Care in Ireland: Provisions and Providers*, Working Papers 10(1), 1–34, Dublin, University College Dublin.

Bartlett, R. and O'Connor (2010) *Broadening the Dementia Debate: Towards Social Citizenship*, Bristol, Policy.

Beaulieu, M. and Belanger, L. (1995) 'Intervention in long-term care institutions with respect to elder mistreatment', in MacLean, M. (ed.) *Abuse and Neglect of Older Canadians: Strategies for Change*, Toronto, Thompson.

Berkman, B. (2011) 'Gerontological social work research in health and mental health', *Generations Review*, 21(1), www.britishgerontology.org/DB/.

Braye, S., Orr, D. and Preston-Shoot, M. (2011) *Self-neglect and Adult Safeguarding: Findings from Research*, London, Social Care Institute for Excellence.

Brennan, J. (2010) 'From community care to residential care: personal social services and older people', in S. Quin and P. Kennedy (eds) *Ageing and Social Policy in Ireland*, Dublin, University College Press.

Cahill, S., O'Shea, E. and Pierce, M. (2012) *Creating Excellence in Dementia Care: A Research Review for Ireland's National Dementia Strategy, Dublin and Galway: Living with Dementia Programme*, Trinity College Dublin and Irish Centre for Social Gerontology, National University of Ireland, Galway.

Charpentier, M. and Soulieres, M. (2013) 'Elder abuse and neglect in institutional settings: the resident's perspective', *Journal of Elder Abuse and Neglect*, 25(4), 339–54.

Clough, R. (1999) 'The abuse of older people in institutional settings: the role of management and regulation', in Stanley, N. Manthorpe, J. and Penhale, B. (eds) *Institutional Abuse: Perspectives Across the Life Course*, London, Routledge.

CSO (Central Statistics Office) (2011) *Census 2011 Ireland and Northern Ireland*, Cork, CSO.

Cummings, S.M., Adler, G. and DeCoster, V.A. (2005) 'Factors influencing graduate social work students' interest in working with elders', *Journal of Educational Gerontology*, 31, 643–55.

Day, M.R., McCarty, G. and Leahy-Warren, P. (2012) 'Professional social workers' views on self-neglect: an exploratory study', *British Journal of Social Work*, 42(4), 725–43.

Department of Health (2012a) *Creating Excellence in Dementia Care: A Research Review for Ireland's National Dementia Strategy*, Dublin, Stationery Office.

Department of Health (2012b) *National Carers Strategy*, Dublin, Stationery Office.

Department of Health (2012c) *Future Health: The Strategic Framework for Reform of the Health Service 2012–2015*, Dublin, Stationery Office.

Department of Health (2013) *National Positive Ageing Strategy*, Dublin, Stationery Office.

Department of Health and Children (2002) *Protecting Our Future*, Dublin, Stationery Office.

Department of Health and Children (2009) *Nursing Home Support Scheme Act*, Dublin, Stationery Office.

Dersteine, J.B. and Hargrove, S.D. (2001) *Comprehensive Rehabilitative Nursing*, St Louis, MO, W.B. Saunders.

Donnelly, S. (2012) Family Meeting or Care Planning Meeting? A Multidisciplinary Action Research Study in a Hospital Setting, unpublished PhD thesis, Trinity College Dublin, Ireland.

Donnelly, S.M., Carter-Anand, J., Cahill, S. et al. (2013) 'Multiprofessional views on older patients' participation in care planning meetings in a hospital context', *Practice: Social Work in Action*, 25(2), 121–38.

Donovan, K. and Regehr, C. (2010) 'Elder abuse: clinical, ethical, and legal considerations in social work practice', *Clinical Social Work*, 38, 174–82.

Duffy, F. and Healy, J.P. (2011) 'Social work with older people in a hospital setting', *Social Work in Healthcare*, 50(2), 109–23.

Emilsson, U.M. (2013) 'The role of social work in cross-professional teamwork: examples from an older people's team in England', *British Journal of Social Work*, 43(1), 116–34.

EPS Consulting (2013) *The Business Case for the Outsourcing of Home Care Provision and a More Efficient Use of Fair Deal Funds*, Dublin, Home and Community Care Ireland.

Ever, H.K. (1981) Multidisciplinary teams in geriatric wards: Myth or reality?, *Journal of Advanced Nursing*, 6(3), 205–14.

Fanning, B. (2009) *New Guests of the Irish Nation*, Dublin, Irish Academic Press.

Gibbons, J. and Plath, D. (2005) '"Everybody puts a lot into it!" Single session contacts in hospital social work', *Social Work in Healthcare*, 42(1), 17–34.

Hall, B. (2012) 'Reflective social work practice with older people: the professional and the organisation', in Hall, B. and Scragg, T. (eds) *Social Work and Older People*, Buckingham, Open University Press/McGraw-Hill Education.

Hawes, C. (2003) 'Elder abuse in residential long-term care settings: What is known and what information is needed?', in National Research Council, *Elder Mistreatment: Abuse, Neglect and Exploitation in an Aging America*, Washington DC, National Academies Press.

HIQA (Health Information and Quality Authority) (2009) *National Quality Standards for Residential Care for Older People in Ireland*, Dublin, HIQA.

Houses of the Oireachtas (2012) *Report on the Rights of Older People*, March, Dublin.

HSE (Health Service Executive) (2010) *National Guidelines & Procedures for the Standardised Implementation of the Home Care Packages Scheme*, Dublin, HSE.

HSE (2012a) *Responding to Allegations of Elder Abuse: HSE Elder Abuse Policy*, Dublin, HSE.

HSE (2012b) *HSE Policy and Procedures for Responding to Allegations of Extreme Self-Neglect*, Dublin, HSE.

HSE (2013) *Open Your Eyes: HSE Elder Abuse Services 2012*, Dublin, HSE.

HSE (2014) *Safeguarding Vulnerable Persons at Risk of Abuse: National Policy and Procedures*, Dublin, HSE Social Care Division.

Jack, R. and Mosley, S. (1997) 'The client group preferences of diploma social work students: What are they? Do they change during programmes and what variables affect them?', *British Journal of Social Work*, 27(6), 893–911.

Jones, A.E. (2000) 'Social work: An enterprising profession in a competitive environment?', in O'Connor, I., Smith, P. and Warburton, J. (eds) *Social Work and the Human Services*, Melbourne, Longman.

Jones, M., O'Neill, P., Waterman, H. and Webb, C. (1997) 'Building a relationship: communications and relationships between staff and stroke patients on a rehabilitation ward', *Journal of Advanced Nursing*, 26(1), 101–10.

Joshi, S. and Flaherty, J. (2005) 'Elder abuse and neglect in long-term care', *Clinics in Geriatric Medicine*, 21, 333–45.

Kerr, B., Gordon, J., MacDonald, C and Stalker, K. (2005) *Effective Social Work with Older People*, www.scotland.gov.uk/Resource/Doc/47121/0020809.pdf.

Lymbery, M. (2010) 'A new vision for adult social care? Continuities and change in the care of older people', *Critical Social Policy*, 30(1): 5–26.

McCormack, J.T. (2008) 'Educating social workers for the demographic imperative', *Australian Health Review*, 32(3), 400–4.

McDonald, A., Postle, K. and Dawson, C. (2008) 'Barriers to retaining and using professional knowledge in local authority social work practice with adults in the UK', *British Journal of Social Work*, 38(7), 1370–87.

Manthorpe, J., Moriarty, J., Rapaport, J. et al. (2007) '"There are wonderful social workers but it's a lottery": older people's views about social workers', *British Journal of Social Work*, 38(6), 1132–50.

Milne, A., Gearing, B. and Warner, J. (2007) *An Introduction to the Mental Health of Older People: Services for Older People with Mental Health Problems*, London, SCIE.

Mullaly, B. (2007) 'Oppression: the focus of structural social work', in Mullaly, B. *The New Structural Social Work*, 3rd edn, Don Mills, ON, Oxford University Press.

Naik, A.D., Burnett, J., Pickens-Pace, S. and Dyer, C.B. (2007) 'Impairment in instrumental activities of daily living and the geriatric syndrome of self-neglect', *The Gerontologist*, 48(3), 388–96.

Naughton, C., Drennan, J. and Lafferty, A. (2013) 'Older people's perceptions of the term elder abuse and characteristics associated with a lower level of awareness', *Journal of Elder Abuse and Neglect*, doi: 10.1080/08946566.2013.86742.

Naughton, C., Drennan, D., Treacy, P. et al. (2012) 'Elder abuse and neglect in Ireland: results from a national prevalence survey', *Age and Ageing*, 41(1), 98–103.

NHS QIS (NHS Quality Improvement Scotland) (2004) *Draft Standards for Healthcare Governance*, www.nhshealthquality.org.

Nussbaum, J. (1985) 'Successful aging: a communication model', *Communication Quarterly*, 33, 262–9.

O'Brien, M., Begley, E., Carter-Anand, J. et al. (2011) *A Total Indifference to our Dignity: Older People's Understandings of Elder Abuse*, Dublin, Age Action Ireland.

O'Donnell, D., Treacy, M., Fealy, G. et al. (2012) M*anaging Elder Abuse in Ireland: The Senior Case Worker's Experience*, Dublin, National Centre for the Protection of Older People University College Dublin.

O'Loughlin, A. (1990) 'Old age abuse in the domestic setting: definition and identification', *Irish Social Worker*, 9(2), 4–7.

O'Loughlin, A. (1993) *Awaiting Advocacy: Elder Abuse and Neglect in Ireland*, Dublin, IASW.

O'Loughlin, A. and Duggan, J. (1998) *Abuse, Neglect and Mistreatment of Older People: An Exploratory Study*, Dublin, National Council on Ageing and Older People.

O'Neill, D., McCormack, P., Walsh, T. and Coakley, D. (1990) 'Elder abuse', *Irish Journal of Medical Science*, 159(2), 48–9.

Payne, M. (2000) 'The politics of care management and social work', *International Journal of Social Welfare*, 9(2), 82–91.

Phillips, J. and Waterson, J. (2005) 'Care management and social work: a case study of the role of social work in hospital discharge to residential or nursing home care', *European Journal of Social Work*, 5(2), 171–86.

Phillipson, C. and Baars, J. (2007) 'Social theory and social ageing', in Bond, J., Peace, S., Dittmann-Kohli, F. and Westerhof, G. (eds) *Ageing in Society*, London, Sage.

Pierce, M. and Timonen, V. (2010) *A Discussion Paper on Theories of Ageing and Approaches to Welfare in Ireland, North and South*, Belfast and Dublin, CARDI.

Post, L., Page, C., Conner, T. et al. (2010) 'Elder abuse in long-term care: types, patterns, and risk factors', *Research on Aging*, 32(3), 323–48.

Postle, K. (2002) 'Working "between the idea and the reality": ambiguities and tensions in care managers' work', *British Journal of Social Work*, 32(3), 335–51.

Powell, J. and Orme, J. (2011) 'Increasing the confidence of social work researchers: What works?', *British Journal of Social Work*, 38(5), 988–1008.

Prince, M., Bryce, R., Albanese, E. et al. (2013) 'The global prevalence of dementia: a systematic review and metaanalysis', *Alzheimers Dement*, 9(1), 63–75.e2.

Ray, M. and Phillips, J. (2012) *Social Work with Older People*, Basingstoke, Palgrave Macmillan.

Ray, M., Milne, A., Beech, C. et al. (2014) 'Gerontological social work: reflections on its role, purpose and value', *British Journal of Social Work*, doi:10.1093/bjsw/bct195.

Richards, S. (2000) 'Bridging the divide: elders and the assessment process', *British Journal of Social Work*, 30(1), 37–49.

Richards, S., Sullivan, M.P., Tanner, D. et al. (2013) 'On the edge of a new frontier: Is gerontological social work in the UK ready to meet twenty-first-century challenges?', *British Journal of Social Work*, doi:10.1093/bjsw/bct082.

Sahlsten, M.J., Larsson, I.E., Sjöström, B. and Plos, K.A. (2006) 'Patient participation in nursing care: towards a concept clarification from a nurse perspective', *Journal of Clinical Nursing*, 16(4), 630–37.

Scharf, T., Timonen, V., Carney, G. and Conlon, C. (2013) *Changing Generations: Findings on New Research on Intergenerational Relations in Ireland*, Social Policy and Ageing Research Centre, Trinity College Dublin, and the Irish Centre for Social Gerontology, NUI Galway.

Statham, J., Cameron C. and Mooney, A. (2006) *The Tasks and Roles of Social Workers: A Focused Overview of Research Evidence*, http://eprints.ioe.ac.uk/59.

Taylor, B. (2012) 'Developing an integrated assessment tool for the health and social care of older people', *British Journal of Social Work*, 42(7), 1293–314.

Timonen, V. and McMenamin, I. (2002) 'The future of care services in Ireland: Old answers to new challenges?', *Social Policy and Administration*, 36(1), 20–35.

Timonen, V., Doyle, M. and O'Dwyer, C. (2012) 'Expanded, but not regulated: ambiguity in home-care policy in Ireland', *Health and Social Care in the Community*, 20(3), 310–18.

Wahl, H.-W. and Lang, F.R. (2006) Psychological aging: a contextual view, in Conn, P.M. (ed.) *Handbook of Models for Human Ageing*, Amsterdam, Elsevier.

WHO (World Health Organization) (2008) *A Global Response to Elder Abuse and Neglect: Building Primary Health Care Capacity to Deal with the Problem Worldwide: Main Report*, Geneva, WHO.

WHO (2014) *Facts about Ageing*, www.who.int/ageing/about/facts/en.

WHO/INPEA (International Network for the Prevention of Elder Abuse) (2002) *Missing Voices*, Geneva, WHO.

Index

CPSIA information can be obtained
at www.ICGtesting.com
Printed in the USA
LVHW061654261118
598242LV00014BA/51/P

9 781137 383204